Gratry's Philosophy

Julián Marías' *La Filosofía del Padre Gratry*

I0894616

Gratry's Philosophy

Julián Marías' *La Filosofía del Padre Gratry*

Translated from the fifth Spanish edition by

Mary L O'Hara, CSJ

with the assistance of

Catherine T McNamee, CSJ

ATF THEOLOGY

Adelaide

2020

Originally published as *La Filosofía del Padre Gratry*
Copyright Julián Marías 1972
Madrid: Ediciones de la Revista de Occidente
Colección El Alción
(The above is the fifth Spanish edition.)

Gratry's Philosophy
Translated by Mary L O'Hara from the fifth Spanish edition
Translation copyright 1991 by Mary L O'Hara
All rights reserved.

ISBN: 978-1-925679-52-6 soft
978-1-925679-53-3 hard
978-1-925679-54-0 epub
978-1-925679-55-7 pdf

Published by:

ATF THEOLOGY

An imprint of the ATF Press Publishing
Group owned by ATF (Australia) Ltd.
PO Box 504
Hindmarsh, SA 5007
ABN 90 116 359 963
www.atfpress.com
Making a lasting impact

In the middle of winter,
season of storms and tempests,
the winds cease to blow and it becomes calm.
These are the days in which, according to the old myth,
the halcyon calmly builds its nest
so that life will continue.

Table of Contents

Translator's Preface

A translation of a work by a Spanish author about a nineteenth-century philosopher may raise a few questions: Why Gratry? Why now? Because 'whatever in the past happens to have been of significance or value ought to be held in memory, insofar as this is possible, so that it can give us guidance' (Marilynne Robinson, Introduction to *The Death of Adam: Essays on Modern Thought,* 1998).

The particular work here presented has been long in coming, having been conceived when the translator first read it as a graduate student. At the time of its appearance in Spanish, its author, Julián Marías, who saw in Gratry an early phenomenologist, intended to show its relevance to the phenomenology current at the time. For us today, Gratry continues to hold the place Marías pointed out, but his advanced thinking on social matters and his perennially useful ideas in theology and philosophy and on the person make him of particular interest.

Alphonse-Joseph-Auguste Gratry (1805–1872) was born into the world of Napoleonic France and lived his entire life in a time of endless revolution. Recipient of an excellent classical education, he decided to pursue a degree in engineering, and was admitted to the outstanding École Polytechnique in France. Despite the cynical view of his parents and teachers toward religion, he experienced as a young man a religious conversion that determined the course of his future life.

Deeply immersed in the Parisian religious scene of the time, he became well known as a distinguished logician, theologian and social thinker, as an outstanding educator and preacher, and also as a spiritual director, especially of young men. He was one of the co-founders of the Congregation of the Oratory in France after the Revolution. His English fellow Oratorian, Blessed John Henry Cardinal Newman, suggested Gratry's name as his possible successor as editor of the outstanding English Catholic periodical of the time. He was also a prolific writer on a broad range of subjects. Gratry's concern for the need to eliminate world hunger, for example, does not accidentally coincide with the feelings of many people today: his influence upon practical politics through the Christian Democratic parties of Europe and upon groups of socially concerned persons like Peter Maurin of the Catholic Worker movement was the result of devoted works by his many young disciples. Gratry's aim was to return to the origins of Western thought, but in doing this, he in fact inspired in his followers an appreciation of the ancient sources and a sense of the need for critically addressing the problems of his day.

Marías points out that, whereas Franz Brentano had numerous followers to carry on his work and to keep his ideas and works current, Gratry for various reasons lacked such a following; therefore, from the time of his death, he ceased to be considered an important philosopher. According to Marías the time is ripe for bringing Gratry into the contemporary philosophical conversation. In numerous ways Gratry's ideas can resonate more with people today than they did in his own time. It is with that in mind that I have undertaken to make the present translation.

The book on Gratry by Julián Marías presented here has enjoyed great success in Spain, having gone through five editions since 1941. When I first read it as a graduate student, it was Gratry's theory of the person, in particular his emphasis upon the idea of a special sense underlying one's intellectual and volitional powers, that attracted my interest because of its originality and power—although Gratry himself claimed to be original principally in going back to the sources of Western thought, especially to Plato and Aristotle. Marías' realisation of the need to understand philosophers' presuppositions exerted a powerful formative influence upon my own thought over the years.

Gratry's recognition of the need to cultivate the body as well as the spirit in the spiritual life sets him apart from many spiritual writers of his day and of ours. His interest in the person as a whole, body and soul, is evident in his little book *Les Sources*, translated into English as *The Well-Springs*. This very influential work, often given as a prize book or a present to young students, offers for someone aspiring to a life of learning an introduction to all phases of the intellectual life, including the spiritual life. It became the inspiration for Sertillange's influential *The Intellectual Life*. The first part of *The Well-Springs*, a portion of Gratry's *Logic*, was brilliantly translated into English by Helen and Milton Singer. The second part, with practical directions and general observations, is not so readily available. It is therefore appended to this book, along with some selections from Gratry's book on social thought and a quotation from Peter Maurin.

The present work of translation has been a labor of love. In carrying it out I have received generous assistance from a number of persons, in particular from Agatha Grossman, CSJ, who read a preliminary version and corrected a number of errors; from the late Mary Henry Nachtsheim, CSJ, who checked translations from the French; from Agnes Ward, CSJ, who checked translations from the Latin; from the late Bernard J Portz, SJ, who corrected the translation of several pages of mathematical text; from the late John H Nota, SJ, who corrected translations from the German; and finally from Catherine McNamee, CSJ, to whom I am most indebted for a meticulous reading of the entire text and for numerous corrections of infelicities as well as of some incorrect renderings of certain Spanish phrases. I am particularly grateful to the following persons for preparing the final manuscript: Benedict C Skemp, Lynn Alcorn Frame, Cyndy Krey, Jeanette Jungbauer, Madonna Clare Adams and, most importantly, Dolores Steinberg. To all of them as well as to the Sisters of Saint Joseph who have enabled me to spend time on this work, I am most grateful.

Mary L O'Hara, CSJ
12 August 2011

Prologue

This fifth edition of the present book coincides with the centenary of the death of Gratry (1805–1872). Written in 1941, it appeared in Spanish bookstores—after not a few vicissitudes, which I shall one day recount at leisure—thirty years ago, in the first months of 1942. It was my second book, a little posterior to my *Historia de la Filosofía*. The present edition includes additions made in 1951 and collected in *Obras*, IV.

The situation of philosophy has changed considerably in the space of two generations. When it was first published, the book encountered the official vigilance of a closed scholasticism that rebuffed the innovative attitude of Gratry, which itself anticipated in so many ways the philosophy that was actually being created—and of a great part of that which has subsequently been done. Now, at the end of three decades, the manifest horizon of philosophy appears to have changed to attitudes very like the positivism that dominated European thought when Gratry wrote his books, something that interfered with his work being understood and assimilated in his own time.

This gives to this study an unexpected currency. When it was written, some thirty years ago, it faced an imposed archaism at the same time as it made manifest the beginnings of what is [now] most current and creative. Now however, the philosophy which is set forth here affirms itself before another archaism: the repetition—without too much change—of the dominant mental form in the presence of which Gratry was able to innovate with genius.

In correcting the proofs of this book I felt its pages agitated by a new drama, inasmuch as it crosses three levels of history, precisely when we commemorate the centenary of the death of the philosopher Gratry.

Julián Marías
1 July 1972

Introduction

I propose in this book to study the most profound nucleus of the philosophy of Father Gratry. With this it remains to be said that the theme of this investigation has a strictly philosophical sense and range, and that I do not have to occupy myself with the personality of Gratry, with his religious activity or his theological ideas, save only in the measure in which these cannot be prescinded from in understanding his philosophy. But this explanation does not suffice. It is necessary, further, to indicate in just what sense I intend to study this philosophical thought of Gratry.

Father Gratry is an almost unknown philosopher in our time. To most of our contemporaries he is altogether unknown, even to his name. In most of the current books that deal with the history of philosophical thought he is scarcely mentioned. In some of them one finds a few lines alluding to Gratry, which usually come down to an indication of his dates, the titles of two or three of his works, and little or nothing more; often, some disoriented and so misleading commentary. No more? Yes, some books and shorter studies, which will be mentioned later, have been written on Gratry. But the interesting point is that they have not succeeded in making him known and putting him into intellectual circulation. Some examples will turn out to be particularly instructive. If we examine the more current books on the history of philosophy, we find that there appears to be no mention of Gratry either in such well-known works as those of Messer,[1] or of

1. *Historia de la Filosofía*, Spanish translation, *Revista de Occidente*.

Vorlander,[2] or in the French of Janet-Seailles,[3] or in that of Russell,[4] or in the Dictionary of Runes.[5]

No allusion, either, in the extensive bibliographies of Gilson's historical studies, nor in Goblot,[6] nor in Roustan,[7] despite their being French books and despite Gratry's having treated extensively the problems of logic and psychology; for the same reason, his absence from Cuvillier's Manual[8] is strange. Nor is he apparently cited in Sigwurt[9] nor in Erdmann,[10] who are so well informed about studies of logic. In Windelband[11] one finds a simple mention in a note; in Brehier[12] one page of his 1700 is dedicated to Gratry; in the enormous heap of Uberweg,[13] mere references. Still more interesting is the fact that in the book of Benrubi,[14] dedicated precisely to setting forth 'the founts and currents of contemporary philosophy in France', which studies more than one hundred fifty French authors of the nineteenth and twentieth centuries, he does not appear among them, and his name appears only twice, cited in passing without elaboration. These examples, which could be multiplied, show superabundantly that the significance of Gratry—his very existence—is not available in any way in our time.

After other works, above all that of B Pointud-Guillemot,[15] a learned German, Emil J Scheller,[16] set out to gather, with Teutonic patience, a bibliography of Gratry, which includes the articles, editions, and simple mentions or citations of him in all kinds of books and review articles; the very fact that this could be attempted and realised in an approximately sufficient manner is especially signifi-

2. *Historia de la Filosofía,* translated by JV Viqueíra.
3. *Histoire de la philosophie.* 'Les problèmes et les écoles'.
4. *A History of Western Philosophy* (1946).
5. *The Dictionary of Philosophy* (London: 1944).
6. *Lógica* (Spanish translation).
7. *Psicología* (Spanish translation).
8. *Manuel de philosophie* (2 volumes).
9. *Logik.*
10. *Logik.*
11. *Lehrbuch der Geschichte der Philosophie* (1935), 559.
12. *Historia de la Filosofía* (Spanish translation), II, 697.
13. *Grundriss der Geschichte der Philosophie.*
14. *Les sources et les courants de la philosophie contemporaine en France.*
15. *Essai sur la philosophie de Gratry* (Paris: 1917).
16. *Grundlagen der Erkenntnislehre bei Gratry* (Halle: 1929).

cant, and a glance at that bibliography shows, furthermore, that for the most part it comes from the time of Gratry or from the years following his death.

All these facts would lead one to suppose that the interest in Gratry would be very slight; this book claims to give a response to this supposition. But something more important must be kept in mind; the allusions to Gratry that the most representative books of those that mention him contain reveal not only a minimal appreciation but a concrete ignorance of his thought. Well now, the fact that a philosopher who had considerable renown and approval in his own time should be unknown indicates something abnormal; in the majority of cases it signifies, simply, an absence of a true philosophy. On the other hand, one can hardly make of them those 'hidden geniuses' without influence in the history of philosophy, without roots or consequences. Those unknown and almost uncultivated thinkers who then turn out to have anticipated all cartesianism or kantianism excite the mistrust of every philosophical mind and end by showing their complete inanity. The discoveries of great philosophers inspire, then, a limitless mistrust, and one need not fear that I intend here to present one more instance of the type to which a certain sort of historical investigation has accustomed us.

The case of Gratry is quite distinct. In the first place, he is not a spontaneous thinker without known roots, but rather the contrary, the most explicitly rooted and founded of his time, to the point that this rootedness is essential to his philosophy and constitutes one of its capital traits and the source of his interest for us. Father Gratry belongs to the line that originates in the Greek philosophers and ends in the great modern systems of cartesian filiation. And further, he gathers and sums up insistently all of this tradition, of which he feels himself the heir and repository. And not in just any way whatever, but rather he presents his own philosophy as an explicitation of the most substantive and common content of the entire history of philosophy. This question will occupy us at length in the following pages.

In the second place, even given the connection of Gratry to the continuity of philosophical thought, there remains the abnormality of his having been lost sight of and forgotten. Why is Father Gratry not known today? We must of necessity find it anomalous; but this need not be in the philosopher, but could be found in the other element that intervenes in his influence and his reputation: the time in which he lived. And so it is, in fact. The importance and the philosophical interest of Gratry have made it fall into oblivion, although that appears paradoxical. It is the fate of the most profound and original thinkers of the nineteenth century: Maine de Biran, Brentano, Dilthey; *today* those names are very well known, but for many the names alone; and, furthermore, this repute dates only from the last few years and has been achieved through the work of disciples who have the task of bringing into relief the meaning of the philosophy of these thinkers. Besides, we could say something similar about the best-known philosophers of the past century, Comte or Nietzsche: their fame has been immense, but it has been usual to overlook the most authentic meaning of their philosophy, and today it would be necessary to call it into question in a radical way, rejecting three-fourths of the image their contemporaries had of them. The second half of the nineteenth century was a time blind to metaphysics, and, for that reason, it could not see it; where there was something else, even though very secondary, as in the last two mentioned philosophers, this was paid attention to, omitting what was most substantive; where scarcely anything but metaphysics was to be found, everything was left in silence and obscurity. Even Maine de Biran remained relegated to the penumbra, to say no more;[17] Brentano alone has been studied and known sufficiently since 1900, that is to say, through his disciples: Kastil, Kraus, Meinong, above all Husserl and the other phenomenologists; with reference to Dilthey, only now is there beginning to be clarity about him, and for the first time in these last years his extraordinary philosophical importance is being discovered. (See the chapters in the book of Ortega, *Guillermo Dilthey y la idea de la vida* [Wilhelm Dilthey and the idea of life], published in the *Revista de Occidente* of November, 1933 to January 1934).[18] Well then; with Father Gratry the same thing occurs in even greater measure. The point of view in which he is located in relation to religion contributed

17. Gouhier is still working on the publication of his works and on his study. See J Marías: 'El hombre y Dios en la filosofía de Maine de Biran', in *San Anselmo y el insensato*, 1944.
18. *OC* [Obras completas] VI, 165–213. See also J Marías: Introduction to the *Teoría de las concepciones del mundo*, by Dilthey. [*Cf Biografía de la Filosifía*, Obras, II.] In the last decade much progress has been made in the knowledge of Dilthey, and it has been translated in Spain, Mexico, and Argentina, and, to a lesser extent, into other European languages.

to making him harder for his own time to assimilate; and, above all, the fact that Gratry centered all his philosophy on the problem of God, a question for this reason, that metaphysics lost all its meaning for more than a century, so that it is only barely beginning to recover it nowadays.

Gratry, as we shall see throughout this study, speaks a language which in its most profound dimension is unintelligible for his contemporaries; for this reason, when the first vogue which the strong personality of its author afforded to his work had passed, his epoch slid over his philosophy and generally passed certain decisive findings that are to be met with in his pages. Since no external reason caused later generations to fix upon his books, and he lacked the following of disciples as devoted as those of Brentano, Gratry remained at the margin of the history of philosophy, and his essential contribution to today's philosophy has not been utilized nor even known until the present. One might think that his influence, in virtue of those hazards or of an historic destiny, had been frustrated, and that the philosophy of our time has done without him; so that the thought of Gratry has been something lost by the living history of metaphysics, regardless of its intellectual qualities. But that is not so, and this is the reason for the present investigation. I believe that even now it is not too late; a series of aspects of the philosophy of our century has been constituted without reference to Gratry's contribution; but in this moment contemporary thought comes to confront some decisive questions, about which we do not find enough light in the contemporary philosophical traditions: the questions of the person and of God. It is precisely the moment in which the thought of Gratry can insert itself into the real movement of philosophy. In such a way now, and only now, it will be able to produce the fullness of its yield, be able to be understood sufficiently and fruitfully. From the present situation, Gratry acquires an extraordinary relief: everything his contemporaries could not see acquires for us an immediate and profound sense that gives us light on these central problems and on the whole of philosophy. Gratry, then, is no longer lost, but can reappear on the philosophic horizon to acquire his greater efficacy. Let us see how.

* * *

The study of the thought of Gratry presents a difficult prob1em. When the history of philosophy encounters any system, it always holds before itself a double element: on the one hand, the work itself that it tries to interpret; on the other, the later resonance of that work in philosophy, and therefore the variable image it has been acquiring over time. The history of philosophy tries then, from the given knowledge of the original work, to interpret it in a way that reveals its authentic sense and bestows light on the philosophy that proceeds from it. For example, if it is a question of studying the thought of Descartes, we must seek the most profound strata of cartesianism, to explicate them from their roots and make clear how from the philosophy of Descartes are born all the systems of rationalism. Here we cannot do this. In the first place, the thought of Father Gratry is not known; in the second, there is no philosophical continuation, at least visible, that comes from him.

We find ourselves, then, in a situation like that at the time when Gratry published his works: at that time there was an unknown philosophy and, naturally, the result of it. It appears, then, that what is to be done today is simply to expound the content of Gratry's philosophy and thus to make contact with him; thus to renew his philosophy, in such a way that this time, it may achieve in comprehensibility and influence what it did not at the time it first appeared. This is obvious; in fact, the first thing needed is to know the work of Gratry; and with this object I have recently published in Spanish translation his major work, *La connaissance de Dieu.*[19]

But this is not enough. The belief that a reading of this book, for example, is equivalent to what could have been done when it was first written, is a pure illusion. Gratry wrote his principal works from 1850–1870; seventy, eighty, ninety years have passed since then. We read in Gratry what his contemporary could not; each sentence has for us a distinct sense. We read Gratry *from* the present situation; the perspective has changed profoundly: much that remained almost unintelligible in 1860, in our time holds a great wealth of meaning; but this shows that it is illusory to claim simply *to read* Gratry; it is not possible to acquire mere *information* about him unless the reading of his books is an *historical interpretation.*

---

19. A. Gratry, *El conocimiento de Dios* (Madrid: Pegaso, 1941).

It is important to take account of this fact, in order not to seek a presumed 'objectivity' that would consist in the mere reproduction of his doctrine. For, what are Gratry's doctrines? This is precisely the problem. *We* need to underline in the pages of this philosopher something that seems to us to constitute more properly the basis of his thought; put in other terms, something that *interests* us, that seems living in his philosophy, and for that reason, that we can understand. And here we have to ask ourselves a new question: this *interesting* content today, capable of being up to date, *why* does it interest us? What do we claim to do today with Gratry? Why do we need him?

The adequate answer to these questions will be found only in the whole of this study; but already it is clear from this that the mere reading of Gratry is not possible without further qualification, unless it must necessarily be a reading *from* our philosophical situation and *in view of* our concrete problem, to resolve what we have flowing from him. For this reason, simple *exposition* is scarcely possible; rather the whole intent of his philosophy obliges us to articulate and dispose the ideas of Gratry according to a determinate point of view; determined by three elements, which are: 1) the reality of his philosophy in 1941; 2) the problem we intend to clarify (therefore, the direction in which we seek to advance philosophy in the immediate future); 3) the idea we hold of the history of philosophy as an integral element of philosophy itself. Therefore, the past and the future of philosophy, in the unity of the present in which they are given, intervene in every intention to set forth and interpret the thought of Gratry: that is to say, the philosophic problem in its integrity.

I shall not attempt, then, to give a complete exposition of the work of Father Gratry, following the plan of his books; I shall simply refer to them and to the personality of their author briefly to supply for their lack of familiarity. But, above all, I shall fix my attention on some points that interest us today, that can be fertile and cast light upon some grave questions preceding those that the philosophy of our day debates. The image of Gratry that will be obtained will be very distinct from that which his contemporaries, including in a certain sense the philosopher himself, could see of him; but it should be—this at least is my intention and my hope—the *true* image, in a very concrete philosophic sense; that is to say, the image of that which was truly *philosophic* in Gratry, and which for this reason can be incorporated in the living history of philosophy, carrying it further, and perdure in it and in that metaphysical movement.

And at the same time, the inclusion of Gratry in the history of philosophy will illuminate for us the meaning of this history and will enable us to understand better the origins and the meaning of the philosophy of our time.

This, then, is what I propose at the beginning of this study. It does not in any way treat of an archeological curiosity, of an interesting find of past thought as such; no more of the joy one experiences in reliving a past historical era; nor even of the usefulness of using a series of valuable ideas. Nothing of this; my intention is to include a necessary element in the history of philosophy of our time, and make it yield its efficacy from the point of view of truth.

Chapter One
Gratry's Place in the History of Philosophy

Gratry's Personality

Alphonse Gratry—Auguste Joseph Alphonse—was born in Lille in 1805 and died in 1872. He received a rigorous scientific training in the Polytechnic School of Paris. Later he was ordained priest and was professor in Strasbourg and in the capital. In 1852, Gratry and the Abbé Pététot, curé of Saint Roque in Paris, thought of organizing a center for promoting the Catholic movement which had been reborn in France. Gratry wanted to found a 'workshop for apologetics' in which various priests animated by a common belief could collaborate freely. In this way the so-called Oratory of the Immaculate Conception was founded, reviving the name and spirit of the old Congregation of the Oratory of Jesus, or Oratory of France founded in 1611 by Cardinal Pierre de Bérulle, to which such prominent intellectual figures as Condren, Thomassin, and above all, Malebranche, had belonged. This French Oratory of the seventeenth century in turn went back to the foundations of Saint Philip Neri in Italy in the sixteenth century. These groups of priests preferred to dedicate themselves to the ecclesiastical ministry and to study, with great freedom, without vows or rigorous rule, without forming an Order, and solely in a spirit of collaboration. The spiritual and intellectual fecundity of the Oratory was very high in its various periods.

Beginning in 1863 Gratry was professor of moral theology at the Sorbonne; he also belonged to the French Academy. He was, then, an outstanding public figure, who achieved great prominence during the polemics of 1870, on the occasion of the [First] Vatican Council, about the infallibility of the Pope. Gratry was not an obscure, unknown figure in his time; on the contrary he was a well-known and esteemed thinker and writer. His works appeared in various editions during his lifetime; *La connaissance de Dieu* [the knowledge of God] had already had seven editions by 1864.[1] This makes more interesting and puzzling the obscurity into which Father Gratry fell later. What superficial dimensions of his thought did his contemporaries perceive? We shall have to touch upon this point in speaking of the reaction to his philosophy by Émile Saisset and Ravaisson. In 1872, after a fruitful life of religious fervor and intellectual power, Gratry died, leaving a few books of uneven scope and value. What are these books?

The Writings of Gratry—The principal writings of Father Gratry make up a *Course of Philosophy*: theodicy, logic, psychology, and ethics. But in no way is it a question of a philosophical classroom manual nor a series of systematic treatises on these disciplines. They are rather the developments of his original points of view, in each of these disciplines, about the central question of philosophy, which is for him the problem of God. I shall give here a brief summary of the content of these important books:

La connaissance de Dieu is the most important work of Gratry. In a certain sense, the whole of his philosophy is included in it; the rest fill out and develop special points, which are nevertheless found already treated in the great book about God. His two volumes include an Introduction and two parts. The introduction is a splendid and surprising analysis of the contemporary spiritual condition, understood as an essential weakness of reason, from which proceed the personal crisis and that of religion. In the first part Gratry sets forth the problem of theodicy, that of the knowledge of God and his attributes, as the central question of philosophy; he goes on to outline the history of theodicy—and thus, at least in its essential nucleus, the history of philosophy—in the philosophers 'of first rank', from Plato to Leibniz; we shall soon see who they are and what are the reasons for his choice; finally, in the last two chapters, he studies the attributes of God and the *infinitesimal procedure* for proving the existence of God; with this, Gratry summarises the essentials of his theory on the two procedures of reason that he was expounding at length in

1. Later I shall emphasize his editions in detail. [Translator's note: English translation by Abby Langdon Alger, *Guide to the Knowledge of God: A Study of the Chief Theodicies* (Boston: Roberts Brothers, 1892)].

his historical investigation. In the second part he explains and develops his doctrine of the degrees of the divine intelligible and of the states of reason, and the entire system of relations between reason and faith. Finally, in an appendix, Father Gratry briefly sums up the capital points of the Catholic faith; this appendix is not extraneous to the book, but rather stands in an intimate relation to its contents.

La connaissance de l'âme [the knowledge of the soul], in two more volumes, which is the second of his important works, is a theory of the soul based upon a fundamental principle: that man is made in the likeness of God and the body in the likeness of the soul. For this reason, it is necessary to study the soul in relation to God, on the one hand, and to the body, on the other, and to discover in the soul a vestige of the Trinity. After these first comparisons, he studies 'word' and constructs a theory of languages, and then he expounds his theory of the three powers of the soul: the sensibility, the power of knowing, and the will. Here Gratry tackles at length the problem of the *senses*, that of the procedures of reason and that of freedom. From this point on, Gratry's work enters ever more into the sphere of theology and religion, first in a theory of sacrifice, then in a long disquisition on immortality, and, above all, the place of immortality, and finally, on death.

In the third place, the two volumes of his *Logique*. Gratry's logic is very original; it is written, as we shall see, from a point of view unusual in this discipline: the point of view of the juncture of philosophy and the human spirit; for this reason it appears in intimate rigorous relation with ethics and with the 'science of God'. After a long introduction on the general method of reason, Gratry expounds his theory of certitude and the causes of our errors. The second book is dedicated to the exposition and refutation of the logic of pantheism, understood as an inversion of the authentic procedure of reason, and as such a destruction of reason; above all, he attacks with great energy and in detail the hegelian system. In the third book is found the theory of the syllogism or the discursive procedure of reason. The fourth book, which is the most original and important, contains the entire theory of induction or dialectical procedure, constructed from its history in philosophy and in the mathematical and natural sciences. The fifth book turns upon 'the inspired intellectual virtues'; and finally the sixth, entitled *Les Sources*, is an intellectual methodology, where principal importance is given to the religious and moral foundations of the activities of the mind.[2]

In the two volumes of his fourth important work, *Ethics and the Law of History*, Gratry attempts to show that there is a general law of history and that this law, which Vico sought in his *New Science* 'and could not know', is the moral law. Concretely, that which Christ formulates in the seventh chapter of the Gospel according to Matthew: 'So whatever you wish that men would do to you, do so to them [RSV Mt 7:12].' [*Omnia ergo quaecumque vultis ut faciant vobis homines, et vos facite illis*]. The law of history, dependent upon this moral law, according to Gratry, is found contained in the words of the Gospel according to John, chapter 8: 'If you remain in my word, . . . you will know the truth, and the truth will make you free [RSV 8:31].' [*Si vos manseritis in sermone meo . . . cognoscetis veritatem, et veritas liberabit vos*]. The fulfillment of the moral law indicated above moves history toward truth and freedom and its violation moves it in the opposite direction. The development of these ideas is of great interest, but more religious and sociological than strictly philosophical.

The remaining writings of Gratry are occasional and polemical books, or of a more religious or autobiographical content and less essential.

Below I have listed a brief outline of the works of Gratry, because this will give an indication of the principal questions he treats. Thus the reader can get acquainted with the external contour of his philosophy, and this will allow me to situate the different problems within the total context of his works and also to limit myself to an in depth study of the essential questions of his metaphysics, without intending to set forth all his teachings in detail.

Chronology of the Writings of Gratry

1824—*De auctoritate sensus intimi et rationalis evidentiae.* (Latin dissertation for the 'concours general' of philosophy in the Collège Henri IV of Paris. Second prize. Published in the *Annales des concours généraux.*)

2. [This part of the *Logique* (translated into English by Stephen J Brown as *The Wellsprings* [New York: Benziger Brothers, 1931]) served as model for Sertillanges' *The Intellectual Life*, translated by Mary Ryan (Westminster, Md: The Newman Press, 1956)—Translator].

1824—*De l'association de nos idées et de son influence sur nos habitudes intellectuelles et morales.* (French dissertation—first prize—for the same 'concours'.)

1833—*Dissertatio philosophica de methodis scientiarum.* (Doctoral thesis. Strasbourg.)

1835—*Sur la vie de Jeanne d'Arc de Goerres.* (Article in the *Revue Européenne*, second series, volume I, 167ff.)

1846—*Thesis theologica de Deo.* (For the degree of Bachelor of Theology in the Faculty of Theology at Aix.)

1846—*Thesis theologica de Dono Dei.* (For the degree of Licentiate).

1848—*Catéchisme social ou demandes et réponses sur les devoirs sociaux* (Paris).

1851—*Une étude sur la sophistique contemporaine ou Lettre à M Vacherot.* (Paris, fourth edition 1863).

1853—*Introduction à la Philosophie.* (Article in *Le Correspondant*, volume 32 (April 25), 112–140.)

1853—*La connaissance de Dieu.* (2 volumes, seventh edition 1864; eighth edition, 1903; ninth edition, 1918.)

1855—*Logique.* (2 volumes, fifth edition 'enlarged with a polemical appendix, and with an introduction on the theory of the inductive procedure', 1868. New edition, 1908.)

1855—*Notes sur un article de M. Saisset.* (Article of October 25.)

1856—*Lettre à Mgr. l'archvêque de Paris sur les derniers instants de M Aug Thierry.* (June 25.)

1857—*De la connaissance de l'âme.* (2 volumes, tenth edition 1926.)

1859—*Le mois de Marie de l'Immaculée Conception.* (fifth edition 1916.)

1861—*La Paix. Méditations historiques et religiouses.* (third edition 1917.)

1861—*La philosophie du Credo.* (third edition, 1864; ninth, 1926.)

1861—*Les Sources.* (Separate edition of one part of the *Logique*, second part, 1862; in 1864 was added: 'A discourse on the intellectual duty of Christians in the nineteenth century and on the mission of priests of the Oratory'; fourth edition 1904; twentieth edition, 1923.)

1863—*La crise de la foi.* Three philosophic conferences at Saint-Etienne du Mont.)

1863—*Commentaire sur l'Evangile selon Saint Matthieu.* (2 volumes, ninth edition 1928.)

1864—*Les sophistes et la critique.*

1864—*Jésus-Christ. Réponse à M. Renan.* (Extract from the preceding. sixth edition 1923.)

1866—*Petit manuel de critique.* (Recasting of *Les sophistes et la critique*, with a letter of Pius IX and a 'Collection of sophistic texts'.)

1866—*Henri Perreyve.* (fourteenth edition 1923.)

1868—*Discours de réception à l'Academie français.* (March 26.)

1868—*La morale et la loi de l'histoire.* (2 volumes, fourth edition 1909.)

1869—*Lettres sur la religion. Réponse à M. Vacherot.* (third edition 1869.)

1870—*Quatre lettres à Mgr. Dechamps à propos du Concile.*

1871—*Les sources de la régenération sociale.* (Recasting of the *Catéchisme sociale.* third edition, 1901.)

1874—*Souvenirs de ma jeunesse.* (Posthumous work, written in 1845. twelfth edition 1925.)

1874—*Méditations inédites.* (Posthumous work, written between 1835–1840 and 1847–1851. Edition 1898, 1921.)

1919—*Elévations. Prières et pensées.* (Posthumous work, published by CL Peyroux)

This enumeration of the writings and editions of Gratry leads to an interesting consequence: three groups of works can be considered: philosophical, spiritual, and polemical; leaving aside the last, whose interest, although lively, was momentary, we see that the important philosophical works—above all *La connaissance de Dieu* and the *Logique*—were re-issued rapidly during the author's lifetime, and very rarely thereafter; on the other hand, the spiritual and religious writings were reprinted frequently in the last sixty or seventy years.

That is to say that the social figure of Gratry experienced a visible change: from philosophy he passes to religious literature; now he is not a metaphysician or a logician, but simply, Father Gratry.

A comparison of the translations into other languages—German, English, Spanish, Italian, Polish—shows the same result. From 1868—with the sole exception of my translation of *La connaissance de Dieu*—none of Gratry's philosophical works is translated; and, certainly, there was none—on any subject—between 1905 and the present. The Spanish translations I know of are:

1863—*La filosofía del Credo*. (Barcelona)

1865—*Los sofistas y la crítica*. Respuesta a la Vida de Jesús de M Renan. Traducida al castellano por C Urquiola. (Paris)

1868—*La moral y la ley de la historia*. (Without the name of the translator. Press of the Diario de Barcelona. Barcelona)

1941—*El conocimiento de Dios*. (Translation by Julián Marías. Pegaso. Madrid)

1950—*Fragmentos* from *El conocimiento de Dios*, *Lógica*, and *Del conocimiento del alma*. (Translation by Julián Marías and Dolores Cebrián, in *La filosofía en sus textos*, by Julián Marías, Volume II, 1995–2039.)

For studies about Gratry, see the Bibliography at the end of this book.

Gratry's Philosophical Tradition

The Situation of His Time—The nineteenth century, around its midpoint, appeared to be an epoch to which philosophy had become alien. In Germany, after the flourishing of idealism, from Kant to Hegel, and in particular of the death of the old Schelling, there is dominant an unbridled and sufficiently irresponsible speculation with very scant philosophical content which produces at the end an insuperable excess of idealism and *a priori* mental constructs, and launches German thought upon the ways of the most insipid and extraphilosophical naturalism. It is the epoch of Strauss, of Feuerbach, etc, and on the other hand of Vogt, Moleschott, Büchner, Haeckel. This is the dominant 'philosophy'; some other currents then begin, subterranean and scarcely visible, and they will appear only at the end of the century.

In England, philosophical activity is divided between the remnants of the 'Scottish School' (Hamilton, etc.) and the Utilitarian tendency (Bentham, Stuart Mill). With Darwin the naturalist currents of an evolutionary tint, which continue to be maintained first in the field of positive science and then will have to invade philosophy, with Spencer, also manifest themselves.

In France there is somewhat greater philosophical richness, but almost all is very second rate. On the one hand, the last stages of Condillac's sensualism and of the idealogues: Destutt de Tracy, Laromiguière, etc. On the other hand, as a reaction against the materialist tendency of sensualism, there is the spiritualism of Victor Cousin, an eclectic and temporizing system, which turns in an insistent way to the history of philosophy, but in a very different way from that which we shall meet later in Gratry: Cousin underlines the word *history* more than *philosophy*, and the repertory of opinions he was studying interested him more than the decision about which might be true. In the third place, there is a group of writers who preferred to occupy themselves with social problems, with utopian flourishes and of great intellectual imprecision, but who prepared the way for positivist sociology and the political-social movements which manifested themselves on the occasion of the revolution of 1848. In addition to this, there is an occasional solitary and obscure thinker, little understood, who passes for an example of mental darkness, like Maine de Biran (see the book of Taine: *French Philosophers of the nineteenth Century*, in which one can realize the ambiance that surrounds him). Also other philosophers of scant prominence, close to Maine de Biran, like Jouffrey, Royer-Collard and some others. Finally, the great philosophic movement of the century, prepared for by almost all the other tendencies, and which from its beginning dominated almost entirely, invading philosophy and the sciences, and even the general style of the spirit of the time: the positivism of August Comte.

Well then: the great philosophical system of the nineteenth century appeared as an explicit negation of philosophy. Metaphysics, according to Comte, is impossible; one must renounce it, as something definitely extinct and past. Philosophy can only have the mission of coordinating the positive sciences and converting itself into a theory of them, into a reflection on scientific knowledge. From then on, philosophy will be understood in Europe as, above all, theory of knowledge, and they will claim to construct this discipline without founding it in ontology, therefore by a psychological route. This state of affairs dominates until 1900, when Husserl published his *Logical Investigations* and showed positivism's essential lack of positivity and rigor. With reference to the deeper and more metaphysical dimension of Comte's philosophy, which is not explicit in his work, if not exactly completely negated, only much later, in our days, will it be realized and a different and even opposed view to that which reigned in the positivism of the last century begin to be held. But in his time nothing of this was realised, and the final watchword is the negation of metaphysics. It is not possible to know *essences* or *causes* of things: facts, data, alone are interesting, as a means to formulate *laws* that govern them. Of course, neither a study of the soul that would be other than experimental psychology, nor much less anything that would claim to be a knowledge of God, is possible. The accusation of metaphysics is enough to reject any doctrine without appeal.

This is the situation of philosophy in mid-nineteenth century. This is what Gratry, in his turn, encountered. Now one can see the radical discrepancy between his preoccupations and points of view and this intellectual ambience. Recall the prodigious exertion it cost Brentano and the phenomenologists, and, on the other hand, Bergson, to overcome positivism and revindicate authentic philosophy. Imagine, then, the philosophical situation of a man who, from 1850, proclaimed in France that the organ of knowing is the reason, that this reason allows one to know with certainty the infinite and the absolute, that philosophy is metaphysics and that its central and decisive question is the problem of God. A man who affirms the connection of the philosophical method of arriving at God with *prayer*; who, alongside external senses, posits an interior sense and, what is more serious, a *divine sense*; who considered *sacrifice* as a philosophical method; who believed that God and the soul, the latter understood as image of the former, are the most proper object of philosophy; who affirms, finally, the moral character of truth and error, and the reference of all this to God. How could he be understood in his time? How could these ideas be taken seriously *philosophically*? Could they appear otherwise than as words of a pious soul, as apologetic exertions of the 'priest of the Oratory'? To whom could it have occurred to inquire about a rigorous and scientific meaning to those expressions? We see, then, that Gratry had to be, necessarily, misunderstood and forgotten. There was too much distance between the style and assumptions of the century and the philosophy of Father Gratry to allow the latter to grow and prosper. Contemporary critics like Saisset and Ravaisson who deal with him, despite the attention with which they study him and their undeniable competence, scarcely see in Gratry more than attacks on pantheism or his theories on method, principally in relation to mathematics. Ravaisson,[3] after citing some sentences of Gratry on God as root of liberty, on love and sacrifice and on the Gospel word about the one who seeks to save his life losing it and only the one who consents to lose it saving it, adds these revealing words: 'By the developments he has given these exalted maxims, full of the most pure spirit of Christianity, even more than by his ingenious but questionable theories on method, the eloquent Oratorian has deserved well of philosophy and natural theology.' That is to say, he treats of 'exalted maxims', full of Christian spirit, which are counterpoised to his theories on method. Gratry made 'developments' of those maxims, moved by the effusion of his religious soul. And when he seeks a paraphrase to avoid repeating Gratry's name, Ravaisson has recourse to a significant one: 'the eloquent Oratorian.' It is a question of this: of an eloquent and pious priest who speaks with unction and apologetic purpose about evangelic maxims. And this is interesting and meritorious, of a high religious and even theological value. What could not have occurred to Ravaisson was to understand those words as propositions of strict philosophy, as expression of a rigorous metaphysics, with the claim to attain scientific knowledge in the highest sense of the term.

This explains to us sufficiently the later fate of Gratry's work. But the glance we have just cast over the philosophical ambience that surrounded him sets for us a more serious question: How could Gratry think in this way? In what other ambience did his ideas germinate? Whence came his philosophy? To these questions we must now respond.

His Personal Formation—Gratry was a Catholic priest; further, as I have already said, he studied at the École Polytechnique. These two facts enter into his intellectual formation in a decisive way. Gratry, in the first place, is a theologian. A few times it has been emphasised—he does it himself—that the knowledge and study of theology is important *for philosophers*. Many times one finds in otherwise brilliant

3. *La philosophie en France au dix-neuvième siècle*, chapter XVI, end.

thinkers lacunas and faults owing to a lack of theological preparation, and even more to the lack of a certain peculiar *habitus* that the study of theology confers. Gratry points out in this respect the inferiority of Descartes and Malebranche in comparison to Fénelon, for example. The profound study of theology produced in Gratry a great familiarity with the medieval thinkers: Saint Augustine, Saint Anselm, Saint Thomas, Saint Bonaventure; these produced in turn the knowledge of the Greek and Latin fathers, and from them he had necessarily to pass to Greek philosophy, from which in part the Patristic period derived its impulse, and, above all, its intellectual instruments. Father Gratry attained, then, a complete understanding of philosophy and theology, ancient and medieval. But, in virtue of this, he realised perfectly that the history did not stop with Saint Thomas, as people have repeatedly wished to make us believe.

Gratry knows very well—in 1850, thus much before the modern works of investigators who have taken up the theme: Grabmann, Koyré, Gilson—that modern philosophy, that of the seventeenth century, is not a current opposed to the Scholastic, nor much less a pure error, but quite the contrary: the rigorous continuation of medieval thought and one of the moments in which the human mind has made very decisive steps on the road to truth. As a good French Catholic thinker, he knew his Bossuet and Fénelon, but also Pascal and Petavius, and the great Oratorian Thomassin, and the Spaniards; and not only the theologians, but those who were no more than philosophers, or philosophers above all: Descartes, Malebranche, Leibniz. The whole history of philosophy from Greece to the seventeenth century formed for him a unity: that is his tradition.

At this time it was interrupted; at least he felt this to be the case; but not by ignorance of it—the great fabricator of exclusions—but by a real divergence. Gratry believes that philosophy lost its rigor and its truth from the beginning of the eighteenth century; and this judgment, which today we would for the most part share, he extends to German idealism and its immediate consequences. For Gratry, that truth exist, error must also exist, and this begins with Leibniz, to culminate, in its most essential and acute form, in Hegel. We shall return to this point at an appropriate place. But in any case, through agreement or disagreement, Gratry includes in his knowledge the entire history of philosophy—and of theology—from the Greeks to his contemporaries.

And there remains yet another element in his formation: that of mathematics and physical science. Gratry cultivated these discipline intensely and had an especially good command of the fundamental steps of their constitution. Kepler, Newton, Descartes, Leibniz, Wallis, Lagrange, up to his friend and contemporary Cauchy, appear in his thought and provide materials of great interest for his philosophy. At the same time he found in physico-mathematical science a stimulus, and a constant check on his logical and metaphysical theories.

We see, then, that Father Gratry was not dependent, rather the contrary, upon the surrounding philosophical climate. His personal tradition is the whole history of Western thought. And this tradition, it must not be forgotten, is above all metaphysics. Metaphysics and theology, in a peculiar unity, constitute the nucleus of his formation and the center of his interest. Notice that almost the entire movement that in the nineteenth century reestablished metaphysics and prepared the philosophy of our epoch proceeds from the Catholic Church. Bolzano in Germany, Rosmini and Gioberti in Italy, Gratry in France, Brentano in Austria.

Naturally, it was not enough to belong to the Church or to have the formation usual for ecclesiastics; along with these names, we have the philosophical—and theological—sterility of the great majority of the neo-scholastics. But it is just this that Gratry was not, as Brentano was not. The two kept open to the whole of philosophy, every time they came to know it, and they did not limit themselves to trivial exegesis of a splendid text superficially understood, or to the 'refutation of modern errors', but rather they felt the problems in a lively, energetic way, and they believed like the great medieval scholastics, and all authentic philosophers, in the spirit and in truth. The formation acquired in Catholic surroundings served to put them in touch with metaphysics and theology and to give them thus the tools to overcome the circumstances of the time and display their genius for a philosophic life.

Attitude toward Tradition—But Gratry did not limit himself to finding in the philosophic past a repertory of questions or an arsenal of intellectual tools for approaching problems that interested him personally. Gratry took account of that tradition and accepted it in its totality: it is a point of departure and constitutes an essential element of his thought; only at the end of that philosophic continuity and in function of it does he expound his personal contribution to philosophy. But it should not be thought that this is a facile eclecticism; on the contrary: Gratry, as has already been said, believes in truth and error; but he believes also in what has been known since the old Parmenides: that only the way of truth can decide about the way of opinion, and even on the impracticality of the *what is not*, of the ὡς οὐκ ἔστιν; error and even the absurd have their place in the history of truth, from which they must be interpreted and understood, and which they serve for demonstration by absurdity. But this will oblige Gratry first to make an issue of the whole of past thought, and then to pose the problem of the history of philosophy. This question, upon which we shall dwell later, characterises Gratry and differentiates him radically from the thinkers of his time. His philosophy, which is of course metaphysics, presents itself besides as determined by the entire history of philosophy, of which he must give an account. We shall have to investigate sufficiently these two dimensions of his thought.

The Turn to Metaphysics

From the perspective of his time, Gratry appeared as an eloquent Oratorian, full of the spirit of the purest Christianity, who commented fervently and acutely upon the Gospel texts and held ingenious—and in sum erroneous—theories on the methods of philosophy and in general of reason. Seen from today's situation, Gratry appears to us as one of the thinkers who have renewed the study of metaphysics and have given back to the philosophy of the nineteenth century the authentic content it had lost with positivism, the culmination of a tendency that began in the eighteenth century. He was, then, in the line of the philosophers of Catholic lineage that culminates in Brentano. Well, now, there are profound differences in the talent and in the very intention of these thinkers, and above all in the assumptions and the style of their thought. The manner in which metaphysics has been approached in our time depends upon what has been the means of access to it, and so our philosophy appears to us conditioned by its antecedents in the past century. The fact that the most substantive and creative metaphysics of today proceeds from phenomenology, flowing directly from Brentano, confers its general character upon the philosophy of the period and predetermines in good part its ulterior fate. If the thought of Gratry had had a fruitful philosophical continuation, that of our day would present different traits from those which perhaps it would be able to integrate into itself if the philosophy of Father Gratry were to be incorporated into today's thought. To simplify things I shall limit myself to comparing Gratry and Brentano, to make evident the points in which they differ, within the unity of significance of their thought.

Opposition to German Idealism—Gratry as well as Brentano considered that German idealism, far from being a moment of fullness for philosophy, was misguided and decadent. But the disagreement each finds in facing it is of a distinct character: while for Brentano the greatest fault of idealism is its aprioristic and constructive method, remote from observation and from the analogy with the natural sciences, for Gratry what is inadmissable is the logic of Hegel: the identification of being and nothing and the Hegelian attitude before the principle of contradiction. Brentano was affirming the thesis that the true philosophic method is none other than that of natural science; [*vera philosophiae methodus nulla alia nisi scientiae naturalis est;*] Kant appeared to him to be the author of all the errors of his successors, and what he condemns above all is the speculative use of reason, which claims to expound all of philosophy beginning from *a priori* principles. Gratry, on the other hand, esteems Kant, and in a certain sense Schelling, though with reservations, but the hegelian principle, being and nothing are the same [Sein und Nichts ist dasselbe], appears as such absurd to him, and as the culmination of all sophistry.

We see, then, that the disagreement with idealism refers in Brentano above all to a methodological question, while Gratry particularly notices what appears to him a radical error of metaphysics; and when he affirms that it is a question of method, and that the problem is the logic of Hegel, he sees clearly that he is moving on the plane of ontology, and that the logical progression of Hegel is the inversion of the 'principal procedure of reason'. From this difference others proceed in the development of their doctrines.

The Relationship with the Metaphysical Tradition—Brentano has in his background the past of philosophy, as far as Greece. But not in so complete and unitary a way as Gratry, but rather in isolated moments: Bacon, Descartes and Leibniz—above all Leibniz—in the seventeenth century; Saint Thomas in the Middle Ages; Aristotle among the Greeks. This line, Aristotle, Saint Thomas, Leibniz, is his.

It is known that Brentano is, with Trendelenburg, the great introducer of aristotelian studies in the nineteenth century; from this contact proceed in no small measure his rigor and philosophic fecundity; philosophy has always felt the profound influence of its encounters with aristotelian thought. Father Gratry takes much more account of the whole of past philosophy, and the current that we have pointed out in Brentano is completed in Gratry by another, which, beginning from Plato and passing by way of Saint Augustine, would arrive at Saint Anselm, Saint Bonaventure, Bossuet and Fénelon. But the most important thing is not that the tradition of Gratry should be more complete, but that it should function in a completely different way. For Gratry, it is not only, as has been said earlier, that there is a content of thought worthy and useful, a way of doing philosophy that has shown itself exceptionally efficacious, but above all a *history of philosophy*. That past *is* philosophy, and it is *one*. All the wise, Gratry repeats, speak with only one voice, faced with the sophists who disagree with the philosophers and among themselves. There is an essential concordance among philosophers 'of the first rank'. It does not make sense to let one's voice be heard separately, but rather to have it linked to this whole chorus of philosophy. For this reason Gratry has to take account of the whole of its history, and he knows that in doing so he is doing nothing other than philosophy. In Gratry we meet one of the few profound intentions to understand the sense of the history of philosophy, and we shall have to study it more later. What concerns us here is to see how the inclusion of his thought in the metaphysical tradition is much more radical than in Brentano, and of much greater significance.

The Reaction in the Face of the Philosophy of His Time—This point must be insisted upon. Already we have seen that Gratry as much as Brentano, in the same way as the other thinkers named above, signifies a break with the reigning philosophic climate and the restoration of a distinct conception of philosophy. But the intellectual attitude in the face of their intellectual surroundings is not the same for each of them. Concretely, Brentano accepts in part the reigning position in philosophy and appears tinged with positivism. His opposition to the German idealists makes him hit upon the point of view of the observation of facts and the approximation of philosophy to the positive sciences. Of course, the most profound stratum of his thought lay leagues away from positivism, and his method has nothing whatsoever in common in the end with that which dominates the nineteenth century; on the contrary, he destroys it, and from his philosophy proceeds directly that of Husserl, which eliminates the last traces of psychologism. Nonetheless, Brentano always calls himself an *empiricist*, no doubt in a sense that sets him apart radically from that of the English philosophers of modern times or of almost all those of nineteenth century Europe; but the fact is that he uses a word currently in vogue and brings his philosophy nearer to the dominant point of view after German idealism; see, for example, his *Psychology from an Empirical Standpoint*. The scientific preoccupation of Brentano, his belief in the identity of the method of science and philosophy, all this makes him share, at least in a first stratum, the philosophical ideas of his time, even though fundamentally he was radically superseding them and substituting for them others of a very different stamp.

In Gratry we do not encounter this situation. His own scientific formation made him turn against the science of mere observation of facts, and energetically revindicate the dominance of *reason in the strict sense* in all the disciplines. Gratry keeps before his eyes, above all, the founders of modern science, from Kepler to Newton and Leibniz, persons of reason, in no way submitted to the tyranny of the simple datum, of the observable *fact*. On the other hand, the empiricism which followed, above all in France, the philosophy of the seventeenth century, appears to him a profound error: it is the exclusion of the great themes of philosophy, the abandonment of reason, the suppression of metaphysics. With the empiricists of the Enlightenment, philosophy ended in Europe; Gratry could not accept the consequences that this orientation held in the nineteenth century. Precisely what he values in Kant and Schelling is the opposition to this empiricism of skeptical and naturalistic tendency. At the same time, the themes that occupy Gratry, above all that of God, are foreign to the philosophy of his time. Abandonment of God *and* of reason, with an *and* that is not simply copulative, but that indicates a profound and essential connection of reciprocal causality; this is the intellectual situation of the period in which it fell to his lot to live. The disagreement is too radical for Gratry to be able to accept it in any sense. He awaits a new 'great metaphysical century', like the thirteenth and the seventeenth; but he succeeds only in situating himself in resolute opposition to his own and in raising it to completely new points of view. This, naturally, must have made even more difficult the comprehension and diffusion of his philosophy.

Nevertheless, it would be incongruous to think that Gratry has no connection with his time. He stands in it, of course, but in the concrete mode of exceeding and surpassing it. In taking up a position opposed to the philosophy of the nineteenth century he includes it, because he did not limit himself to condemning or depreciating it from a distant ignorance, but he penetrated into it to be able to make its error clear. Therefore, he affirms it, insofar as it is erroneous, as a confirmation, by absurdity, of the truth. And, on the other hand, Gratry has an acute sensibility for perceiving the rare contemporary doctrines in which a metaphysical preoccupation flourishes. The ideas of Royer-Collard about induction, some ideas of Cournot and Joubert, of Bordas-Demoulin and, above all, the great figure of Maine de Biran, cross his pages with a positive evaluation; and not only that, but he uses this positive content of contemporary philosophy and finds himself linked with it, as with the metaphysicians of the past, in the higher unity of philosophy and truth.

Explicit Metaphysics—I have many times defined the role played by Gratry and the philosophers near him as a *restoration of metaphysics*. But this is not altogether univocal. In the first place, at no time, even in the full flowering of positivism, were there lacking nuclei that affirmed the legitimacy of metaphysics and occupied themselves with it; on the other hand, in the tendencies that proposed to renew it, it does not appear always in a way equally rigorous or clear; finally, we should not forget that *all* philosophy, in the measure in which it is such, is metaphysics, although it does not know it and does not desire it, and so we can today see the original metaphysical significance of the philosophy of Comte. We intend, then, to explain this question with some rigor.

Of course, neo-scholastic philosophy has always cultivated metaphysics, and this is one of its titles to appreciation. The circles linked to the medieval systems, especially to thomism, have not fallen into the error of separating themselves from all ontology to construct, for example, a 'theory of knowledge' or experimental psychology; only, very much at the last minute, in an extraneous and tardy manner, some nuclei have allowed themselves to be excessively influenced by these positivist tendencies. But this neo-scholastic metaphysics, in general, was not original and creative, but usually reduced to the transmission and the commentary of the great medieval thinkers. Furthermore it did not include the effective history of modern metaphysics, concretely since Descartes; the majority of the time it ignored it, considering it a 'mistake' that had incomprehensibly snatched control from the only true philosophy, namely, the medieval. For these reasons, then, neo-scholastic metaphysics could not resolve the problems really posed nor could it make philosophy walk the road of ontology. It could only conserve the deposit of the medieval and Greek tradition, which provided a means for other thinkers, emerging from the neo-scholastic point of view, to insert metaphysics into the philosophy of the nineteenth century.

But, even in the non-scholastic currents that intended to re-establish ontology, for example, in Brentano, this did not appear in an explicit manner. It has cost much labor to make metaphysics as such penetrate into the domain of scientific thought, from which it seemed excluded without possible recall. Even at the beginning of this century, in French philosophical circles, it sufficed to condemn a theory absolutely, as one of my teachers used to recall, to say, 'Ah, but that is metaphysics!' And everyone knows the resistance of Husserl himself to admitting anything that could have a metaphysical sense; it is the last survival of positivism in its most radical conqueror, who could not, nevertheless, escape all its influence.

Brentano occupies himself, above all, with two particular philosophic disciplines: psychology and ethics; his most substantive contribution is, on the one hand, the idea of intentionality, which had been so far removed from the philosophy of the present, and, on the other hand, his *empirical* method, founded on the evidence of intuition, which entailed as a consequence the rediscovery of essences and of ideal objects. In this way he arrived at a conception of man as a being defined by intentionality, and this posed the problem of metaphysics; further, the objectivity of values and of ideal objects in general is recognized, and finally, the concept of essence has once more been posited in today's thought and it has come to be seen that philosophy has as its mission the knowledge of essence. All this has determined the splendid metaphysical flourishing of our days; but in Brentano it does not appear in an explicit and manifest way as ontology. There still persist, in external appearance, and even in his project as such, excessive remnants of positivism.

In Gratry the matter is quite different. He underscores the scholastic influence more than Brentano and remains more attached to the traditional hierarchy of problems—not only in the Middle Ages, but also in the seventeenth century—; but he is not a scholastic. We have seen that his philosophic attention involves equally Greek philosophy, the medieval and the modern, and that he affirms its essential unity. The point of view at which he places himself is not that of a definite school, but that of philosophy as a whole, understood as the conjunction of the thinkers 'of the first rank'. And, starting from these suppositions, he occupies himself wholly and explicitly with metaphysics. More than that, he not only tackles the great traditional questions of ontology, like the problem of God or that of the soul, but he also takes his stand rigorously from the point of view of being; and besides, all the disciplines, for example, logic, have for him the strictest metaphysical content. See how he expounds the problem of pantheism in the greatest detail in his *Logique*, in studying the logic of Hegel, which he understands as an ontology in which the legitimate procedure of reason is inverted.

Therefore it can be affirmed that metaphysics, in all rigor and in the most explicit manner, is already found in Gratry. Perhaps too quickly; the human spirit perhaps needs to relax this tension that philosophy imposes upon it and which it appears unable to bear for long. The German idealist speculation was too near; philosophy had perhaps to drain off the error of positivism, of the supposed servitude before facts, until it could find, at the end of its road, that it had been doing metaphysics despite itself. Thus it imposed itself upon him with its necessity. Without this perhaps it could not have arrived at that way of approaching philosophical problems that we know by the name of phenomenology, and would have lacked its decisive intellectual tool.

God and Man—This metaphysics of Gratry is centered in theodicy; the problem of God is his capital question. A question that philosophy had relegated—and still does—to an extraneous oblivion. Since Hegel few philosophical books have dealt in a serious and original manner with the problem of God. Apart from Gratry, perhaps we could cite only the lectures given by Brentano about the existence of God in the universities of Würzburg and Vienna, from 1868–1891, and published after his death, in 1929, by his disciple Alfred Kastil, with the title, *On the Existence of God*.[4] Even today, the problem of God, except for some luminous and fugitive intention to pose it on

4. See my study, 'El problema de Dios en la filosofía de nuestro tiempo', in *San Anselmo y el insensato*, 1944.

new bases, is eluded in philosophy. At the time when we are confronted with the great question, it is important to take account of Gratry's splendid contribution.

But there is still more. Gratry does not separate the problem of God from the problem of man, nor this latter from that of the world. Above all, he considers that the demonstration, and in general, the knowledge of God, supposes a real elevation of man in his integrity. Therefore, theodicy involves at the same time the problem of the person, and Gratry presents it in a dimension that today turns out to be most timely. In the moment in which philosophy, in possession of its rigorous phenomenological method, convinced of its metaphysical character and dominated by the ontological analysis of existence or of life, feels the implacable urgency of posing the radical problems of God and of the person, in a peculiar unity, the philosophy of Gratry, which moves in just this dimension, acquires its most living timeliness, and makes plain its position in the history of philosophy. This is the reason for the present study.

Chapter Two
The Historical Point of View in the Philosophy of Gratry

The History of Philosophy at the Beginning of the Nineteenth Century

I have already alluded on various occasions to the attitude of Gratry toward the history of philosophy. We have seen how he knows it in its general lines and essentially depends upon it. We now need to investigate what idea of the history of philosophy he holds, and what is the use he makes of it. This use has, of course, as its presupposition, the interpretation Gratry gives of the philosophic past. The philosophy of our time is determined in one of its dimensions by the history of philosophy, to the point that at times it seems that all philosophy is reduced to it, and this produces a strange discomfort; one wonders whether it is not going to be converted into a perfect knowledge of the past as such, with omission of the decision about truth and error. This uneasiness has cut across all the epochs that have experienced historicism up close.[1] This is what happened, to a certain degree, at the moment in which the history of philosophy became a philosophical discipline, in the first years of the nineteenth century. Gratry represents an original point of view, which holds the greatest interest for us. But we should first glance at the diverse interpretations of the history of philosophy that Gratry found in effect in his time, so as to consider the novel position the Oratorian philosopher took in regard to this problem. Let us examine briefly three examples, of very

1. See the general introduction to my anthology, *La filosofía en sus textos* (1950). *Cf* also my *Introducción a la Filosofía*, chapters III and IV, and *El método histórico de las generaciones*, chapter I.

unequal importance, that sum up the fundamental types of interpretation: Degérando, Cousin, and Hegel.

Degérando—At the beginning of the century, Degérando published, in 1802, a thesis entitled, *On the Generation of Human Knowledge*, which was awarded a prize by the Berlin Academy of Sciences. In 1804, he published a further development of this theme, *Comparative History of Systems of Philosophy, relative to the principle of the Human Sciences*, in three volumes, with a total of more than 1,500 pages. It is a great history of philosophy from its beginnings to the moment when he wrote: up to Schelling.

Degérando was born in 1772 and died in 1842. He is identified with the sensualist movement that proceeds from Condillac, although he attempts to go beyond empiricism with a 'philosophy of experience'. Degérando shares certain similarities with the point of departure of Maine de Biran, who also arrived at his metaphysics of the *sens intime* [intimate sense] from his initial position of sensualism, which dominated the French philosophy of the period. Above all, for Degérando philosophy has one first and fundamental question, 'which is like the axis of all philosophy'. And he adds: 'This question is the one that has for its object to establish *the principles of the human sciences*.'[2] The theory of knowledge is the first and principal issue which philosophy has to decide, because 'before deciding about *God, the Universe, man*, these three great objects of philosophical doctrine, it is necessary above all to examine in virtue of what title man decides on something'.[3] Starting with this assumption, he divides his treatise into two parts: the first is 'a simple historical exposition of the systems imagined by philosophers concerning the principles of human knowledge'; the second is 'a critical analysis of these same systems'.[4] In the first place, then, he classifies, divides and defines the teachings; in the second, which is the truly important part, 'we grasp', he says, 'these facts as so many great data which can, by the methodic comparison of motifs, of proofs, of effects produced, cast a new light on the fundamental question itself, and fix our choice upon the system that, at the end of this test, will show itself the best'.[5]

2. *Histoire comparée* I, xviii–xix.
3. *Histoire comparée* I, xx.
4. *Histoire comparée* I, xxi.
5. *Histoire comparée* I, xxii.

The text is explicit enough. It is a question of *comparing* the systems methodically in order to try to clarify the primary problem of philosophy with all its implications, and *choose* the *best* of those systems. In another place Degérando says that his work is a treatise of philosophy, according to a new method: 'As it were *an essay in experimental philosophy*.'[6] His history is, he adds, an 'inductive or comparative history'. The history of philosophy appears, then, as a series of systems causally linked by reciprocal influences, that he has to try to order and classify; this attempt at philosophic taxonomy must be realised from a directive point of view, which is that of the principles of knowledge; and the purpose of this study is, in the first place, the balancing of what history has to say about this question, and above all the determination of which is the best of the teachings. Degérando understands the history of philosophy, then, as a repertoire of solutions and as the experimental justification of the true principles of a doctrine. After an enumeration of facts, he makes a typology of systems; then, through a comparison of these latter forms and of their consequences, he decides which is the best and thus formulates his position with respect to the problem itself. The ultimate object he proposes to himself is 'to discover how the comparison of the different systems of philosophy can serve to found a good theory of the generation of knowledge'.[7]

This idea of the history of philosophy could appear trivial and lacking in rigor today; but if one takes account of its time (1804), one must recognise it as very interesting, like the whole of Degérando's book, which would be worth an extended study.[8] If one examined it in detail, one would notice, in the first place, that Degérando is concerned only about the problem of knowledge; in writing of Aristotle, for example, after expounding his theories about ideas, about sensation, faculties, language and logic, he covers his metaphysics in little more than a page. The Middle Ages is scarcely treated, and in a form that indicates a profound ignorance of its meaning. On the other hand, empiricist philosophy since Bacon is studied with special predilection. I shall point out, finally, one apparently secondary and

6. *Histoire comparée* I, xxvi.
7. *Histoire comparée* II, 337.
8. Some interesting details can be seen in my Introduction to the *Teoría de las concepciones del mundo*, by Dilthey (1944), 27–30. (In *Biografía de la Filosofía*, *Obras*, II).

external detail: the erudition that abounds on all its pages; it is a book that enumerates and describes, with greater or less precision, almost all the cultivators of philosophy, including those of the third or fourth order, in all countries. This fact should be kept in mind for comparison with Gratry's criterion.

Cousin—Victor Cousin, a philosopher who filled the mid-century with his activity and achieved an extraordinary influence in the intellectual life of France, lived from 1792 to 1867. Cousin inherited the tradition of Maine de Biran, although with considerable loss of its metaphysical depth. He also retrieved elements of the German idealists and of the Scottish school, which he confronted with the still prevalent tendency of sensualism so rooted in France. Cousin is a *spiritualist*, but above all an *eclectic*. His intent is to bring together opposed philosophic systems, to find in this reconciliation the deposit of truth that each contains; in this way, some are corrected by others, and the truth remains free and manifest.

Cousin occupied himself largely with the history of philosophy; this was obligatory; he is the principal cultivator of this discipline in the first third of the nineteenth century, and he dedicated various university courses and a series of monographs to it. Let us consider, then, what Cousin means by the history of philosophy.

Cousin begins from psychological analysis, which he considers as the great discovery of philosophy. But he observes that human nature manifests itself, not only in the individual, but also in the species, on a greater scale and in a more visible way. The species develops in time and space, and that is history. This development implies the idea of *progress*, and that progress is *civilization*. Human nature can be known, then, in the vision on a grand scale which is history, 'and historical analysis is the supporting evidence of psychological analysis.'[9]

Thus the history of philosophy cannot be separated from the whole of human history. 'A true history of philosophy, at the same time as it must be specific, must then be universal and link itself to the whole history of humanity. Nothing human can be alien to it; for nothing human escapes the history of humanity, and all the travail of the history of humanity passes into the history of philosophy.'[10] For

9. *Cours de l'histoire de la philosophie*, 1828. *Oeuvres de Victor Cousin*, 1840, I, 12 (lesson 2).
10. *Cours de l'histoire de la philosophie*, 28.

this Cousin demands of the historian of philosophy a quality, almost a virtue, he says, before any other: the love of humanity. 'The true love of humanity ought to attach us to all that is human. If you love human nature, you must take it not onesidedly, but as it is, in all its aspects.' And he does not shrink from the old inevitable slogan: 'I am a man and I consider nothing human alien to me.' This is his motto. Here, it is evident, all Cousin's eclecticism slips away.

One must forcefully admit all that is human; nothing can be rejected or expelled. All forms part of civilisation, of the progressive development of the human spirit, and the nineteenth century has to integrate and reconcile it: it is the eclectic period, which finds the point at which opposite tendencies coincide and merge. And this, Cousin notes, extends to everything: to methods, to philosophic disciplines and even to what goes beyond philosophy: to literature, which must reconcile classicism with romanticism, to politics above all which must coordinate the monarchic with the popular element; the result is an agreement, a pact between king and people: constitutional monarchy, symbolized in the constitution. One must not forget that this is said in 1828, on the eve of the July Revolution, of the politics of the proponents of the *juste milieu*.

But a grave problem arises: that of method. What method should the history of philosophy follow? It appears at first glance that it is the experimental method. One would trace and describe the systems, and then look for their relationships, to find the general laws. This is approximately the procedure that Degérando suggests. But Cousin realises that this method is impossible. If one follows a rigorously empirical method, one cannot begin by speaking of periods, nor even of schools: only individual systems exist; all the rest is an *a priori* introduced surreptitiously. But, further, one would have to study *all* systems equally, because we cannot begin by assuming that some are important and others not, and precisely in the way mankind has distributed glory. One must then seek all the books, all the fragments. Supposing this task accomplished, we have a chronological history of facts; but, is that enough? From pure facts one cannot pass without further ado to causes, reasons, necessary laws; we would remain in purely factual contingency, without being able to go further. For this reason, the 'simple historical exposition of systems' of which Degérando speaks, contrasting it to 'critical analysis', is not possible. The first already presupposes the second, presupposes principles that are not obtained by pure empirical consideration of historical facts. The empiricists also employ *a priori* principles, only without knowing it, and this is the greatest error.

What sort of method is the true one? Where can we find the governing principle? The elements of history are infinite; herein lies the difficulty; but who is the central character of history? Humanity. And Cousin says, 'If we could, before entering into history, be in possession of all the elements of humanity, we would have gained much.'[11] We must, then, investigate the elements of humanity; to begin with, reason itself has a law; reason is rational: 'It is necessary in itself that the human reason develop reasonably, and consequently that it form in its development something regular, harmonious, systematic, philosophic.' And Cousin adds: 'The identity of philosophy and its history is certain.' The history of philosophy, which is the development of reason, is also rational, is philosophy. The ruling principle of that history is, therefore, that which rules reason: 'One must seek out what are the elements of human reason.'[12] Here it is that as if by different routes, we return to the point of view of Degérando: the first thing is to study reason, the generation of knowledge. Cousin lapses into this position, with greater consciousness of it; systems will appear to him to be developments of that human reason, and as such all are admissible, if not in what they have of the partial and exclusive, then in the unity of their reconciliation. This is the true foundation of his eclecticism.

But the identity that Cousin affirms between philosophy and its history is external and unexpected. According to him, the philosophy of each period, once achieved and completed, turns toward the past to understand it with its spirit.

> If it is true that the new philosophic movement which is being accomplished secretly in Europe is an eclectic movement, it follows that eclecticism will be the foundation of the new history of philosophy, because it is a necessary law that each philosophy that comes to rule in its turn, after having exhausted its theoretical development, turns its gaze toward the past, interrogates it with the spirit that is within it, and ends by coming up with a history of philosophy that conforms to itself.[13]

11. *Cours de l'histoire de la philosophie*, 30.
12. *Cours de l'histoire de la philosophie*, 31.
13. *Cours de l'histoire de la philosophie*, 106.

Philosophy, then, needs its history radically only to turn toward it 'after having exhausted its theoretical development';[14] the history of philosophy is, then, curiosity, however elevated and perhaps necessary it may appear, but no more than that. Despite the identity previously formulated, which only signifies the rationality of the development of thought, the history of philosophy is for Cousin *history*, and not, in the end, rigorously, *philosophy*.

Hegel—We cannot enter into an investigation of the hegelian idea of the history of philosophy, which would carry us too far afield and oblige us to consider the general presuppositions of the system. On the other hand, it is not likely that Hegel influenced Gratry on this point, although the French philosopher knew the great German idealist well; he nearly always cites the *Logique*, and one does not find in his works any allusion to the interpretation of the history of philosophy expounded by Hegel. I shall therefore limit myself to indicating some of its capital points, as Hegel formulated them in his *Vorlesungen über die Geschichte der Philosophie* [*Lectures on the History of Philosophy*] published by Karl Ludwig Michelet.

'What the history of philosophy shows us', says Hegel, 'is the series of noble spirits, the gallery of the heroes of reason thinking, who in virtue of that reason have penetrated into the essence of things, of nature and of spirit, into the essence of God, and have conquered for us the supreme treasure, the treasure of rational knowledge.'[15] But Hegel warns us that what matters here is not the individual personality and character, but rather the thought itself and the general character of man as man. These facts of thought appear historical and, as such, as a thing of the past, alien to our reality; but what we are, says Hegel, we are at the same time historically: the imperishable is indissolubly linked with the historical.

But there appears a contradiction: philosophy has the truth as its end, and the truth is contained in thought (*Gedanke*); thought, then, is eternal, in and for itself; and history exhibits what is variable, past, that which no longer exists. How is it possible then that philosophy has a history? What is meant is an internal and intrinsic history, not of external and contingent occurrences of philosophers and of the

14. *Cours de l'histoire de la philosophie*, 106.

15. Introduction to *Vorlesungen über die Geschichte der Philosophie* (Ed Glockner. Stuttgart:1928, I, 27).

transmission of their thought.[16] One would have to show that the historical content itself belongs to the science of philosophy (*zur Wissenschaft der Philosophie*): the history of philosophy is scientific, and it turns into the science of philosophy. This is the problem.[17]

Hegel examines and rejects as insufficient the usual conceptions of the history of philosophy: as repertory of opinions, as something that destroys or proves the nullity of philosophic knowledge, etc. If philosophers have followed, contradicted and refuted one another, the history of philosophy proves no more than the nullity of all this past; it could be said, says Hegel, like Christ, 'Let the dead bury their dead, and follow me'; or, better, in this case, 'follow yourself', hold fast to your opinion, and do not be swayed by those of others. But this idea also leads one to think that one's own philosophy will be equally refuted, and that one could say, with Saint Peter: 'See at the door the feet of those who will carry you off [Acts 5:9].' On the other hand, every philosophy claims to be the truth, and as the rest are different, they must be in error.

To overcome these difficulties Hegel has recourse to the concept of development (*Entwicklung*);[18] in the Spirit, this development is the march toward itself; the Spirit itself knows itself and makes itself more free. What is it that evolves? Hegel says that the idea is always *concrete*, a unity of distinct determinations. The truth is never abstract, but concrete. In a flower there is form, color, scent, and so forth; and these are as if distinct, but nevertheless joined in the concrete unity of the flower. In the Spirit, which is concrete, are found at once liberty and necessity; furthermore, concrete liberty is only found in necessity, and necessity in liberty. Philosophy is the knowledge of the evolution of the concrete. The idea is an organic system, a totality that contains in its concrete evolution a multitude of degrees and moments: 'The idea is thus—concrete in itself, and developing—an organic system, a totality, which contains in itself a wealth of steps and moments' [*Die Idee ist so—koncret an sich, und sich entwickelnd—ein organisches System, eine Totalität, welche einen Reichtum von Stufen und Momenten in sich enthält.*].[19] Philosophy is, then, *a system of development*, and so

16. Introduction to *Vorlesungen über die Geschichte der Philosophie*, I, 31–32.
17. Introduction to *Vorlesungen über die Geschichte der Philosophie*, I, 33.
18. Introduction to *Vorlesungen über die Geschichte der Philosophie*, I, 38ff.
19. Introduction to *Vorlesungen über die Geschichte der Philosophie*, I, 56.

is the history of philosophy.[20] The ultimate end of philosophy, Hegel says, is the reconciliation of the concept with reality, the reconciliation of the Spirit which has conceived itself in its liberty and in the richness of its reality. For this reason, he says, *philosophy is the true theodicy*.[21] And he interprets the history of philosophy as a series of moments that are preserved and overcome; philosophy is always a *result*, and with it the entire philosophic past is present. Everything possesses its *truth* as a dialectical moment of the absolute, which must include even error. 'The final philosophy', Hegel adds, 'is the result of all the earlier ones; nothing is lost, all principles are preserved. This concrete idea is the result of the efforts of the Spirit for almost 2500 years (Thales was born 640 years before Christ), of its most serious work, to make itself objective, to know itself: What toil it was for mind to know itself' [*Die letzte Philosophie*—Hegel says—*ist das Resultat aller früheren; nichts ist verloren, alle Principien sind erhalten. Diese konkrete Idee ist das Resultat der Bemühungen des Geistes durch fast 2500 Jahre (Thales wurde 640 vor Christus geboren), seiner ernsthaftesten Arbeit, sich selbst objektiv zu werden, sich zu erkennen: Tantae molis erat, se ipsum cognoscere mentem*].[22]

The Hegelian interpretation of the history of philosophy, which I have just described in its briefest and most summary formulation, would require a long study of its philosophic assumptions and would call for an exposition of the whole Hegelian system. Here we can content ourselves with these approximations, sufficient for comparison with the thought of Gratry on this point, reserving the right to return later on to the philosophy of Hegel, when it may cast more light on these unadorned declarations.

The History of Philosophy in Gratry's System

We must now study Gratry's idea of the history of philosophy. We shall find in it, as its foundation, the idea of what philosophy itself is. Gratry did not write any book in which he thematically expounded that history; but, as already indicated, the greater part of *La connaissance de Dieu* was dedicated to the exposition of the theodicy of the

20. Introduction to *Vorlesungen über die Geschichte der Philosophie*, I, 58.
21. *Vorlesungen über die Geschichte der Philosophie*, III, 684.
22. *Vorlesungen über die Geschichte der Philosophie*, III, 685.

great philosophers, from Plato to Leibniz. And in this connection Gratry observes: 'The history of the philosophers who have just been cited is nearly the entire history of philosophy. Now, one knows a philosopher by his theodicy. The theodicy of an author contains his method, implies his logic, his ethics, is his metaphysics and his theory of ideas, and so also his psychology. In this sense the whole philosophy is in the theodicy. So, in treating successively of the theodicy of all the great minds, we give at the same time a precis of philosophy and a summary history of philosophy' [*L'histoire des philosophes qui viennent d'être cités est à peu près l'histoire entière de la philosophie. Or, on connaît un philosophe par sa Théodicée. La Théodicée d'un auteur renferme sa méthode, implique sa logique, sa morale, est sa métaphysique et sa théorie des idées, donc, aussi, sa psychologie. En ce sens la philosophie est toute entière dans la Théodicée—Donc, en traitant successivement de la Théodicée de tous les grands esprits, nous donnons à la foi un abrégé de philosophie et une histoire sommaire de la philosophie*].[23] Therefore, we can find, not only the theory about what that history is, but also its very realisation.

Unity of Philosophy—For Gratry, the whole history of philosophy forms a unity. All the geniuses 'of the first order' are in agreement although it does not seem so. The differences among them are a matter of words, or, at most, of method, but there is fundamental agreement. Socrates, Plato, Aristotle, Saint Augustine, Saint Anselm, Saint Thomas, Descartes, Pascal, Malebranche, Fénelon, Petavius, Thomassin, Bossuet, Leibniz: this is the great series of the minds *of the first order*. We shall see soon the role one who escapes from that unity plays in this history of philosophy.

The foundation of this unity of philosophy is the unity of *truth*. 'The human mind is one, and truth is one. By the goodness of God, man faces truth, and the light enlightens every man coming into this world. All those who see, see the same thing, and all that a man has seen is true . . . At bottom, all the geniuses of the first order agree; and there is one universal human philosophy, which, in fact, has been accepted, elevated, consecrated, crowned by Christian theology' [*L'esprit humaine est un, et la vérité une. Par la bonté de Dieu, l'homme est en face de la vérité, et ceux qui voient, voient la même chose, et tout ce qu'un homme a vu est vrai . . . Dans le fond, tous les génies du*

23. *La Connaissance de Dieu* (seventh edition 1864), I, 73.

premier ordre sont d'accord; et il y a une philosophie humaine universelle, qui, par le fait, a été accepté, élevée, consacrée, couronnée par la théologie chrétienne].[24] As truth is one and confronts us, all we see in it is true and must agree; at most, one can distinguish the point of view, and the appearance may be diverse; but falsehood does not fit: there can be no *false vision*, but falsehood and error are lack of vision, darkness in place of light. Therefore error, far from being the great presupposition—attitude of almost all modern philosophy—is a problem it is necessary to explain. What is normal is to see, given that reality is here and we have the reason for it; falsehood supposes an abnormality of that for which a reason will need to be given: philosophy must set forth the problem of sophistry, as Plato and Aristotle already saw clearly.

There is then a unity between the philosophy of Greece, that of the Middle Ages, and the modern. Philosophy is anterior to Christian revelation and independent of it; for this reason the Christian philosophers could accept the Greek thought, purifying and elevating it, but without altering it; the philosophy of the new age, from the Fathers and, above all, from St Augustine, incorporates what is fundamental in Greek thought and makes it its own. In its turn, the seventeenth century will gather up all the earlier tradition and *renew wisdom*, but always illuminated by the same unique light. Therefore the major division of philosophy is the passage from Greece to Christianity, much more than the transition from the medieval to the modern epoch; Gratry holds this conviction, which the research of our present day has justified. 'We pass', he says, 'from the ancients to the moderns, from the Greek philosophers to the Christian doctors, considered as philosophers' [*Nous passons—he says,—des anciens aux modernes, des philosophes grecs aux docteurs chrétiens, considérés comme philosophes*].[25] The *moderns* are all Christians. At this moment there is produced in philosophy an explicitly revealed light that does not destroy it, but illuminates it still more. Revelation does not suppress the natural light, as grace does not annul nature, but perfects it. Philosophy in the hands of Christians must always think what Saint Thomas says (*Summa Theologiae* III, q. 9, a. 1, ad 2) about the two kinds of knowledge in Christ, divine and human, which are not reduced to

24. *La Connaissance de Dieu*, I, 187.
25. *La Connaissance de Dieu*, I, 193.

one alone, but one of which is made clearer and more powerful by the other: 'The light of knowledge is not dimmed but rather heightened in the soul of Christ by the light of the Divine knowledge' [*Lumen scientiae non offuscatur, sed magis clarescit in anima Christi per lumen scientiae divinae*]. The presence of revelation introduces a new element into reason and causes fruits to be produced in it superior to those that naturally correspond to it; it is a *graft*; and so Gratry speaks felicitously of *grafted philosophy* [*philosophie greffée*]. And this is the sense of the lemma with which he begins the exposition of augustinian philosophy: what Plato says lives in Saint Augustine [*quidquid a Platone dicitur, vivit in Augustino*]. With reference to the seventeenth century, Gratry interprets it, justifiably, as a reestablishment of the true continuation of philosophy. In the moment in which one tries to forget tradition and think on his own account, to seek truth, the mind finds itself in the same line as earlier philosophers. It is a phase, with its own unity, within the superior unity in which all philosophy moves.

Discontinuity—But philosophy does not manifest an uninterrupted tradition. Aristotle said that probably the arts and philosophy were discovered and lost many times; Gratry remembers that and believes that philosophy was discovered in Greece, with Plato and Aristotle; in the century of the Fathers; in the Middle Ages, with Saint Thomas; finally, in the seventeenth century; and that it was lost in the intervals. In the periods in which philosophy loses itself, the monuments of ancient thought are preserved; but those monuments without the tradition that vivifies them have no meaning and turn into pure matter of curiosity or erudition. That is when history of philosophy is done from the point of view of history, and it falls into eclecticism. This is, says Gratry, what has happened since Leibniz: philosophy is lost, and there is only obscurity since the eighteenth century. This engenders the loss of confidence in minds who in this time of darkness have the sense of the light, and, as they do not see it, wonder whether it is possible. The first thing that would be needed to return to philosophy would be to reestablish the living sense of the tradition and to actualize the philosophy of the past, which is not something past, but the very essence of philosophy. For this reason Gratry must return above all to that line of traditional metaphysics, discontinuous in time, but one in truth, to insert into it his own philosophy. This makes it clear that preoccupation with the history of philosophy is not in any way extrinsic for Gratry, but constitutes the first element that can get his own thought started.

On the other hand, that interruption of philosophy over time is accompanied by a division even within the very periods of fullness. Joined to the unanimous voices of the wise are found those of the sophists who disagree with them and also among themselves. This produces a discussion, a movement of refutation and of discord, and makes one think that philosophy supports both the pro and the contra of everything and lacks internal unity. This is the common view of philosophy, which is born, Gratry thinks, of the fact that it is not rigorously distinguished from sophistry. If everything is taken as philosophy, then, effectively, contradiction exists in it, and there is no real knowledge; or everything is taken as good, in a total renunciation of truth. Thus, as Plato and Aristotle already knew, the sophist looks like a philosopher, but is not, and sophism looks like real wisdom, but is not; the sophist is a man whose being consists in non-being. Soon we shall see the profound interpretation Gratry gives to this, to explain that double discontinuity.

Truth and Error—Gratry is not an eclectic; he carefully distinguishes truth from error and speaks of the character of truly philosophic minds or centuries which, having knowledge of truth, also have an understanding of the false, and, being persons of light, they chase the darkness away. 'Only the night', he writes, 'favors an equality of systems and an equal respect for error and truth'.[26]

There is, then, such a thing as error. But within it one must carefully distinguish partial error which is merely a wandering within the truth, a defect of vision, and something else which consists of the inversion of the very procedure of reason. Gratry speaks of 'the eternal sect of error, which, by a satanic method, comes to withdraw itself from reason, and to turn its head so as not to see' [*la secte éternelle de l'erreur, qui, par une satanique méthode, parvient à se soustraire à la raison, et à tourner la tête pour ne pas voir*]. It is a question, therefore, of a *method*, with a root in the will—we shall soon see how far reaching this is—which escapes reason and destroys it, so as not to see. Reason produces truth; it is the organ capable of seizing the truth; far from leading us astray, reason keeps us from falling into falsehood; to do this last [i.e., to fall into falsehood] requires inverting it, directing

26. *La Connaissance de Dieu*, I, 357.

it backwards, [*à rebours*] and thus not seeing, as a consequence. This is what sophistry, which remains rigorously opposed to philosophy, does. For Gratry, there are not some philosophers who stand in the truth and others who stand in error, nor still less does he believe that truth and error are indissolubly mixed, nor that all is equally true, but simply that there are philosophers and sophists; the first use reason to arrive at the truth, and indeed do reach it; the second invert reason and turn toward nothingness, instead of seeking being.

This then makes it evident that sophism consists in a destruction of the legitimate procedures of reason; it is, thus, a question of logic. Sophism destroys the principles of reason so as to be able to turn it upside down; only in this way can it arrive at nonbeing and at nothingness in place of being and God.

Gratry does not intend to *refute* sophism, because it is not susceptible of refutation. Refutation presupposes a previous common assumption, that is, that of reason, on the basis of which error can be pointed out to the one who suffers from it. In the case of the sophist, this is not possible, because what he denies is, in the final analysis, reason itself. No dialogue is possible. Aristotle already said that the principle of contradiction cannot be demonstrated, because it is the foundation of all demonstration and even of all speech; its truth can only be shown indirectly, because the one who denies it cannot even speak: he would be like a vegetable, says Aristotle. Gratry intends to expose the logic of sophism, whose greatest example is that of Hegel, only to show its absurdity; and this helps make evident that sophism signifies the destruction of reason, and for that matter serves to demonstrate legitimate procedures, by way of contrast with the absurd. Gratry follows Aristotle in trying to show the impossibility of hegelian logic; he believes that the Greek thinker had already done it by anticipation, and that this reveals the identity of the sophistic tendency, which always consists in following the procedure of reason, but *by inverting it*. And thus, what constitutes the unity of philosophy in truth produces equally the unity in error of the sophistry of all times.

This is not the place to expound Gratry's theory about sophistic thought; that will have to be done in treating of his logical ideas. The sole intention here is to highlight the *relation* of sophism to philosophy so as to explain the concordance of this latter, once rigorously distinguished from the former. It is only necessary to point out one more thing, leaving its development to another context: truth and error, for that matter, philosophy and sophism, have a moral sense. Underlying the two positions is a free act of will, a choice; and this choice springs from the very depth of the human being, and so bears a strict relation to the problem of God. 'Excited by the *divine sense*, which pushes toward the absolute in one way or another, the human being determines the direction in which he will be pushed, and he chooses his conclusion. One concludes to the infinite Being, the other to non-being; the one affirms the Good, the other evil; the one says God, the other nothingness. This is what really, historically, takes place in the bottom of the heart of all men' [*Excité par le sens divin, qui pousse à l'absolu d'un coté ou de l'autre, l'homme détermine le sens où il sera poussé, et il choisit sa conclusion. L'un conclut à l'Etre infini, l'autre au non-être; l'un affirme le Bien, l'autre le mal; l'un dit Dieu, l'autre néant. Voilà ce qui se passe réellement, historiquement, au fond du coeur de tous les hommes*]. (*La connaissance de Dieu*, I, 371.) This question is not, then, a simple problem of *knowledge*; it affects the reality of man and, in that way, the radical dimension of man, his very *roots*. In the problem of sophism, as in that of philosophy, are found joined that of God, that of man, and that of reason, which is precisely the key to the relation between the human creature and the Divinity. The question of the history of philosophy is essentially included in the unity of the metaphysical problem of Gratry.

The Inclusion of the Philosophic Past in the Present—For a history of philosophy, *unity* is not enough; something else is needed: that this unity be *historical*. That is to say, it does not treat of a simple concordance of philosophers, of a dead coincidence, nor even of a chorus of voices that complement each other. Gratry indeed uses this image of a chorus to apply to the seventeeth century; thus, to *one epoch*, to a group of contemporary thinkers, but not to the philosophical continuum across time. On the other hand, this history cannot be that of the frustrated attempts to acquire truth or find the true road of philosophy, as would have been, for example, the opinion of Kant; nor is it a simple intellectual reflection of the march of the general history of humanity; nor, finally, that of a dispute between two tendencies—sensualism and rationalism, for example—which it would be necessary to reconcile. Gratry believes that philosophy stands in a secure path from the time it achieved its maturity in Greece, and that it moves from that time in the truth; further, he does not insist excessively on the relation of philosophic thought to history, except at certain very deep levels, such as the step from the pagan to the Christian world or the contribution of modern natural science; although, as we shall see farther on, the *moral* factor, to which Gratry concedes such an important role in philosophy, is in itself at the same time, an *historical* role; apart from this, sophism being excluded, there are not in philosophy two discordant tendencies, according to Gratry, but rather, at the most, two procedures equally legitimate and necessary, which complement one another and have distinct spheres of application. What is, then, the character of the history of philosophy as such?

For Gratry, a philosophy *includes* those of the past. The word he uses most often, in an almost automatic manner, is *renfermer*. 'One can say', he writes, 'that Saint Thomas Aquinas includes Saint Augustine, Aristotle, and Plato' [*On peut dire*—he writes—*que saint Thomas d'Aquin renferme saint Augustin, Aristote et Platon*].[27] And a little later he adds: 'Saint Thomas Aquinas, as philosopher, includes the entire substance of his three great predecessors' [*Saint Thomas d'Aquin, comme philosophe, renferme toute la substance de ses trois grands prédécesseurs*]. We can see, then, that there are many modes of inclusion. If we have two realities and one of them contains or includes the other, nothing more, we can simply content ourselves with the former, and it is enough. That is to say, when Saint Thomas is known, we should be able to overlook his predecessors, given that their results are already there in him. This idea, which has been, in fact, much used—and certainly applied to Saint Thomas—approximates the historic situation of the sciences, but it has little to do with the history of philosophy. In positive science each period collects the fruits of the earlier ones and distinguishes itself from them. It consists in a cumulative work, more than historical, and for this reason mathematics or physics can be pursued by collecting the results of *past* research in mathematics or physics, but without worrying about them, nor, for that matter, studying their history. (This principle is true in each concrete case, and this approximation suffices for us for our present purpose; if one wished, however, to apply it to the whole of positive science in all the moments of its evolution, it would need to be taken with a grain of salt.) In philosophy, on the other hand, we cannot prescind from the past; Saint Thomas Aquinas *includes* not

27. *La Connaissance de Dieu*, 302.

only the *results* of his predecessors, but their *philosophy*. Aristotle and Augustine, *as such*, are present in Saint Thomas, and without them one cannot understand him. The content of philosophy is inseparable from the radical situation from which it springs, and philosophy as a whole remains incorporated in the history of philosophy in later thinkers. In what way?

The 'Universal Man'—Gratry must utilize a mode of inclusion that supposes an effective *conservation* but also an *increase*; in the third place, a *temporal* structure, in such a way that there is really a present from which the moments preserved exist as past. Gratry has recourse to a *human* way of being: growth, advancement in *ages*. This provides us with a fourth essential character, which had not appeared necessary even to us: the articulation of stages within the temporal continuity; in fact, a person grows in a continuous manner, instant after instant and year after year; but at the same time one is first a child, then a youth, then an adult, and finally old. In human life the past is conserved, and not only conserved, in fact and accidentally, but it consists essentially in the conservation of the past, one is the child and the youth *one has been*; therefore, they are already past; and this signifies an augmentation, a growth and enrichment of the developing person. And one cannot understand a person in a simple present; the only way to understand *this* person is to see him as the effect of the past which has produced him, and at the same time the past is intelligible only as the past of *this person*, something present here, on the basis of which the past must be comprehended. On the other hand, the present of a person is constituted in an essential dimension by what one proposes to be, by the *future* profile one anticipates and which gives one a sense of oneself: those ends *in view of which* I do and am right now what I am and do. The future, then, which at each instant is making itself present by being supplanted by another and changed into the past, is the third element that integrates the *present being* of the person.

When Gratry then wishes to compare Plato with Saint Augustine, nothing better occurs to him than to consider them as *one same man*, the first 'in his early and poetic youth; then, in the strength of his mature age'. Saint Augustine, after a life of work and prayer, would have come to possess the knowledge he had sought and desired as a youth, 'when he was Plato'.

To clarify this interpretation, Gratry appeals to the idea of the 'universal man' of whom Pascal spoke. 'The human mind', says Pascal, 'is like the mind of a universal man in whom the effects of reasoning grow incessantly, because the whole succession of men, during the course of so many centuries, must be considered as one same man who subsists always and who continually learns' [*L'esprit humain—he says—est comme l'esprit d'un homme universel en qui les effets du raisonnement augmentent sans cesse, parce que toute la suite des hommes, durant le cours de tant de siècles, doit être considérée comme un même homme qui subsiste toujours et qui apprend continuellement*]. The human mind, then, is like one sole man; it has in itself a radical unity, but a unity in time, with history. Gratry in a certain way compares the history of philosophy to biography. This unity then is ideal; in fact it is realised in different men, and some of these, the most eminent, are the real bonds of unity; in them the unity is most existent and most manifest; they possess it more than ordinary intelligences, they express it and develop it, often, Gratry says, unknowingly. This brings into relief for us the meaning of that expression of Father Gratry which we have recalled at various times: geniuses *of the first order*. They are the minds in which the unity of the human spirit appears, in which it is manifestly displayed; they are the men who in each century grasp the idea of the time and develop it in different directions in accordance with its own roots; thus, for example, in the seventeenth century, with the idea of the infinite.

In this way Gratry considered the history of philosophy as an essential root of all systems. Each one enfolds or includes the earlier ones, as its living past, as its earlier biography, which is constructing it. For this reason, to try to understand any one of them, or simply the development of philosophy at a given period, it is necessary to begin by going back to the beginnings, and reviewing its major stages of development, those in which the explicit unity of the spirit is seen, the entire philosophic past. It is this idea of philosophy that obliged Gratry to dedicate about 500 pages of *La connaissance de Dieu* to tracing the history of theodicy in the philosophers *of the first rank*. Here there is not a question of accumulating more or less interesting erudition; he does not even approach an historical survey *before* his philosophic labor; but rather those pages are an integral part and—literally—fundamental to his philosophy.

This means that Gratry does not consider the problem of originality with excessively 'modern' eyes. Gratry is not a rationalist—we shall see later the meaning and the range of this expression—; the manner of arriving at the truth does not matter so much to him as the truth itself, nor does the most interesting thing appear to him to be who first discovered it. For this reason he has the highest regard for the most *complete* even though less original philosophers. Into his assessment of Saint Thomas there enters in good part the fact that he makes ample and wise use of ideas developed in an original way by Aristotle and Saint Augustine; in the seventeenth century he admires most Fénelon and Bossuet, even knowing that they are cartesians, who receive from Descartes the principal nucleus of their ideas, because they appear to him centered in the truth, complete and without errors, with the precision that theology adds to philosophy, and that is missing in Descartes or Malebranche; and his predilection for Thomassin is based upon the fact that the Oratorian sums up very carefully the ancient and medieval tradition, and anticipates in a certain sense the work of Gratry himself. And for this reason also, when at the end of his *Logique* he indicates the three thinkers who seem to him indispensable for study, he indicates Saint Augustine, Saint Thomas and Bossuet, for the reason that they seem to him the most concise summary of philosophy and theology, from the Greeks, including the Christian doctors, up to Descartes and Leibniz, all integrated in their essentials into the work of Bossuet.

The Use of the History of Philosophy—This means that Gratry uses the history of philosophy in a very peculiar way, which is very like what characterizes our time. Gratry—as I have said—dedicated the greater part of his principal work to expounding the history of theodicy; in each moment of this history he seeks the central point, that in which all philosophers coincide and which is the nucleus of his own thought. This supposes, naturally, the belief that past philosophy has attained truth and shows an essential concordance. But it also supposes, on the other hand, that his own doctrine is not simply new, but that it goes back to the major intuitions of philosophy, to Greece. Gratry does not pretend to originality, but to truth; truth matters more to him than the novelty of his theories. Speaking of his doctrine about God and about the principal procedure of reason, Gratry writes some revealing words that make his position clearly manifest: 'At first they will oppose us; but as that will not succeed, I hope they will turn soon to say that these things have been known all along, especially in the seventeenth century, and that there is nothing new in all that. We shall hasten to agree, reserving for ourselves only the honor of having put in a clearer light this central point of philosophy, where all the rays come together' [*On nous le contestera d'abord; mais comme ce sera sans succès, je l'espère, on se tournera bientôt à dire que ces choses ont été connues de tout temps, surtout au XVIIe siècle, et qu'il n'y a en tout cela rien de nouveau. Nous nous empresserons d'en convenir, ne nous réservant que l'honneur d'avoir mis en une plus vive lumière ce point central de philosophie, où aboutissent tous les rayons*].[28] Instead of hiding his own sources, then, Gratry expounds his ideas following the thread of the classics of philosophy. It was a question of discovering in the past the forms, more or less explicit, of the fundamental truth. Something like what Aristotle does at the beginning of his *Metaphysics*, when he tracks in the works of his predecessors looking for clues of his theory of the four causes. In the one as in the other case, the discovery of the antecedents is an indirect proof of the truth of the thesis being presented, and then they are an indication of the fact that man, confronted with reality, sees himself obliged to explain it in a more or less perfect way, but in ways that coincide.

In Gratry, then, this becomes doubly justified, because his great discovery is that of a procedure of reason, the principal one; and he must show, first, that effectively reason has used that procedure, with greater or less consciousness, throughout history; second, that that procedure achieves one same truth, seen with different degrees of clarity and expressed in different ways, but essentially one. For this he must expound his personal philosophy following the thread of the past, and try to find it, even in a veiled form, in the classics. His task is, then, twofold: on the one hand, to bring past philosophy up to date in the present, in such a way that every stage of it would be intelligible from what comes later, and, in effect, from the metaphysics of Gratry himself; on the other hand, to present a summary of contemporary philosophy from the authority of the past; but it is necessary to understand this expression *authority* in a very concrete sense: it is not in any way a question of a respect that the philosophy of the past would exact for its simple antiquity or its traditional character; it is the appeal to the testimony of human reason, to show the essential

28. *La Connaissance de Dieu*, 72.

agreement of the philosophers who have used it in a legitimate way, without putting obstacles to it nor inverting its process. The rooting of his own system in the history of philosophy is the indirect proof of its truth, showing it to be included in the unity of the wise, who 'have but one voice', unlike the sophists who always disagree. All a man *sees*, says Gratry, is truth, and conversely, the truth is seen, from one or other perspective, with greater or less clarity, by every man who uses his reason. If a system is true, it will have to find itself, at least in its roots, in the authentic philosophy of the past, and it will be necessary to understand it in its progressive real maturation all through the history of philosophy. This is the double meaning of the appeal to the classics in Gratry, and if in him, on the one hand, the history of philosophy is rigorously philosophy itself, on the other, contemporary philosophy has full reality only when understood as end of its history.

Perennial Philosophy—Everything leads Father Gratry to a perfectly unitary idea of philosophy as a whole. We can call it by a famous but frequently misunderstood term, *philosophia perennis*. It is not a question, however, of a philosophy—that is to say, of a system of philosophy—which would perdure inalterable through all the centuries; nor of a series of exegetical commentaries surrounding this system and within its limits which suppose a mere explication of it, or at most its completion, but never a radical transformation or surpassing, nor a change in point of view. For Gratry, the unity of philosophy means something very different. 'There is one philosophy', he says. 'Which is it?' someone will ask. 'We answer that it is the philosophy of Socrates, of Plato, of Aristotle, of Saint Augustine, of Saint Thomas Aquinas, of Descartes, of Leibniz and of all the geniuses of the first rank without a single exception.' And he adds: 'I do not say that philosophy has already achieved its entire development, or even that its organs are completely developed; I do not say that it is as yet entirely conscious on every point of its method . . .; but I say that it has existed, in the human race, for long centuries, and independently of the Christian revelation' [*Je ne dis pas que la philosophie ait encore toutes ses forces, ou même tous ces organes complétement développés; je ne dis pas qu'elle ait encore de tout point, conscience de sa méthode. . .; mais je dis qu'elle existe, dans le genre humain, depuis de longs siècles, et indépendamment de la révélation chrétienne*].[29] This *one* philosophy is that of the

29. *La Connaissance de Dieu*, 195–96.

totality of the past and, on the other hand, it is not altogether finished and developed, but it lacks *forces*, *members*, *consciousness* of its own method. These deficiencies have a name that encompasses them all: *immaturity*; philosophy is still somewhat immature, growing, developing, and its history is that of its maturation. Perennial philosophy is constituted by the totality of the effective steps of this process of maturation: it is the whole biography of that 'universal man' to whom the human mind can assimilate itself in its unity.

But as the living unity of a man is not determined by any finished past stage, but by his life in each instant, which includes not only the past, but is held between the past and the anticipated future to which he tends, so perennial philosophy is not exhausted in any stage, but in the integral process of its history, *indefinitely* prolonged. This is the point of view of Gratry in reference to the history of philosophy.

Chapter Three
The History of the Problem of God

The Meaning of Theodicy

Gratry accepts the definition of philosophy that Bossuet gives: 'Wisdom consists in knowing God and in knowing oneself.' The knowledge of God and of the human being, then, appear united; and as the latter cannot be known without the visible world, philosophy includes also the knowledge of visible and corporeal nature. Thus the three traditional themes of philosophy, God, human beings, and the world, appear in a peculiar unity, the meaning of which will be revealed to us throughout this study.

Theodicy, Gratry says, implies all philosophy; it presents its aggregate, its unity; it contains its roots. For this reason he chooses it as his point of departure. The theodicy of each philosopher implies his logic, his ethics, his metaphysics, his theory of ideas. All philosophy is found implied in one unique question, that of the demonstration of the existence of God and of his attributes. But this requires an explanation. Gratry does not mean by theodicy, simply, *the science of God;* it is at once, and essentially, the science of the *human spirit that raises itself to God.* The proof for the existence of God is never a simple piece of reasoning; it supposes a journey of the human being toward God, a real elevation of the soul to God; and not only of thought, but of the entire soul, in its totality. It is, then, a moral act at the same time as a mental process; for Gratry, logic is inseparable from ethics; the raising of the soul to God requires reason as much as liberty. In this way, man as such remains involved in the problem of the demonstration of God; it is necessary to explain that demonstration from the ontological possibilities of man, in which we meet the root of his possibility. And in doing this it will be necessary to pose the general problem of the knowledge of the soul in its radical dimensions, and especially to touch upon two primary questions: that of logic and that of the moral presuppositions of the knowledge of God. Thus theodicy, at the same time as it is a theory of God, is also a theory of the person.

The Proof for the Existence of God—Gratry starts from the fact that there are atheists; otherwise the demonstration would have no sense; atheism is the *fact* [*factum*] that obliges one at one time or another to tackle the subject of the demonstration that God exists; this is the starting point of every authentic attempt at a proof. It should not be forgotten that Saint Anselm presents his ontological argument faced with a concrete denial of the *fool* [*insensato*], according to the words of Psalm 13: 'The fool has said in his heart: there is no God' [*Dixit insipiens in corde suo: non est Deus*].

Gratry thinks, then, that if there is a true proof for the existence of God, this must be within the reach of everyone, since, according to the Gospel text, the divine light illuminates *every one* who comes into this world. That proof must be, then, the philosophical translation of some everyday and ordinary operation of the human mind, practiced habitually without knowing or recognising its scientific value. This operation, moreover, cannot be simply intellectual, but must also include all the essential dimensions of the human being, and it is nothing other than *prayer* [*oración*]. Gratry means concretely by prayer the movement of the soul which elevates itself from the finite to the infinite. From the finite and imperfect, from the visible world and from the limited and narrow soul itself, from the insufficient reality that he encounters, one raises oneself to the idea of something higher and more perfect, in which everything positive is raised to its extreme and all limit is suppressed. This movement, instinctive, sentimental and poetic, which is found in the everyday life of the simple, humble, and ignorant, is for Gratry the foundation of the scientific, philosophical proof of the existence of God.

What is the justification of that ordinary procedure? What scientific validity does that step from the finite to the infinite have, which the feelings of any ordinary person could verify? In what measure does it put us into real contact with the Divinity? It would be necessary to make a logical analysis of that operation of the human mind to discover in it a power of demonstration if, in fact, any such power exists. But the fact is that the logic we have does not serve us; it is incapable of interpreting that movement of the soul as a philosophical process, and for the same reason it is incapable of arriving at an effective demonstration of the existence of God. It is necessary, then, to address the problem of logic itself to discover, along with the known procedure of reason, another, equally legitimate, but even more important, that puts into relief the meaning of the elevation of the mind to God and shows its strictly scientific and probative value.

Syllogism and Dialectic—Gratry develops a very interesting theory of logic that will occupy us at greater length later. I need not enter into it here, since it is a question of setting forth the interpretation Gratry gives of the history of theodicy. I shall indicate only two or three main points, required to understand that exposition.

Reason has two procedures, says Gratry, of equal rigor and legitimacy, but one of them is well known and the other almost unheard of. Rather, people hold vague and erroneous ideas of it, which have served to hide its real meaning and scope. The first of these procedures is the *syllogism.* Its foundation is the principle of *identity,* on which it depends to bring about its deductions. This process, which proceeds always from identity to identity, is not capable of raising us to God, because there is no possibility of passing through identity from the finite to the infinite, from the world and human being to the Divinity. In general terms, it is a *deductive and analytic* procedure, not an *inventive* one.

But along with this there is another procedure, which has been called *dialectic* or *induction.* When one says 'induction', one is not to think of what Bacon called by that name, that is, the logical method that proceeds from a series of particular cases to a universal law that is simply *probable,* but rather of the aristotelian ἐπαγωγή. Induction so understood takes its point of departure from a finite given and proceeds, rigorously and with complete certitude, to the infinite, by means of the suppression of limits and the affirmation, without restriction, of perfections. This procedure is, as Aristotle already knew, what yields the major premises which the syllogism then uses to obtain its conclusions.

The theory of induction remains to be worked out; one finds in some philosophers, above all Plato and Aristotle, profound ideas about it, which show that they were aware of it; but they have fallen into oblivion and more attention has been paid to the syllogism or certain trivial applications of the inductive method. Gratry will have to present an ample and rigorous theory of dialectic or induction.

But how is it possible for the *principal procedure of reason* to have remained unknown for long centuries? This would be absurd. And, in fact, Gratry affirms that the philosophers have used dialectic precisely to arrive at God and that one can find their results in the entire history of philosophy. At times, without much realization of it; in some cases, even trying to expound syllogistically what is discovered by dialectic; in others, like Plato and the seventeenth century, in an explicit and thematic manner. The theory of induction, then, is lacking; but not its practice. And at certain times the attempt has been made to justify it scientifically, above all in the case of its application to mathematics in the infinitesimal calculus.

Dialectic, then, which is an inventive procedure, one of discovery, needs an impulse that not all possess. There are minds for whom the syllogism alone serves, and others that have a propensity always to return to it. The mind can have that dialectic force or lack it; the reason is that it requires a *moral spring*, a movement of the entire soul, that can be realized only in conditions of plenitude. This spring is what Gratry calls the *sense of the infinite* or *the divine sense* or also the attraction of the greatest good upon the soul. But not only is it possible for the soul to lack that impulse; the dialectical procedure can work inversely, backwards [*à rebours*], and be directed in a contrary sense, from the finite to nothingness, instead of arriving at the fullness of being, and so at God. Dialectic, inverted by a moral perversion, can suppress being and affirm limits to the infinite; thus, instead of achieving God, it achieves nothingness, and is converted into sophistry. Philosophy and sophistry, then, are born of the direction given in the depths of the soul to the principal procedure of reason.

Gratry must seek first in the history of philosophy the reality of the inductive procedure, to derive from it his own justification and theory.

Plato

I shall briefly analyse the interpretation Gratry gives of the theodicy of the great philosophers. Gratry studies the problem of God in the principal Greek philosophers, Plato and Aristotle, and then in the medievals—Saint Augustine, Saint Anselm, and Saint Thomas—to end with the thinkers of the seventeenth century; and among them, not only the great strictly philosophical figures, like Descartes, Malebranche and Leibniz, but also those who were even more theologians and religious thinkers, Pascal, Fénelon, Bossuet, Petavio and Thomassin. These are the major moments of that history, upon which he pauses in a thematic way. And, naturally, there are exclusions: Locke, an 'opaque mind', hardly metaphysical, and above all Spinoza; Spinoza Gratry does not consider as a philosopher, but rather as strictly a sophist, who disagrees with the great unanimous chorus of voices of the century to fall into pantheism, identified rigorously by Gratry with sophism.

But it is not a question of treating of the problem of God in *isolation*—which would be impossible—but of the fact that theodicy, as we have seen, rigorously implies the whole of philosophy. Gratry presents, then, a history of philosophy, following the thread of the problem of God, with developments found in other books, especially in the *Logique*. This history is, at the same time, that of the *principal procedure of reason,* that of induction or dialectic. And the necessary starting point is the platonic metaphysics which is essentially determined by dialectic and is the moment in which the human mind acquires consciousness of that basic procedure and rises with it, first, to the ideas, and then to that which brings those ideas into being: the Good, which for Gratry is nothing else than the God of Plato.

Plato is, at the same time, the first theorist of dialectic. After him, only at rare moments are there decisive additions to the knowledge of this movement; in general, he uses and even accurately describes the procedure, but without making it much of an express issue. The seventeenth century is the time when the theory of induction took some decisive steps to unite itself explicitly with the theme of the infinite and to apply itself amply to mathematics. As the end point of this history, Gratry will see himself obliged to pose formally the theoretical problem of induction, and this constitutes the central nucleus of his logic, which is founded, like his own metaphysics, upon the reality of earlier philosophy.

Platonic Dialectic—The movement of the soul which leads to the infinite, to the immutable, to the necessary, in brief, to God, departing from the finite, the variable and contingent, that is to say, from things, has two parts, two distinct elements which must be joined together: a moral element and an intellectual and logical one. The elevation to the knowledge of God is not accomplished by the mind alone, if that is understood in the abstract sense of pure knowledge, but by the *whole* soul.

What is the soul like, then, for Plato? There is a threefold life in the soul, or, if you will, three parts of the soul, according to the well-known platonic doctrine; and the principal one is the *demon* [δαίμων] which God has given everyone. Gratry skillfully puts this idea into relation with the Socratic demon, which is the *voice of God*, as Socrates shows in the *Apology*. This divine principle or genius lives in the most elevated region of ourselves, and, by its affinity with the heavenly, raises us from the earth and brings it about that one is rather a heavenly than an earthly plant. And in this highest point, where there is the *first origin of our soul* [ή πρώτη τῆς φυχῆς γένεσις], the *divine* [τὸ θεῖον] holds suspended from itself our head and our root [τὴν χεφαλὴν καὶ ῥίζαν ήμῶν], and in this way raises the whole human being and gives one an upright posture.[1] There is, then, a divine *contact* in human beings, and this contact is the root of the soul, in the rigorous sense that God holds us suspended from himself. Human beings, therefore, are inserted into God, are rooted in the Divinity. And this part of the soul, as Plato says in the first *Alcibiades*, is to the soul what the pupil is to the eye, the center, the luminous and divine, which opposes itself to the *atheistic* and gloomy part of the soul, that is to say, the part in which God does not reside.

Gratry calls this the *divine sense*, the first radical discovery of Plato, from which the whole moral and logical procedure of his dialectic will take its origin. There is, then, a divine given, according to Plato, and this is the principle of the soul, its very root, and at the same time source of its light, that which allows it to arrive at a vision of the Ideas and of God himself. It is the primary condition of the dialectical process. And Gratry, already from the first moment, puts this platonic doctrine into relation with that of the Christian mystics, with that of Pascal and Bossuet, including also the threefold life which, departing from a very different sensist position, Maine de Biran discovers at the beginning of the nineteenth century.

That divine contact, says Gratry, is the first cause of all movement of the spirit towards God; the second cause is the human power to suppress the obstacle to that impulse. To see God it is not enough to turn the reason alone to him, but it is necessary to *turn* the whole soul. Without a total *conversion* of the soul, from passing things to being itself, knowledge of the Ideas is not possible, and even less

1. *Timaeus*, 90.

knowledge of the Good. The obstacle that impedes that vision is double: desire [ἐπιθυμία] and pride [φιλονειχία]; one who is caught in that double slavery cannot raise himself to the higher region, and can have only *mortal thoughts.* This means that Plato begins with a situation of *disorder* in human beings. In spite of possessing divine contact and the faculty of elevating himself to contemplation of the ideas and of the very idea of the Good, one cannot do it without a previous moral force which dominates pride and sensuality and, this obstacle overcome, allows the sense of the divine and immortal to be developed. Therefore, to the first element, which is rootedness in God, who holds us suspended by our very roots, there is added, according to Plato, the human being's effort to remove all obstacles and to turn the mind—not alone, but with the whole soul—toward the divine. Only at this moment will the dialectical process properly so called be able to begin, the march of reason toward being, which includes essentially the previous steps as its *foundation.* Thus does Gratry interpret the moral aspect of the Platonic dialectic.

The Logical Process—For all research, a point of departure is needed. But there can be two very distinct types; in one case it is a question of a *principle of deduction,* from which derive new understandings, implicitly contained in the principle; in the other case the point of departure is rather a *point of support for reason,* from which the latter can raise itself to knowledge that altogether transcends it. In the first, the reason proceeds *syllogistically,* with a method founded in the principle of *identity;* in the second it raises itself *dialectically,* in virtue of the principle of *transcendence,* to something that exceeds the point of departure. This last is the procedure of platonic logic, which Gratry considers the principal procedure of reason.

The starting point is always the spectacle of nature, that is to say, *things,* limited, changing and perishing. Instead of remaining in simple identity and proceeding deductively, then, from one thing to another, Plato *remembers* God; that is to say, goes out from things to discover them; this is the sense of the Platonic *reminiscence* or *anamnesis.* Things, then, allow us to arrive at God; but not by his identity with them, naturally, but by his likeness, and even more, by his *contrast.* The sight of things, their mixture of being and non-being, their reality and their limitation, makes us think of the ideas. The likeness and the contrast *together* are what stimulate the intelligence and raise it to the ideas, first, and then to the Good itself.

The syllogism [συλλογισμός] has as principle [ἀρχή] its point of departure [ὑπόθεσις]; dialectic, on the other hand, goes from the point of departure to a principle which is not *assumed* or contained in it [ἐπ' ἀρχὴν ἀνυπόθετον ἐξ ὑποθέσεως ἰοῦσα]. According to Plato, the first method is proper to geometry, and the second to philosophy. But Gratry will find the most obvious proof of the legitimacy of the second procedure in its rigorous application to mathematics, in the seventeenth century, in the discovery of the infinitesimal calculus. Dialectic, *supported* simply by things and transcending them, arrives at an absolute principle, and from it alone it descends again to things already contained in that principle already possessed. To *deductive* or *immanent* logic, which does not go beyond its assumptions, Plato opposes an *inductive, inventive,* or *transcendental* logic, which arrives at an effective view of being and of the intelligible world.

The Degrees of Knowledge—Plato distinguishes two degrees of being, and thus, two degrees of knowing: the visible or sensible [ὁρατόν] and the intelligible [νοητόν]. We arrive at the visible by the senses; it is the world of things, multiple, variable, passing, which do not have true being. In the myth of the cave, told in the *Republic,* these things correspond to the shadows things cast upon the walls of the cave illumined by the light of the fire. This is always the necessary point of departure; Plato insists strictly[2] on this, that knowledge can begin through sensation alone. But it is only a beginning, for the sake of elevating itself to true being, to the ideas, to the intelligible world. And in this, in turn, there are two degrees that correspond to the two modes of knowing: διάνοια and νόησις. The διάνοια is discursive thought, and it follows the syllogistic procedure, which traces the roots of its identity to the necessary and immutable truths, but without referring them to their *principle.* The νόησις leads to ἐπιστήμη, to knowledge in the strict sense, by means of which the mind contemplates *that which illuminates being and truth.* In this intelligible world, which corresponds to the free and real world in the myth of the cave, there are two regions or, even better, various successive steps: first the shadows are seen; then the images of things in the water; afterwards the things themselves, first at night, by the reflected light of the moon, and, finally, in full sunlight. Shadows and reflections correspond to the first degree of knowledge of the intelligible, and true things to the second degree of knowledge.

2. *Phaedo*, 75.

But this is not all. Something more is still needed: the *sun* itself. The final step of the vision of the free human being, escaped from the cave, after having overcome the pain that the unaccustomed presence of light produces, and having made a painful *effort* [γυμνασία] to run through the various aforementioned steps, is the direct contemplation of the sun in itself, not in images and reflections. Above that which being and truth illumine, stands that which illumines being and light themselves. Above all ideas stands that which brings them into being. When, by dialectic, one knows the truths of science, which are no more than *divine phantasms and shadows of that which is* [φαντάσματα θεῖα καὶ σκιὰς τῶν ὄντων], one can think that these shadows and images are produced by a floodlight, by a sun that brings them into being. Thus he can arrive at knowledge of the Good itself, difficult to see, but accessible to the mind that achieves all the force needed and arrives at the *term of the dialectic.* Gratry insists at length upon the importance of this distinction between the indirect vision, by means of shadows, reflections, phantasms or images, and the direct vision of the light itself. Gratry notes in speaking of this that it is 'the most important point of all philosophy'. We shall soon see, in fact, its consequences. In the judgment of Father Gratry, Plato did not see that distinction, which is found in its fullness only in the Christian thinkers, clearly enough. The most important thing is that Plato realises that the knowledge one possesses naturally is only an image of God, but not the vision itself. Geometry, for example, is *the dream of being, not its waking vision.* But human beings seek and must seek, according to Plato, to elevate themselves and not be detained until they arrive at the vision of being, at the knowledge of the Good, or the Divinity.

God and the Good—Plato raises himself to God, in the *Laws*, X, by means of a dialectic process, seeking the likeness and contrast with the finite. If in us there is some virtue, God has all virtue; if we have some power, God can do all; if we have goodness and evil, God has no evil and all good. The procedure consists, then, in affirming to infinity the positive qualities and suppressing the limits and the negative. In this way one arrives at the infinite and supreme good. This procedure, Gratry says, is the ordinary everyday dialectic of common sense, of poetry and speech; but in Plato there is also a scientific process.

And the God at whom Plato arrives is absolute, living, intelligible and perfect, in whom are all the Ideas, *eternal substance* [ἀΐδιος οὐσία], who has not been nor will be, but who *is*; thus God who always is. This God, maker of all beings, is the supreme Good; he is—Gratry says—the true God.

Philosophy and Sophistry—Already in the first stage of the history of theodicy, in Plato, Gratry finds posed the problem of sophistry. In the first moment in which dialectic appears, the procedure of reason which raises it to being, the contrary movement arises, which goes toward nothingness. Sophistry, Plato and Aristotle say, turns upon nonbeing, and the sophist himself consists in not being. The philosopher, by means of a great effort, by a pruning of the sensual appetites and a purification, manages to *turn* the whole soul toward the truth and to know the Ideas; and at the end of the process, know the sun itself which illuminates them, being itself, God. The sophist, on the other hand, goes in the opposite direction, affirms the negative and the limits, and, instead of arriving at being, arrives at nonbeing. But Gratry observes that the procedure is *the same,* the principal procedure of reason, the dialectic, but *inverted* and directed in the opposite sense. The duty of reason is to know God through visible things, according to the phrase of Saint Paul, to the point that one is *inexcusable* who does not do this. But this can be achieved only by sane and free reason; there is a perverse and enslaved reason, that chooses nonbeing in its very roots and inverts the dialectical procedure, destroying itself in the process: this is sophistry.

Plato, then, utilizes dialectic amply. He knows the divine contact in the depths of the soul, the moral obstacle proceeding from the state of disorder in which one finds oneself, the need to remove it by an effort of the whole soul, to *turn it back* toward being; he knows also the stages of knowledge of the intelligible world, and its *end* in the vision of the idea of the Good. Despite some obscurities, it seems to Gratry inadmissible to think that Plato does not speak of an effective knowledge of God; he believes that in any case he knows God in fact, and his dialectical procedure, rightly used, raises him to God.

But Plato is, essentially, a beginning; one finds in him in germ almost all the elements that will have to develop later, first in Saint Augustine, then in the seventeenth century. Reason, from the moment in which it begins to function dialectically, arrives at the knowledge—certainly immature—of God. The rest of the history of philosophy will be the maturation of that first knowledge.

Aristotle

Syllogism and Induction—Gratry affirms the fundamental accord between Plato and Aristotle. This means agreement in regard to results; the difference between them lies in the method, or at least—Gratry underlines—in the method of exposition.

We have seen how Plato uses the dialectical procedure; Aristotle is not ignorant of it, far from it, and he treats it brilliantly under the name of *induction* [ἐπαγωγή], as we shall see in another place. Aristotle says that the syllogism is the method of demonstration, but that induction provides the majors of these syllogisms. In other words, the syllogism deduces consequences, demonstrates truths, that is to say, *from* principles that are primary and, as such, indemonstrable. Those principles are not attained through the syllogistic method, but through induction. And the point of departure of induction is an experience [ἐμπειρία]. And to this Aristotle adds a profound theory of induction, to which Gratry will need to have recourse when he wishes to consider it metaphysically, to oppose it to the trivial procedure usually called by this name and used in the positive sciences. Aristotle, then, knows the two procedures of reason and clearly delineates their respective roles.

But Aristotle, Gratry says, always forces himself to stick to the deductive method, even denying the legitimacy of the platonic procedure, at times. Gratry supposes that Aristotle, for twenty years a disciple of Plato, knew the use of the dialectic and the results at which it arrived, but then intended to use the syllogism to expound those results, which in reality could never have been obtained by deduction. Gratry compares him with Lagrange, who tried to reproduce the discoveries of Leibniz, obtained through the infinitesimal calculus, algebraically, without realizing that he was at times forcing the proofs, to arrive by means of enormous quantities of equations, not always legitimate, at the truths Leibniz obtained with supreme simplicity, nor, above all, that it might perhaps be possible to reproduce painfully the leibnizian results, once known, but that it was impossible to discover them algebraically. In the same way, Gratry says, by continuous or identical reasoning, by the syllogism, one can never get from the finite to the infinite, from things to God.

Gratry expounds the aristotelian proof of the existence of God, deduced from the fact of movement, as it is found in the *Summa Contra Gentiles*, Book I, chapter 3, of Saint Thomas. There one will find an intricate series of reasonings, complicated and obscure, the truth of which does not appear evident, and about which one does not dare to make a firm decision. The point of departure is a fact of experience: *there is movement*; the conclusion which Aristotle reaches is this: *therefore, there must be a first immovable mover, whom we call God.* Between the one proposition and the other are abysses that syllogisms cannot fill; in other words, one cannot pass from one to the other by the way of identity. One does not go from the variable to the immutable, from the imperfect to the perfect, from the finite to the infinite, syllogistically. Immobility cannot be *deduced* from movement. Aristotle strives to prove it syllogistically, but he bases his reasoning upon two major premises that cannot evidently be obtained syllogistically. In the first place, that everything that is moved is moved by something else, that is, that it is not moved by itself; in the second, that there cannot be an infinite series of [moved—Translator] movers, and, therefore, there must be a first mover. Aristotle attempts this proof, without achieving sufficient evidence. But Gratry affirms that, in any case, those syllogisms are ineffective; that it is not they that discover the great truth they contain, but that it is arrived at by the other procedure of reason: by induction or dialectic. According to Gratry, Aristotle used this latter in his meditation, and through it came to his knowledge of God; but then he was inclined to expound his results didactically in syllogistic form, apparently more accessible and convincing. We must see what are the effective discoveries of Aristotle, according to Gratry.

The God of Aristotle—There are, says Aristotle in the twelfth book of his *Metaphysics,* three substances, two natural and one immobile. Nature [φύσις] for Aristotle is the principle of movement [ἀρχή τῆς κινήσεως]; the immobile substance, which is eternal, is not natural, and it remains outside the physical; and this substance is pure actuality, with no mixture of potentiality: it is *pure act.* And this substance is *principle,* because one cannot begin with a possibility: according to the whole of aristotelian metaphysics, act is prior to potency, which is the same as claiming, Gratry says, that there is no effect without a cause. For this reason God is never an *effect* [effectum], an actualized reality or *entelechy,* strictly speaking, but *enérgeia*, pure act.

In God all is real, all is actual. There is no mixture, as in things, of possibility and reality, of virtuality and actuality; there is not in him anything that could come to be, but all already *is*; he is not in any way *effect* [*effectum*], but *perfect* [*perfectum*]. For this reason there is not in God anything accidental, but all is essential; his being is his essence, and therefore is necessary; his knowledge, his will, his beatitude are his essence. God is an eternal and perfect living being, because in him continuous and eternal life is given, and that life is God. This is the *first unmoved mover.*

Unmoved, we already see why he is this. As he contains in himself no potentiality nor matter, he can have nothing in himself that can be moved, that is to say, that passes from potentiality to act. But how is he mover? How does he move, being himself immobile? God moves without being moved, as the object of love and of desire. The desirable and the intelligible, says Aristotle, move without being moved. God moves as the loved. That is to say, it is a question of an attraction; God is the *end* [*fin*], the τέλος of all beings. God is the principle, and Aristotle says of him: 'Upon this principle depend the heavens and nature'. Gratry puts this affirmation into relationship with the platonic one according to which the divine holds us suspended by the roots; there is a fundamental identity in Plato and Aristotle; the roots and at the same time the end of all things are in God. In Plato, the contemplation of things raises us to the realm of ideas, and this in turn to that of the Good, to the one who brings the ideas into being, the Divinity; in Aristotle, the things themselves tend toward God. In Plato, love, ἔρως, is the prime mover of philosophy; one raises oneself through an erotic impulse to the vision of the higher world, to the intelligible and to the Divinity itself; in aristotelian metaphysics this reappears, in an even more radical mode: God is at once the desirable and the intelligible [ὀρεκτὸν καὶ νοητόν], and functions concretely as the *beloved* [ἐρώμενον]. And so it is that the world depends upon God, who is equally the Good itself, the fullness of being, without mixture of any potentiality. This is what *pure act* means.

The Method—By what procedure does Aristotle arrive at this knowledge of God? Man, says Aristotle, has a passing happiness; God has it eternally; this human happiness consists in staying awake, in thinking, in sum, in living; and in God this happens in an absolute way and without limit: there is nothing in him asleep nor implicit, but all is actual, there is nothing that is *still* not being or is not *already* being, but all always *is*; if a human being possesses wisdom in any instant, God alone has it in an absolute and full manner; his thought does not momentarily surmise the intelligible, but he possesses it totally, since the same God is the intelligible; his activity, his 'eternal and perfect' life—which is not movement, which latter, in the aristotelian sense, supposes composition of potentiality and act—is the most adequate *theoría*, thought thinking itself: νόησις νοήσεως.

Aristotle, then, raises himself to God by means of that which he finds in things and, above all, in himself. But he needs to free himself of all limitation and raise himself to the absolute. He affirms in the infinite—Gratry says—the finite qualities that we find in ourselves. And Gratry recalls the leibnizian principle: 'The perfections of God are those of our souls, without the limits found in them.' This is the dialectical procedure, not the syllogism. And this method culminates, with a maturity that Plato himself did not achieve, in the ontological notion of the *pure act.* All things are composed of matter and form, of potency and act; everything grows, develops, has possibilities not realized, tends to a higher unattainable limit. And from here, from this mixture of reality and limitation, suppressing the latter and raising the former to the extreme, Aristotle raises himself to God, to a being who is actually all that is, who is the sole reality, who is immobile and eternal. And, in spite of the difficulty for the Greek mind of thinking the infinite in any other way than as simple indetermination, he uses this attribute in a positive sense in referring it to God: 'He moves an infinite time', he says, 'and nothing finite has infinite force'. (*Metaphysics* XII, 7).

Aristotle passes, then, from things to God, not by way of identity, syllogistically, but dialectically or inductively: raising himself from the contemplation of a limited reality to the absolute of the Divinity. Act is anterior to potentiality, because potentiality is always such through a certain actuality; *enérgeia* is already present in *dynamis*, because the *dynamis* is the possibility *of something,* that is, of something *in act.* Thus every potency raises us to an act, which is precisely its principle, that which gives it its potential being. But it is necessary to note the manner of the presence of *enérgeia* in *dynamis*; it is not that something is *included* in it, but rather the contrary, *excluded.* Put more explicitly, we cannot find the act in the being in potency by *that which it is,* but by *that which it is not,* which means, by that which it is not *yet*; in the being in potency, actuality is *negated,* which is not equivalent to a simple *non being.* The boy *is not* a man, and also *is not* a tree; but he is not those two things in two very distinct ways: he simply *lacks* the being of a tree, while that of a man is negated in the boy as a *not yet;* concretely, the act is present in the being in potency as *privation,* as στέρησις. Thus, in the being in potency, understood as such, there is a *lack* of the actual reality; but not of just any actuality, but of a determined one, that is, of that for which it is the potency. That is to say, the limited and deficient realization of the being in potency, in manifesting itself as *possibility of,* as a *privation of,* sends us back to the actual reality which it demands, to that which confers its being upon it. The being in potency *leads* us to think of the actual being, but not because this is contained in the former, but rather because it is deprived of it; not by way of identity or deduction, but by way of transcendence, raising us to something that exceeds the concrete thing on which we lean. This is the meaning of the aristotelian ἐπαγωγή.

Since every finite and concrete substance, then, even those we understand as *actual*—a stone, a dog, a man—is composed of potency and act, is not altogether real, it sends us back always to the being which is fully, without mixture of possibility, to pure act. For this reason aristotelian metaphysics, which is the science of being as such, that is, of things in so far as they *are* [τὸ ὄν ᾗ ὄν] turns out to be identical, in virtue of the analogy of being, with the science of substance [περὶ τῆς οὐσίας], given that substance is the primary sense of being, that which is at the base of all the rest; but at the same time this science, in studying substance, turns back to the substance which is fully, totally in act, to God, and culminates in a theological science [θεολογικὴ ἐπιστήμη.]

This is the ultimate meaning of the interpretation Gratry makes of aristotelian theodicy, although he does not express in so explicit a manner the relation of potency to act. With it he shows the meaning of the ontology of Aristotle, with a profundity unknown in his time, and discovers in it the use of the principal procedure of reason. But a question would have to be posed about this aristotelian method of induction: from what concrete reality does Aristotle begin in raising himself to God? Does it make any difference whether he takes one or the other? And, above all, in what dimension is it necessary to take it? These questions remain open in philosophy; we shall see what sort of replies have been attempted, and in what measure they are insufficient. And we shall also see how in this question are involved the gravest philosophical issues in a sense that has scarcely been generally suspected.

The noûs—To complete his exposition of aristotelian theodicy, Gratry uses the most obscure and important chapter 5 of the *De Anima*, Book III, referring to the distinction between the passive and the agent intellect. Aristotle distinguishes, in fact, between that which is in potency, and that which, already in act, produces the passage from potency to act. In the soul is found this difference, and so there is a passive intellect—that is called νοῦς παθητικός—, which can come to be all things, and the agent intellect—νοῦς ποιητικός—capable of producing all. And of this agent intellect Aristotle says that it is *like the light;* this also makes colors actual from those that were only such in potency. And the agent intellect is eternal, immortal, and without it, which is what makes one think, there could be no thought.

This *noûs* is distinct from the soul and is not to be confused with any of its operations, but rather, these are possible because the *noûs* gives life to human beings; it is a substance that comes upon people from outside, or, as Aristotle says expressively, θύραθεν, through open windows; it is divine, separable from the soul, 'as the eternal from the perishable', and is like a light that animals lack and that does not seem to be equally present in all men.

For Gratry, this is the distinction between the *illuminating* [*lumen illuminans*] and the *illuminated light* [*lumen illuminatum*]. The light in us would be one thing and the divine light in itself, another. That *noûs* eternal and divine would signify the term of the intellectual process, of which Plato was already speaking, in that the intelligible is seen *touching it* and making it *one thing with itself;* that is, to see the intelligible as it sees itself. But this, which is precisely what God does, continuously and essentially, is given to man only in rare moments, and that is happiness. Our sight, before this degree of light, is blurred like the eyes of the owl before the sun; and the soul, in the measure in which it sees it, is *not entirely natural*: οὐδὲ γὰρ πᾶσα φυχὴ φύσις. To this point does the theodicy of Aristotle reach.

Saint Augustine

Plato and Saint Augustine—The most profound change the history of philosophy manifests is that produced by the passage from Greece to Christianity, from the ancient to the modern world. The appearance upon the philosophical field of the idea of the Christian God and of the concept of creation, which alters essentially the relation of God with the world and, thus, the meaning of the two, and affects the problem of being itself, is an event that divides into two stages the history of philosophy. But it is well to note that the latter does not lose its unity; the Christian philosophers are careful to make clear their descent from the Greeks, and they situate themselves in the tradition that proceeds from them. Saint Augustine, concretely, in whom Christian metaphysical speculation begins in a mature way, believes that throughout the centuries a true philosophy has come to be established: *una verissimae philosophiae disciplina.*

Apart from revelation, Saint Augustine feels himself inserted into a purely human philosophical tradition, which is that of the natural light of reason, and, above all, that philosophy is the platonic. Saint Augustine tries to take the results of platonism and make them live a higher life, which is found in the soul of the Christian. For this reason Gratry says, in summing up his comparison of the two philosophers, that everything *said* by Plato *lives* in Saint Augustine: *quidquid a Platone dicitur vivit it* [*sic*] *Augustino.*

Plato distinguishes two steps in the vision of the intelligible world: the vision of the necessary and eternal truths, of the *divine phantasms,* of the *shadows of that which is*, and, on the other hand, the vision of God himself. To this *vision,* however, Plato does not attain. From the contemplation of the shadows he infers or concludes, conjectures the existence of the sun and of its beauty; but he does not attain to seeing it in itself, such as it is. In the natural state of the soul, this can be only the *light* of the soul, diffused by itself and by things, but not the sun itself. There is needed a conversion or rebirth, which cannot proceed from man alone, but must be given him by God himself. After this supernatural rebirth one can see God, and this vision begins, in this life, with *faith*, intention of vision or vision begun, as Bossuet and Saint Thomas call it.

Gratry, as we have seen, considers Plato and Saint Augustine as the same man, in two stages of his life; in other words: he understands Plato *from* Saint Augustine, who represents actually what in Plato was only a tendency or possibility. Saint Augustine is the one who has fully realized the moral purification Plato considered to be the necessary condition for raising oneself to God. The soul of Saint Augustine is—Gratry says—that of Plato, 'matured by the sun of God'.

The Interior Man—Saint Augustine introduces a capital modification into the dialectical process. In Plato, things were the point of departure, the world of bodies; the soul was little known by the Greeks, and considered only in a secondary manner. Saint Augustine, on the other hand, starts out from bodies *and from the soul,* above all from the soul; he has a knowledge of it that the ancient mind could never attain; he knows it not as one more thing, but he knows it *intimately*. Saint Augustine discovers the *interior man*, and this becomes, effectively, his point of support; from it, which already represents a position far superior to bodies, he will elevate himself to God. It is the course of Christian mysticism: 'From exterior things to the interior; from the interior to the higher' [*Ab exterioribus ad interiora; ab interioribus ad superiora*].

For this reason Saint Augustine does not expound the dialectic procedure didactically, but presents it in action: he narrates his life. And thus the journey of the mind to God is converted into a *confession*. Saint Augustine, leaving aside the lower stages of sensuality, considers the soul as something divided, dispersed, ill. The soul swells with pride, and this is the same as going forth from itself, as becoming empty and being each time less. To go to the exterior is the same as throwing out one's inmost parts, [intima projicere] and this signifies 'distancing oneself from God' [*longe a se facere Deum*]. And, conversely, to approach God is to enter into oneself: 'truth lives in the interior man' [*in interiori homine habitat veritas*]. Things are mutable, passing, insufficient; they take us to God, and in him alone do they remain, preserved, and thus do not move us: 'they shall stand with thee, and they shall remain forever as long as God is and remains' [*stabunt tecum, et permanebunt ad semper stantem ac permanentem Deum*]

Saint Augustine describes (*Confessions*, VII, Chapter 17) the steps in this elevation. First he goes from bodies to the soul—which perceives through them ('from bodies to the soul sensing through the body') [*a corporibus ad sentiantem per corpus animam*]; from here to its interior force [*ad ejus interiorem vim*], to which the senses announce exterior things; and here, Saint Augustine notes, the animal ends. From this internal power of the 'soul he rises to reason' [*ad ratiocinantem potentiam*], which is the judge of the senses. But reason, raising itself by its intelligence, abandons the dream of custom and the tumult of the phantasms, to encounter the light that makes it luminous, and then proclaims without any doubt [*sine ulla dubitatione*] that the immutable is preferable to that which changes, and this supposes already a certain knowledge of the immutable. Thus, by the contemplation of created things and through them, the soul raises itself to the comprehension of the invisible, according to the word of Saint Paul (Rom 1:20): 'Ever since the creation of the world his invisible nature has been clearly perceived in the things that have been made' [*Invisibilia enim ipsius a creatura mundi, per ea quae facta sunt intellecta conspiciuntur*]. But the soul can maintain itself in this state for only an instant, and it falls back on its own weakness, without taking with it anything more than an amorous memory and as it were a scent of the divine food not tasted. This is the way that leads to God, not directly from corporeal things, but from the interior of man.

The Augustinian Dialectic—Saint Augustine employs the same platonic term, 'dialectic', to designate the procedure by means of which one elevates himself to God; this process consists, not in not seeing the sensible world and prescinding from it, but in seeking in it the traces of reason [*vestigia rationis in sensibus*]. But this is not enough; the reason does not content itself with knowing itself, but tries to elevate itself to contemplation of divine things; but, says Saint Augustine, so as not to fall from the height, it seeks rungs or steps to support itself [*quaesivit gradus*]; it wishes to see something that without the senses it cannot achieve; but, on the other hand, the senses obstruct it; to overcome this difficulty 'the soul turns its regard a little' [*paulum aciem torsit*] toward sensible things. That is to say, it cannot leave off looking at the sensible, because from it alone can one elevate oneself to the divine; but if one looks too much, exclusively, one remains in it and does not go higher; one must look, but little, turning the glance only a little. It is enough, says Gratry, to make comparison, but sufficiently little to be able to see the other term of the comparison also. Things have to be seen, then, but not for themselves nor for vain curiosity, but as steps or rungs to elevate oneself to the immutable and immortal.

The soul thus knows the immutable truths, the laws, and also numbers, figures, geometry, astronomy. But all this is still not the knowledge of God; the eternal truths are immutable and absolutely true, but are not God; their knowledge does not give me the happiness the divine vision would give me. Between God and those real specters [*spectamina*] there is the same difference as between heaven and earth. They are truths of absolute certitude, they are intelligible, like God, but they are so only because *another sun* illuminates them.

Saint Augustine distinguishes, thus, two steps in the *intelligible* world: that of the truths illuminated and that of the light that illuminates them; that of the things lighted by the sun and that of the sun itself.

Gratry observes that so far Saint Augustine coincides with Plato, although he expresses himself with more precision and rigor. In Plato it appears at times that the method consists in departing from the sensible, and it is not easy to see what is the point of support for the reason in its dialectic procedure; it is not clear that it treats of the sensible world, nor of the soul; Saint Augustine, by contrast, indicates clearly the need of things 'so as not to fall from the height', of points of support or *steps*, which one must look at soberly without pausing over them, to see their likeness to and difference from the divine, of which they are images. To Saint Augustine Aristotle could not make the objection that he leads only to an abstract unity; as Aristotle requires for metaphysics. Saint Augustine starts from physical things in order to lift himself to that which stands above them. But there is still an even more important point, Gratry says, in which Saint Augustine radically rises above Plato.

The Divine Sense—What is it that impels man to seek that sun that illuminates the eternal truths? According to Plato, the divine part of our soul, its *root*, by which God touches us and holds us suspended; this gift is that which man can exercise and develop, or else drown it by concupiscence and pride. Saint Augustine makes even more precise that presence of God in the soul: God is in the innermost part of the heart and makes the soul live; thus the withdrawal from God is equivalent to casting forth one's innermost parts [*intima projicere id est longe a se facere Deum*], constantly becoming 'more and more vitiated and diminished' [*inanescere, minus minusque esse*].

But this is not all. There is an intimate contact with God in the depth of the soul; but is it known? Besides the divine contact, is there a *divine sense*? Saint Augustine affirms it. The soul senses the attraction of the sovereign good by a sort of hidden memory [*memoria oculta*]; there is a secret trace [*secreto vestigio*] of the unity which is in us, an *impressed notion* of God: I know not what *interior sense* ('I know not by what interior consciousness God must be sought') [*interior nescio quae conscientia quaerendum Deum*]. Through it, in the midst of time, people seek eternity. If one were not suspended from God and had not in addition reminiscence of him, one would not search for him. But, moved by the divine sense, one sees in each thing, on the one hand, something that imitates God, of whom it is the image; and, on the other, something that differs. Similarity and contrast, then, are the motors of the dialectic.

But not all rise to God by the contemplation of the world. That is because many are subjected to it and cannot interrogate it; only souls not subjected to the world can dominate and judge it, and use it as a ladder to rise above it. The soul raises itself by means of its natural reason to the eternal truths, and then realizes that there is a light that produces these shadows and seeks it. But here, Gratry says, all philosophy pauses; the philosophers who have sought to contemplate the source itself of the light have erred and have abandoned the true way. Here begins another order of things, another world, which Christianity calls *supernatural*; to enter into it a radical rebirth is needed, which permits the entire soul to turn to the origin of the light itself; a rebirth, Gratry says, that follows the death Socrates and Plato refer to when they say 'to philosophise is to learn to die'.

The divine sense is a vague attraction of the desirable and the intelligible to which the soul must respond. The imperfect responses raise us to the earlier point; but the rebirth of which we speak is the work of God, it is a response that God provokes in us. The natural faculties of man, the *depth of his being*, the *intelligence* and the *will*, unite him to the eternal being, to the light of God and to his will, by means of *faith*, *hope*, and *charity*. Without these three things, says Saint Augustine, 'no soul can be healed so as to see God' [*sine tribus istis anima nulla sanatur, ut possit Deum suum videre*]. With them one arrives at the term of the vision; it is the reason coming to its term [*ratio perveniens ad finem sum*], and of it Saint Augustine says that it is 'perfect virtue' [*perfecta virtus*]. It is then that one has a living and real knowledge of God which Saint Augustine calls 'experiential knowledge of God' [*experimentalis Dei notitia*]. But this knowledge is not purely human; it is not simply revelation, it is effective human science, but illuminated by a divine science, which does not destroy but augments it. This is the distinction of the two regions of the intelligible; it is one thing to see God reflected, as in a mirror, and another thing to see him in himself. The latter supposes an intervention by God, and it is possible only when the human reason is raised to the supernatural. We shall have to return to this question in greater detail later.

The Infinite—Gratry notes that with Saint Augustine clarity is reached about one of the most important points of philosophy: the idea of the infinite. The Greek mind is incapable of comprehending the infinite other than as indeterminate; even in the moments in which Plato and Aristotle appear to understand it in a positive mode, there is often confusion. The infinite [ἄπειρον] is the indefinite, that which does not have a true being, and is joined to the evil and imperfect. Saint Augustine, on the other hand, understands the infinite in potency, not in indetermination. God is not indefinite, but entirely the contrary; one cannot place limits upon him. And this explains, says Gratry, two things: the distance of God from things and the meaning of creation.

Plato tended to deny being to things; Saint Augustine, on the other hand, affirms their being and calls them *the things that are less.* Things are, because they have a finite being created by God; but, *compared with God*, they are not. 'My substance is as nothing before you', [*Substantia mea tanquam nihilam ante te*] declares Psalm 38. Gratry seeks a mathematical meaning for this truth and notes that a finite quantity added to infinity does not increase it, and that a finite quantity divided by the infinite tends to zero:

$$\infty + \mathrm{A} = \infty; \frac{\mathrm{A}}{\infty} = 0.$$

In the same way it is certain that from nothing nothing comes, that is, if there is not an infinite power; this alone can produce from nothing. Zero multiplied by any finite quantity, however great, is always zero; but multiplied by the infinite it gives any quantity. Thus the being 'created from nothing' [*ens creatum a nihilo*] supposes an infinite creative power, from which it receives its finite being.

But to say that God has created the world from nothing means that it has been produced by the infinite action of God, but that it does not go forth from its own nature, but from nothing; that the world and God are of distinct natures, and that God has created the world freely, because he loved it. Saint Augustine says: 'When it is said that God made what is made from nothing, nothing else is said but that it is not made from itself' [*Cum dicitur Deus de nihilo fecisse quae fecit, non dicit aliud, nisi quia de se ipso non fecit*]. And in another place: 'This is what it is for any nature to be made from nothing, that the nature not be God' [*Hoc est quique naturae de nihilo factum esse, quod ut naturam Dei non esse*]. And finally: 'When it is said: God made from nothing, it means nothing other than: it was not whence it was made, and yet because he willed it he made it' [*Cum dicitur: Deus ex nihilo fecit, nihil aliud dicitur, nisi non erat unde faceret, et tamen quia voluit fecit*].

Saint Augustine eliminates, then, rigorously, all possible pantheism. God and the world are distinct in nature; the creation is free. This strict position emanates from the precise distinction of the finite from the infinite. God is infinite; the world is finite, but it is. The world is not annulled, by being converted into a simple manifestation of God, the unique reality, nor is it made infinite in any sense, divinized. By either of these ways one ends up in pantheism. Gratry discards it with the greatest energy, in virtue precisely of his capital idea about the infinite: *infinite being*, he says, *is infinite in every sense; finite being is finite in every sense.* This eliminates all partial identification of the world with God.

Saint Anselm

The Ontological Argument—Gratry centers his interpretation of Saint Anselm upon the ontological argument to demonstrate the existence of God, which the archbishop of Canterbury expounds in the first chapters of the *Proslogion*. From there, he goes on to recognise that the ontological proof is not a piece of reasoning, or, at least, it is not reasoning alone; it is, he says, like the intersection of ontology, psychology, and logic, and, as a reasoning process, it is a process of induction.

The point of departure is a sense of God; the soul experiences his attraction; but it has only an implicit vision; one feels God as something *lost*, as a radical *privation:* 'I have never seen you' [*numquam te vidi*] says Saint Anselm, 'Lord my God, I do not know your face' [*domine Deus meus, non novi faciem tuam*]. And then: 'I have been made to see you, and I have not yet done it, because I have been made' [*Ad te videndum factus sum, et nondum feci, propter quod factus sum*]. It is a privation that affects the very being of man, made to see God and who has never yet done it; it is a situation of *blindness*, of privation of vision, in which the mind feels confusedly what is everywhere, but cannot see it. Why? There is an obstacle to vision, a moral obstacle, which is sin, that obscures the sight; the image of God is obfuscated by the smoke of sins [*offuscata fumo peccatorum*], and sin, before it is even obscuring, is *fall*; God hides his face from a person, and the person, without light, falls; where? into himself: 'I was stretching toward God and I stumbled into myself' [*tendebam in Deum, et offendi in me ipsum*]. Thus the starting point for Saint Anselm is strictly *religious*, it is the same as *prayer*. The whole of Chapter I of the *Proslogion* is essential, even though it has nearly always been unnoticed, including in Barth's book[3]—in other respects also most inadequate—; this chapter is a call to God; thus, it supposes that one has not attained him, but that one nevertheless has some sense of him. 'I believe that I may understand' [*Credo ut intelligam*]; this is the attitude of Saint Anselm; more precisely: 'faith seeking understanding' [*fides quaerens intellectum*]. When the faith stops being lazy and dead (idle faith) [*otiosa fides*], and by means of love or *dilectio* becomes living and active (operative faith) [*operosa fides*], then it tries to know God in whom it believes, and it is a question of an effective *knowledge*. We have then in the first place, a vague and confused sense of God; in the second place, the moral *obstacle* of sin, the removal of which is the necessary condition for knowing God; and in the third place, the moral *spring*, which is love, *dilectio*, which heals the soul and raises it to God. Saint Augustine had already said: 'Truth is not entered into except through charity', [*Non intratur in veritatem nisi per caritatem*], although probably with reference to the supernatural order, and so to the truth of the *catholic religion*, and finally also to the triune God, not to God the Creator alone; for Saint Anselm there is equally necessary a loving impulse to God, as mover of the dialectic that brings us to know him. What now is the process of the faith that seeks understanding?

Gratry notes that the obstacle is twofold; not only the moral evil of sin, but also the limitation of the infinite; there is needed, he says, a sacrifice of evil as obstacle and a second sacrifice of humility, the vision and the sentiment of the narrow limitations of finite nature. Then, the mind understands that it cannot conceive a limited good without conceiving a greater, and another still greater, and so it arrives at an end that it reaches in one sole stroke: the idea of a being such that one cannot think a greater: 'that than which a greater cannot be thought' [*id quo maius cogitari nequit*]. And the mind then recognizes the existence of this being. There is, however, Gratry says, a first moment in which setting out from the desire or the vision of limited goods, one conceives the *name* and the *formula* of the being

3. Karl Barth: *Anselms Beweis de Existenz Gottes*, 1931.

than which one cannot think a greater, that is to say, of Being; and a second moment in which one recognises immediately the real and actual existence of this Being, given that one cannot say: *Being is not.*

At this idea of the supreme Good he arrives by means of the vision of limited goods mounting from lesser goods to greater [*de minoribus bonis ad majora conscendendo*]; from the idea of a good such that one can think a greater, he passes to that of a good such that one could not conceive of a greater; from *finite* goods he comes to the idea of the *infinite* good. Every lesser good, as good, says Saint Anselm, is like the greater. Thus there is a point of support from which [*unde*] to raise oneself to the infinite. There is, then, a real basis for the argument, which is the vision of finite things, although neither Leibniz nor Kant, Gratry says, saw this.

Why, then, does the *idea* of the infinite imply its real and actual existence? This is, says Father Gratry, the core of the argument. And he explains it by showing the significance of the idea. The modern pantheists, he says, believe that the idea is the object; those who have no philosophy believe that an idea, on the contrary, can be without an object; the truth is in the middle: 'the idea, the idea properly so called, is a certain vision of the object'. There is no idea without an object; the idea of God, *if it is an effective idea,* supposes a certain vision of him, and this proves his existence. If he did not exist, there would not be a being such that a greater could not be conceived, because, far from being infinite, he would be *nothing.* The non-existence of the being such that one cannot think a greater is contradictory. This is what the formula of the ontological argument expresses. The argument, then, is not valid for anything but God, because he is the unique necessary being; for no matter what other being, its idea does not show anything else than its essence or possibility; only in God does the essence imply his existence.

But Gratry does not see sufficiently a point that seems to me capital for the interpretation of the proof of Saint Anselm: the role of the *fool,* of the atheist who denies in his heart that God exists: 'The fool has said in his heart: there is no God' [*Dixit insipiens in corde suo: non est Deus*]. Saint Anselm starts out from precisely this denial of the fool; the demonstration of the existence of God makes sense only in face of a negation and it is founded precisely upon it. We saw before that the supposition, the point of departure, was God himself, not known, but sensed and missed; it is a question, then, of *knowing him,* but in a mode of *demonstrating his existence*. This is necessary only when someone *denies* it, and this someone is the fool, the person who does not have *sense*, who does not know what he says when he denies God. Thus the one who has no authentic *idea* of God. Saint Anselm distinguishes two modes of thought: one is to think the *word* which signifies the thing; the other is to understand *that* itself which the thing is. In the first sense it is possible to say that there is no God; in the second, no. But then the negation of God is a pure equivocation, because one is not thinking of him, one does not have an authentic idea of him; when one possesses this, when one has a vision of what God is, one sees that he necessarily exists. He who denies the existence of God has not the sense of what he says, he is *insensate*, [that is, a fool—Translator] in all rigor. Saint Anselm, depending upon what the fool says, upon the *word* 'God' which he uses in negating, obliges him to face the *meaning* (that is, sense) of what he says, and thus, to turn back to himself and enter into his mind, to leave off being *insensate*. When he encounters his very self, image of God, a person encounters the authentic *idea* of the Divinity, and with it the assurance of his existence.[4] But the problem—which will reappear in Descartes—is whether the vision of things and of oneself is sufficient to have this *idea* of God, equivalent to a *vision* of him.

The Attributes of God—In all things, and especially in the soul, I see at the same time the created thing and the light of God, the absolute perfection of God and the relative qualities of the creature. And it is necessary to discern what corresponds to each one of these, in other words, to know what attributes can be predicated of the Divinity.

Saint Anselm follows the dialectical procedure already mentioned: to obliterate the limits: One must wipe out all that comes from imperfection and nothingness. Thus, he affirms of God no attribute which is less good than its negation, and he affirms infinitely every attribute greater than its negation. Thus he affirms of God life, wisdom, beauty, goodness, omnipotence, happiness, eternity, etc. This is, says Gratry,

4. No interpretation of the ontological argument that I know of insists sufficiently upon the role of the *insensate*. This deprives the proof of its ultimate basis, and makes it not entirely intelligible. Neither Barth nor Koyré has noticed this; both pass over this essential point. One will find an exposition of this point of view in my essay, 'San Anselmo y el insensato', published in the second number of the *Cuadernos de la Facultad de Filosofía y Letras*, Madrid, 1935, included in the volume of my *Obras*, IV, of the same title.

what the pure and religious soul does spontaneously, what prayer does. And these attributes are found, above all, in the soul; the soul, unique being that can elevate itself to seek God, is the object in which one can find his traces: thus the primordial condition for the knowledge of God is the entering in to oneself, the turn to the interior of the mind: 'enter into the chamber of your mind' [*intra in cubiculum mentis tuae*] is the imperative of Saint Anselm.

The Vision of God—What is the knowledge that suffices for attaining God? Is it possible to know God in himself, as he is? Saint Anselm, from the beginning of the *Proslogion*, notes that God lives in light inaccessible: 'but surely you live in inaccessible light' [*sed certe habitas lucem inaccessibilem*]. Into this light one cannot penetrate; Saint Anselm does not try to do it, because there is no proportion between it and human possibilities, except only by hearing the divine truth in some way: 'I do not try, Lord, to penetrate your greatness, because in no way do I compare my intellect with it; but I desire in some way to understand your truth, which my heart knows and loves' [*Non tento, domine, penetrare altitudinem tuam, quia nullatenus comparo illi intellectum meum; sed desidero aliquatenus intelligere veritatem tuam, quam credit et amat cor meum*]. Thus he treats only of a vision of the divine light, 'even though it be from far away, from the depths'; 'I am permitted to look up to your light, from far away or from a depth' [*liceat mihi suspicere lucem tuam, vel de longe vel de profundo*]. It is, then, an enigmatic, mirrored vision of God, like the image in a mirror. But this vision is absolutely certain and evident; the knowledge of God thus obtained admits no doubt. When one understands that God exists, one cannot stop thinking it; up to the point that, although one does not wish to believe that God exists, one could not fail to know it. The knowledge of God that starts from an active faith [*operosa fides*] to which it appears negligence not to be able to understand what is believed, ends in an understanding, in an illumination that makes itself independent of faith itself: 'what before I believed by your gift, now I understand with your illumination, so that if I did not wish to believe you exist, I could not fail to understand it' [*quod prius credidi te donante, jam sic intelligo te illuminante, ut si te esse nolim credere, non possim non intelligere*]. Faith [*fides*] arrives at understanding [*intellectus*], and the way to achieve this is to seek [*quaerere*], the seeking moved by the moral spring that is the presence of God in the depth of the soul. But he does not lose sight of the fact that although faith can indeed *lead* us to know God, it is merely a matter of effective *knowledge* of the natural and rational order, and as such independent of faith. Modernism has interpreted this erroneously, from a sentimental and irrational point of view, which is a hundred leagues away from Saint Anselm and Gratry, although it has used them abusively and some authors have with levity confused positions radically distinct.

But this is not all. Besides the natural knowledge of God, which raises us only to an indirect mirror image of him, there is a direct and supernatural knowledge of him. The divine light is inaccessible for man, but the blessings of God can elevate him to it: 'it is inaccessible to our powers, but can be reached by divine gifts' [*inaccessibilis est viribus nostris, sed acceditur ad eam muneribus divinis*]. Saint Anselm also distinguishes, then, two steps of the divine intelligible, one natural and the other supernatural. Only in the second can one arrive at a vision of God in himself, no longer in a mirror.

But, if one looks closely, one sees that Saint Anselm speaks, above all, of the human science that rests on the light of revelation. Thus, if in the *Monologion* it is a question only of rational thought, in the *Proslogion* he starts from faith, which is precisely the assumption: 'Faith seeking understanding' [*Fides quaerens intellectum*]. From faith, which is a supernatural gift, and which is already an attempt at vision, a vision begun. Thus, if one who first *believes* already participates in God ('I believed through your gift') [*credidi te donante*] one does it also in the result, when one arrives at *understanding* ('I understand through your illumination') [*intelligo te illuminante*]. Reason and faith, the two principles of light, says Gratry, always radically distinct, remain profoundly united. This is the method of Saint Anselm.

Saint Thomas Aquinas

Syllogism and Dialectic in Thomism—Gratry considers Saint Thomas as the moment in which Plato, Aristotle and Saint Augustine are reunited in a superior state of maturity. But his mind, he says, is that of Aristotle, and he is to Saint Augustine as Aristotle is to Plato. In other words: as each mind uses, above all, one of the procedures of reason, Aristotle and Saint Thomas use mainly the syllogism, while Plato and Saint Augustine, as we have seen, use dialectic above all. The latter proceed more by way of transcendence, the former by that of identity.

The reason for this, Gratry says, apart from a certain intimate natural disposition, lies in the position each one occupies in philosophy. Saint Thomas deduced and operated by means of the syllogism, because he already possessed the majors, discovered by preceding philosophers; he set out from the discoveries of the Greeks and of Saint Augustine, revised and proved scrupulously, but already possessed, and descended from there, from idea to idea, to the consequences. But this syllogistic procedure is applied in Saint Thomas to ideas, not just to what is perceived by the senses; he deduces from heaven, says Gratry, not from the earth.

But Saint Thomas, who uses the syllogism *more*, also uses dialectic, and he distinguishes it carefully, as an inventive science: 'The *dialectic* science of reason is one thing, ordered to inventive acquisition, and the *demonstrative* science determinative of truth is another' [*Alia rationalis scientia dialectica quae ordinatur ad acquisitionem inventivam, et alia scientia demonstrativa quae est veritatis determinative*]. Saint Thomas uses with all rigor the dialectic method to discover truths and raise himself to the knowledge of God. Even more: he gives a most clear theory, and one congruent with the whole tradition on this point, about this principal procedure of the mind.

The Proof of God's Existence—Gratry cites the whole of Question Two of the *Summa Theologiae*, 'Does God exist?' [*An Deus sit*] in order to comment on it and extract from it the thomistic doctrine about the existence of God and our knowledge of it. The point of departure of Saint Thomas is the idea of Saint Paul: The invisible God is demonstrable through his effects. This is the traditional foundation of the proof, which rises from the finite to the infinite, and at the same time is the meaning of the elevation to God in poetry, in prayer, in the daily life of the soul. But, naturally, it is not a question of a *deduction*, of obtaining a conclusion through a syllogism, but of going by *induction* from an effect to a cause *not contained* in the effect, but which transcends it. From things one cannot go deductively to God, by identity, nor can one even know the Divinity completely through creatures, because they are not proportionate to it, but one can prove that this cause exists.

Saint Thomas does not admit the ontological argument of Saint Anselm, understood as an *a priori* syllogism; he believes that there is also need for *a posteriori* knowledge that there exists a being such that no greater can be thought. How, then, can one arrive at this knowledge? By the way Saint Anselm himself indicates, by consciousness of imperfection, which always aspires to something better and greater. People feel an interior attraction to the highest Good. This attraction, this desire for happiness, is an *obscure* knowledge of God, which all human beings possess naturally, and it signifies the experiential basis for the clear and distinct knowledge. It is the divine sense, the sense of the infinite, which resides naturally in all human beings, unless, says Saint Thomas, they snuff it out by their perversity; *iniquity* is what chokes the knowledge of God; thus Saint Paul says (Rom 1:18): 'They hold truth captive in injustice' (They detain truth in injustice.) [*veritatem in injustitia detinent*].

God is, then, despite everything, unknown; one knows *that he is*, but one does not know *what he is*. Seeing things cannot give us the divine essence; but it raises us to the knowledge of God by three ways; first, the way of causality [*via causalitatis*]; as things are changeable and defectible, we have to refer them to an immutable and perfect principle; second, the way of excellence [*via excellentiae*]; when we refer things to their principle or cause, since it is a principle not contained in them and which absolutely exceeds them, we know that God exists beyond all things; third, the way of negation [*via negationis*]; as the cause is greater than its effects, nothing of them can be attributed to it, but rather denied of it; this is the foundation of negative theology, and the reason for our saying of God that he is infinite and immutable, whereas creatures are finite and variable. The procedure consists, then, in seeing the perfection [*excellentia*] in the imperfect being, but not positively *in it*, but, on the contrary, by *denying* [*via negationis*] the limits of the created quality. In this way the invisible perfections of God are known but not in their unity, but dispersed through the traces we find in creatures and which *induce* us to raise ourselves to know him.

By the way of negation the *divine essence* is known; by the way of causality, its creative power, understood as the principle of all; by the way of excellence or eminence, his divinity, and he is known as the end to which all beings tend. This is the procedure of *transcendence*, founded, at once, on similarity and contrast; but Saint Thomas notes that negation of created qualities in God does not signify that he lacks them, but on the contrary, that he possesses them to excess: 'these are not removed from him because of his defect, but because he super-exceeds them' [*haec non removentur ab eo propter ejus defectum, sed quia superexcedit*]. The *inventive* method of Saint Thomas, then, is, as in the other philosophers, *dialectic*.

The Moral Element—We have already seen how Saint Paul affirms that the cause of not knowing God (which is inexcusable) is *iniquity*. Saint Thomas, in his commentary on Saint Paul's text, expounds his doctrine about the moral element in the knowledge of God. The human spirit must *lean on* God; if not, it becomes shallow and *empty*, and the heart becomes shrouded in darkness; the light no longer illuminates it and it is each time more *insensate*. Man can only escape vanity, emptiness, by leaning upon God; if he departs from him and turns to himself and his own support, he loses the 'light of the spirit' [*spiritualiter obscuratur*] (he is spiritually obscured). Then man falls into the reprobate sense [*sensus reprobus*] of which Saint Paul speaks, and this *mystery of iniquity* is rigorously, according to Saint Thomas, *an inversion*: 'they turn the first into the last' [*converterunt primum in ultimum*].

Such a person considers himself as root and origin; he believes that the light comes from himself and from the corporeal world, that reason comes from the senses. In practical life, consequently, reason remains hostage to sensual impulses. It is a general inversion, in speculation as in practice. Gratry affirms that the doctrine of pantheism and of atheism, of the radical error about God, is rigorously a doctrine of inversion: the methodic and scientific inversion of the dialectic procedure. There is required, therefore, a moral force to conquer the obstacle and turn us to God, to be able to raise us to him, departing from the spectacle of creatures. Only thus does one step out of that foolishness that causes one to deny God, to deny one's own reason; from that culpable stupidity that, in the words of Saint Thomas, is sin: 'stupidity is sin' [*stultitia est peccatum*].

The Two Steps in the Vision of God—The theodicy of Saint Thomas Aquinas culminates in his doctrine of the two steps of the divine intelligible. Saint Thomas speaks of a 'twofold way of truth' [*duplex veritatis modus*]. Reason arrives at the first step through the natural light; at the second, through the supernatural light. In what is one distinguished from the other?

Saint Paul said that God can be seen 'in a mirror' [*per speculum*] (through a mirror) or 'face to face' [*facie ad faciem*]. One can see the light itself 'which is present in the eye' [*ipsa lux quae praesens est oculo*], says Saint Thomas, or its reflected image. God sees himself in the first mode, that is to say, his essence is present to his intelligence, because his intelligence is his essence. In this life we know God through created things; creation is for us like a mirror: *tota creatura est nobis sicut speculum quoddam* (every creature is to us like a kind of mirror). This, then, does not give us a vision of the *thing itself*, of God such as he is, but only of the image. In the vision face to face of which the Apostle speaks we shall see the very essence of God; as God knows mine, so I shall know his. If one could not see God more than in an image or a mirror, the natural desire to arrive at the first cause and contemplate him in himself would be in vain. Thus, as Plato and Saint Augustine already saw, beyond the vision of eternal verities [*fantasmas divinos*], there is the vision of the Good itself.

The first step is known to us through natural reason. The vision of things raises us to their cause, which exceeds them absolutely, of which one has to deny all the created, because it altogether transcends them. At the second step, on the other hand, the intelligence cannot arrive through its natural powers alone [*per sua naturalia*], nor in this life, save through a miracle. This is the rigorous distinction, through which both Saint Thomas and Gratry avoid the error into which Malebranche falls. But in this life, can one know God more profoundly than in the first step? Can one not penetrate, as Plato and Aristotle believe, into the second step, and arrive at knowledge of God in himself, even though obscurely and with difficulty?

Saint Thomas distinguishes in his turn, within the higher step—that of the essence of God—two further steps; one full, which can only be attained in the other life [*in patria videntium*], and the other less elevated, at which the soul can arrive in this life during its journey [*in via videntium*].

There are two distinct lights that illumine the mind: one, first, that is the light of grace [*lumen gratiae*], and the other that is the light of glory [*lumen gloriae*]; the first is also called the light of faith [*lumen fidei*], and the second, the light of vision [*lumen visionis*]. It is not a question of the simple natural reason, abandoned to itself, but of the natural reason with the help of divine grace. Faith is the beginning of vision; it is a beginning, an anticipation of the beatific vision that we shall enjoy in the next life: 'faith is a certain foretaste of that knowledge that makes us happy in the future' [*fides praelibatio quaedam est illius cognitionis quae nos in futuro beatos facit*]. The simple natural light is a created truth, a light reflected in a created object, an image of the divine truth; the object of faith, on the other hand, is the uncreated truth. That is to say, the *object* of faith and of the supreme vision is *the same*; in both cases it is a question of the same God, not of his images or creatures; only the *mode* of the vision differs: in the next life the object seen is the first truth as luminous; in faith, this same truth, but as obscure. 'The first truth is the object of vision in the fatherland, as appearing in its own likeness, but of faith as not appearing' [*Veritas prima est objectum visionis patriae, ut in sua specie apparens, fidei autem ut non apparens*].

There are, then, two steps in the divine intelligible; to the first, the mirror vision, the reason naturally attains; here, Saint Thomas says, natural reason stops; the philosophers suspect the existence of the superior region, but do not enter into it; they see the light, but are not in it. [*quidam vident lumen, sed non sunt in lumine*]. Reason by itself cannot penetrate into the supernatural plane; it will arrive at it only in the next life; but there is room for a vision in this world, confused, implicit, clouded, which is faith, the light of grace, before arriving at the full vision of the light of glory. This is the theodicy of Saint Thomas, whose unknown profundity, amid so much reading and so much commentary, Gratry underlines. We have the monuments, he says, but we do not know the language nor can we penetrate its meaning.

Descartes

The Seventeenth Century—The passage from medieval to modern philosophy does not consist, according to Gratry, in a rupture from the former, except in appearance. The philosophy of the past was rebuffed, and it was ignored or depreciated; but, in reality, it was continued. The tradition remained obscured; one tried, says Gratry, to see for oneself; one sought the truth more than its tradition. But the light is the same; the seventeenth century does not change it; it only *renews wisdom,* completes and makes more profound the truths discovered by the Middle Ages; but this wisdom is *ever old and ever new.*

Gratry considers the seventeenth century, as I have already said, to be like a chorus of unanimous voices, in spite of some dissonances that can be reduced to a harmony. Naturally, to do this he has to eliminate *radically* [*a radice*] Spinoza, 'false and evil mind' [*esprit faux et mauvais*], and prescind from Locke, 'opaque mind' to whom the great geniuses of the century did not speak, except Leibniz, 'who was too good', says Gratry. The seventeenth century is the example of the truly philosophical periods that keep awake the sense of truth, and, because of this, also the sense of error; it is exclusively in the light, he says, and it stands enclosed in the unity of truth. To what extent this exclusion of Spinoza and Locke in the name of philosophy and truth is justified, and, on the other hand, to what point it is impossible to include them in the higher unity with the rest of the thinkers of the time, are questions into which I do not have to enter here; it is enough to note them as problems.

The theme of the century, says Father Gratry, is God. But these men do not merely seek with their demonstrations to prove that God exists, but they know that in this question is encountered 'the center of philosophy, the depth of metaphysics, the whole question of method, the science of the soul, the point of contact of logic and ethics, the basis of physics, and the meaning, so long sought, of geometry'. For Gratry, the whole seventeenth century, from theology to mathematics, with its idea of the infinite, turns toward God.

First, the orthodox mystics, the 'secure mystics' of Bossuet. They sustain the abstract and isolated reasoning by the practical and immediate sense of God, by what Gratry calls, with a word full of danger and equivocation, *divine experience.* After the saints—Saint Philip Neri, Saint John of the Cross, Saint Teresa, Saint Francis de Sales—come the wise. And these are they who pass scientifically from the finite to the infinite, setting underway, with a rigor unknown previously, the dialectical procedure. They place in relief and in full light some moments that are found already, but only noted, in the Middle Ages, principally in Saint Augustine and Saint Thomas. Above all, two points: one, that God is all *eminently*, that is infinitely; the other, that to know God one must use a method of *elimination*; 1. 'God is all eminently' [*Deus est omnia eminenter*]. 'Whatever of being, goodness, perfection is in whatever creature, the whole is more eminently in God' [*Quidquid entitatis, bonitatis, perfectionis est in quacumque creatura, totum est eminentius in Deo*]. 2. To know God the way of removal [taking away what is bad—Translator] is needed [*Ad cognitionem Dei oportet uti via remotionis*]. These principles are the ones that determine the philosophy of the seventeenth century, and in it they acquire their utmost rigor and the justification, including the mathematical justification, of their legitimacy.

The Cartesian Proof—Descartes uses various proofs of the existence of God, which come down in the final instance to two: one, the ontological argument, that is, the proof (*a priori*) from the idea of God; the other, the proof from the presence in me of the idea of God, idea of something infinite and perfect, which I cannot have put into myself, but which must come from him. These two proofs, in their turn, have an intimate connection that makes them reciprocally support one another and converts them into only one. As we see, in the two, the point of departure is the *idea* of God, even though taken from two distinct points of view; here is where the common root and nerve of the double proof is found.

Gratry interprets the cartesian proof, then, as only one, and finds its point of support in what he calls the *natural prayer*, which is an impulse of the soul toward God; more concretely, of the imperfect and limited soul toward the infinite which it conceives and desires. Descartes says:

> Not only do I know that I am an imperfect thing, incomplete and dependent upon others, who tend and aspire incessantly to something greater and better than I am; but I know also at the same time that the one upon whom I depend possesses in himself all those great things to which I aspire, the ideas of which I find in myself, not indefinitely and only in potency, but that he in fact enjoys them actually and infinitely, and thus that he is God [*Non-seulement je connais que je suis une chose imparfaite, incomplète et dépendante d'autrui, qui tend et qui aspire sans cesse à quelque chose de plus grand et de meilleur que je ne suis; mais je connais aussi en même temps que celui duquel je dépends possède en soi toutes ces grands choses auxquelles j'aspire et dont je trouve en moi les idées, non pas indéfiniment et seulement en puissance, mais qu'il en jouit en effet, actuellement et infiniment, et ainsi qu'il est Dieu*]. (*Meditation III*)

These words, Gratry says, contain in a restrictive way the conditions of a true proof of the existence of God: in the first place the *point of support*, which is the *finite being* [*ente finito*] that we see and are; in the second place, the *moral condition*, which is the moral life, the incessant *aspiration* toward the highest Good which attracts us; in the third place, the *procedure* consisting in the *elevation* to infinite perfection, by means of *negation* of the imperfect and finite. I doubt, vacillate, ignore, deceive myself; I am limited, imperfect, finite; I see and I feel this, that is to say, I see at the same time, contrasted, the infinite and perfect, and I aspire to it; my life, Gratry says, is a tendency toward the infinite. This lacks, surely, a moral condition, because the perverse reason tends to the lesser being or to nothing; but if there is no moral obstacle, man feels the attraction to God, who is at once desirable and intelligible, to use the aristotelian phrase. This is what is usually called the innate idea of God, or, better, the *divine sense*. In this moment, in possession of the gift of God which is the sense of him, man freely *chooses*: his reason takes him to being and to God or to nonbeing and nothingness; his will raises him to good or evil. 'It is in that interior history of the relation of the soul to God', [*C'est dans cette histoire intérieure du rapport de l'âme à Dieu*] says Gratry, 'that one must always read and study the proof for the existence of God' [*qu'il faut lire et étudier toujours la prevue de l'existence de Dieu*].

But here is the center of the proof. This idea is a vision of God; thus it permits us to reach the conclusion that he exists: he exists, because we see him. *The idea is the thing itself conceived* [*L'idée est la chose même conçue*]. This is the meaning of the word *idea*, taken in its strict sense, for Descartes and for all the philosophy of the time. It is not something that occurs to man, simply; nor even something he thinks and which should *coincide* with reality: it is the reality itself, *seen*. This is the key to the double cartesian proof and what is most problematic about it.

The Idea of God—The idea is a vision; but of what sort? How does one see God? In himself or indirectly? The idea of God, Descartes says, is God and the soul at the same time; the soul, seen in the light of God; God seen in the reflection of his light. But we could not hold in ourselves the idea of God if we were not more than finite beings and did not have God as our cause. Man has the idea of God, which does not proceed from himself nor from nothing, but which is 'like the mark of the worker imprinted on his work' [*comme la marquee de l'ouvrier empreinte sur son ouvrage*]. But this sign is not distinct from the work, but man himself is a trace or mark of God; he is, as Christianity knows, according to *Genesis*, an image and likeness of God. There are, then, two elements: a finite, which is the soul, and another, infinite, which is the light of God present in it. *The idea of God is God seen in the mirror of the soul.*

The two proofs of Descartes have a common element: *I possess the idea of a perfect being, therefore, he exists.* What changes is the reason for which the idea proves the existence; in the first case, in the *a priori* or ontological proof, one argues that the idea of God implies his existence; in the second, it is affirmed that God alone can put his idea into me. Gratry thinks that these two proofs, *in themselves*, are true and sufficient separately; but that in fact and relative to us they are one sole proof and mutually support one another. It is certain, he says, that God is the necessary being, and being this, his essence implies his existence and his idea is his existence. The argument concludes, and is only valid, with reference to God, naturally; of any other being whatsoever one could only prove the possibility; in God, his possibility or essence coincides with his reality or existence, and so we say that he is necessary. To say, then, that God exists, Gratry adds, is equivalent to saying that *Being is*. But this truth holds in itself, *for us*, a supposition: that we possess the *true idea* of God. Without it we cannot know that the essence of God implies his existence; this true idea, living, real, is not something that merely occurs to us, nor something that comes from nothing, but it is produced in us by God; it is the divine *sense*, the obscure presence of God in the soul, with the name that wishes to give itself. It is only, however, with the second proof that the first acquires its sense for us.

But, on the other hand, the simple divine sense, with the confused light of the idea implicit in us, is not enough. This immediate contact is only a germ of knowledge, and it is necessary that it germinate, principally under the influence of *the word of one's neighbor*, when the mind removes the moral obstacle and responds by an act of intellectual and moral consent, Gratry says, to the light of God. Then the mind raises itself to the knowledge of God, and the obscure contact in the depth of the soul is converted into light and knowledge. Then, when the idea is clear and distinct, when one knows about it that it is a vision of God and that it implies his existence, that is to say, when it is joined to the first proof, that is when it constitutes a proof for us. Thus, Gratry interprets the two cartesian proofs—valid in themselves separately—as one, resulting from the mutual support of the two, and unique, which is *for us* effectively demonstrative.

Descartes' Procedure—The cartesian method, as Gratry understands it, is the same as that of Plato and Saint Thomas: dialectic, the way of eminence and elimination. Descartes says in a restrictive way:

'To know the nature of God, to the extent possible for my nature, I have only to consider, of all the things of which I find in myself some idea, if it would be a perfection or not to possess them, and I would be sure that none of them that lacked some perfection would be found in him, but that all the others would be there' [*Pour connaître la nature de Dieu, autant que la mienne en était capable, je n'avais qu'à considérer, de toutes les choses dont je trouvais en moi quelque idée, si c'était perfection ou non de les posséder, et j'étais assure qu'aucune de celles qui marquaient quelque imperfection n'était en lui, mais que toutes les autres y étaient*]. And elsewhere: 'I conceive God actually infinite in so high a degree, that nothing could be added to the sovereign perfection he possesses' [*Je conçois Dieu actuellement infini en un si haut degree, qu'il ne se peut rien ajouter à la souveraine perfection qu'il possède*]. Finally, Descartes adds that nothing of what we encounter in the world or in ourselves and attribute to God, even perfection, is in him and in creatures in a *univocal* manner. Gratry puts into relief, then, that Descartes rises from the finite to the *actual infinite*—not to the indefinite—denying the limits and affirming the positive qualities in an unlimited way, but transposing them in his turn by a procedure of *transcendence*, which eliminates all possible univocity or identity with creatures. In this way, Descartes abandons the exterior world and enters into himself. Gratry says that this is the progress of prayer. But soon we shall see how this abandonment and this entrance into oneself pose for us a grave problem.

Father Gratry encounters in Descartes a lacuna: the reference to the distinction between the two regions of the intelligible world. There is not in him any mention of the two steps of divine knowledge nor of the *final step of reason*, of which other philosophers speak. Descartes remains in natural reason; but he does not fall into the error of supposing that this can give us the direct vision of the Divinity.

Gratry believes that Descartes knew to what point Christian reason could go, but he sought to separate rigorously the rational order from that other in which supernatural help intervenes. Before the attacks upon reason by the Protestants and Jansenists, and the attacks on faith by the *libertines*, Descartes wished to present as unassailable and rigorous the purely rational procedure. Gratry, then, observes that this is not an activity peculiar to Descartes, but rather to his era. At the same time as he, many theologians make a sincere effort to present a theology founded in authority and revelation, conceding a minimal place to reason and avoiding philosophical proofs. Gratry cites textually passages of Regis in his *Concordance de la foi et de la raison*. Cartesian philosophy, Gratry says, did for one side what the Sorbonne did for the other.

But what he does not say is that this was already old—it goes back to the fourteenth century—and involves a great change from the attitude of the thirteenth century, of Thomism, for example. Already since Scotus, and above all in Ockham, theology and philosophy had been separated, converting the latter[5] into speculative, rational, and natural science. This proceeded from the evolution of the idea of *reason* in the Middle Ages, and it had grave consequences, to which Gratry adverts in part, though not in the greatest profundity. And this is why Descartes, despite his evident connection with medieval thought and his agreement with the whole Greek and Christian tradition represents a decisive turn in philosophy: *rationalism* becomes *idealism*.[6]

Pascal

Pascal's Point of View—In a certain sense, Pascal represents the contrary of Descartes; the latter occupies himself solely with natural philosophy and prescinds from theology and every supernatural element, whereas Pascal insists especially upon the practical aspect of the knowledge of God and understands his interest from the point of view of salvation. On the other hand, he gives the greatest and almost exclusive attention to knowledge founded upon the supernatural help of God.

The point of support for elevating oneself to God is, above all, an experiential knowledge of our existence; but also of our imperfection, of our poverty. This is the horizon within which pascalian speculation moves. To know imperfection as such supposes a certain sense of perfection: this is what we have been calling, under different names, *the divine sense*. This sense, then, can develop or be destroyed, according to the *choice* of a human being. He has a natural sense for God, a necessary condition for his lively and fruitful knowledge; but he

5. In a 1995 letter the author corrected the Spanish text, which read 'former', to 'latter'—Translator.

6. See my *Historia de la Filosofía* (*Obras*, I). [Julián Marías, *History of Philosophy*, translated from the Spanish by Stanley Appelbaum and Clarence C Strowbridge (New York: Dover Publications, 1967).—Translator].

can surrender himself or not to this sensibility, and thus increase or quench it.

But Pascal launches out at once toward the *end of the process*, says Gratry, and forgets the intermediate steps. He knows that the last step of reason ends in faith, and he goes to this faith and to the supernatural knowledge of God through Christ. The knowledge of natural reason seems to him not impossible but sterile; he means sterile for salvation; a clear echo of the spirit begun in the fifteenth century still reaches to this point, a spirit that has a famous representative in Thomas à Kempis. There are three ways of knowing God, says Pascal: as pagan, as Jew, and as Christian; for the pagan, God is author of the truths of geometry and of the order of the elements; for the Jew, he exercises his providence toward men through giving a long and happy life to those who adore him; but for the Christian he is a God of love and consolation: 'He is a God who fills the soul and the heart which he possesses.' Hence the inefficacious character of the metaphysical proofs for God, complicated and remote proofs, which do not convince, or at most only for an instant, while the reasoning takes place, only to return a little later to fearing that one has deceived oneself, and which, besides, can give only a sterile speculative knowledge of God.

For this reason it has been said, with extreme oversimplification, that Pascal is a skeptic and that he denies reason. But it would be necessary to ask first what is meant by reason and, above all, what Pascal means by it. And then one will find that he speaks of reason [*raison*], but at the same time of what he calls the heart [*couer*]. What is the heart for Pascal?

The Heart—Since Pascal contraposes heart and reason, he has been thought to be an irrationalist, proclaiming, instead of the rational, the importance of sentiment, that is, understanding with the heart. But one should not forget, above all, the famous phrase, usually so poorly understood: 'The heart has its reasons which reason does not know' [*Le couer a ses raisons que la raison ne connaît pas*]. The heart is what senses God, not reason, and this is faith: God, sensible to the heart. All this makes us see that the heart is, in some sense, *reason*, and that it has not much to do with *sentiment*; rather it pertains—something altogether different—to the *sense*, to the divine sense, which, as we have seen at some length, is what gives us immediate contact with God in the depth of the soul.

And Pascal adds explications that do not leave room for doubt. The heart is *the first of the faculties of the soul, which implies the roots of the intelligence and the will*; that which clings immediately to the first principles of the desirable and the intelligible. And Gratry notes that in Pascal the term *reason* [*raison*] almost always means reasoning, understood as *syllogism*. The distinction between *reason* [*raison*] and *heart* [*couer*] then would move within the *reason* in a higher sense, which would include the divine sense and its unfolding. And so Pascal writes: 'We know the truth, not only by reason, but also by the heart: it is in the latter way that we know the first principles and it is in vain that reasoning, which lacks a foundation, tries to combat them. . . .' [*Nous connaisons la vérité, non-seulement par la raison, mais encore par le couer: c'est de cette dernière sorte que nous connaissons les premiers principes et c'est en vain que le raisonnement, qui n'y a point de part, essaye de les combattre. . . .*]. The knowledge of first principles is as firm as any of those [conclusions—Translator] that our reasoning gives us. [*La connaissance des premiers principes est aussi ferme qu'aucune de celles que nos raisonnements nous donnent*]. And it is upon this knowledge of the heart and of instinct that reason must depend and that it founds all its discourse [*Et c'est sur ces connaissances du couer et de l'instinct qu'il faut que la raison s'appuie et qu'elle y fonde tout son discours*]. 'The principles are felt, to the propositions one concludes; and the whole with certitude, although by different ways' [*Les principes se sentent, les propositions se concluent; et le tout avec certitude, quoique par différentes voies*]. We see, then, that the heart knows truth in a rigorous sense, but with even greater firmness than reason; it is thus the *basis of reason*. When Pascal opposes reason, he intends to speak only of reason isolated, separate from its origin in the ground of the soul and in God.

Thus he also believes that the knowledge of God must be founded, not only in the *mind*, but in the *whole soul*. Like Augustine, Pascal believes that the truth is inseparable from charity, and that without this it is an idol. What does this mean? Something that for us is already very clear. One must not confuse the eternal truth, divine image [*fantasma divino*], with God himself, who is the one who makes the truth be true, who is the sun that produces the shadows. Pascal says: 'One makes an idol of truth itself' [*On se fait une idole de la vérité même*]. For truth outside of charity is not God; it is his image, and an idol one should not love nor adore' [*Car la vérité hors de la charité n'est pas Dieu; elle est son image, et une idole qu'il ne faut aimer ni adorer*]. The text is most clear: without charity, that is, with pure natural reason, one comes to know God only in a mirror, in his image, not God himself; if we take it to be a knowledge of God in himself, as he is, that is idolatry. And as a summary of this doctrine, Pascal says: 'Two excesses: to exclude reason, to admit reason alone' [*Deux excès: exclure la raison, n'admettre que la raison*]. Thus Gratry interprets the thought of Pascal. An interpretation that is merely a sketch, since much would have to be said about the complex mind of Pascal. Gratry, at least, orients the research and undoubtedly sets one on the right way toward understanding him. In this way Pascal, instead of being a skeptic outside the main stream of his century, appears as an essential participant in it, in agreement with the rest of the thinkers of the time at the most profound and radical level, and in some sense goes before all of them and discerns truths that are almost intuitively within him.

For Pascal, if one does not have the divine sense, if one does not rely on the heart, the reason proceeds slowly and sluggishly, among so many distinct principles, that at every instant it goes astray. With the heart, on the other hand, at the least reasoning the soul raises itself immediately and with full rigor to God. Gratry sees here described with precision both syllogism and dialectic, the latter like a sentiment, a prayer.

The error of Pascal, which Gratry interprets as Jansenism, lay in his idea of the relations between reason and faith. He denies too much to natural reason, and also believes that supernatural light is an arbitrary gift of God for which no effort can prepare us. Neither thought, nor books, nor even sacred things, neither sacrifice, nor the use of the sacraments have *any* efficacy, not even to *begin* my conversion, without the *extraordinary* help of grace. Between the two grades of the divine intelligible there is not, according to Pascal, any other intermediary than the arbitrary decree of divine grace. Gratry indicates that this teaching obviously contradicts that of Saint Augustine, according to whom God gives us the power to believe, but does not oblige us, and faith lies within our power.

Malebranche

The Role of God—The entire philosophy of Malebranche is founded on two principles of the new law: the first, that which affirms that we live, move, and have our being in God [*in Deo vivimur, movemur et sumus*]; the second is the word of Christ according to which he is the principle of all things, 'who speaks with men'. For Malebranche God is united in the closest way possible with souls, is present in them in such a way, he says, that one might say that he is the *place of spirits*, as space is in a sense the place of bodies. And the Word of God, who is called at times Christ and at other times Reason, Gratry observes, speaks always to every man. Reason is the interior speech of God and the human capacity to understand his meaning. This is the starting point of Malebranche's thought.

Human beings have an impulse that moves them to know God. Desires oblige God to answer, but God 'wishes to be asked'. What is this asking? 'Your desire', [*Ton désir*] writes Malebranche, 'is *a natural prayer* that my spirit forms in you' [*est* une prière naturelle *que mon esprit forme en toi*]. 'It is the actual love of the truth that prays, and that obtains the sight of the truth' [*C'est l'amour actual de la vérité qui prie, et qui obtient la vue de la vérité*]. Prayer is the point of departure that leads to truth.

Malebranche's Proof—The demonstration Malebranche gives of the existence of God coincides fundamentally with the double cartesian proof. He begins by saying what he means by God: 'God *is he who is*, that is to say the Being who contains in his essence all there is of reality or perfection in all beings; the infinite Being in every sense, in one word, Being' [*Dieu est celui qui est c'est-à-dire l'Etre qui renferme dans son essence tout ce qu'il y a de réalité ou de perfection dans tous les êtres; l'Etre infini en tous sens, en un mot l'Etre*]. God does not have any restriction, any limitation, anything negative; rather, he has all the reality of all beings, but infinitely. He is the necessary being, because Being exists necessarily. This is the proof of Saint Anselm, the proof of Descartes through the idea of God.

But one can make the traditional objection, which is that which corresponds to the position of the fool: the idea of the infinite contains the idea of being; but the infinite does not exist. To this objection Malebranche answers that it is the same thing to think about nothing and not to think, to see nothing and not to see. All that the mind sees immediately and directly, exists. If it did not exist, it would not be seen. I see the infinite immediately, so it exists. Nevertheless, even conceding that the idea is a vision, as Descartes thought, one can make a second objection: that the immediate object of the mind, when one thinks of the infinite, is not this, but the mind itself, and this proves nothing. Malebranche replies—in a cartesian manner—that a finite mind does not have enough reality to see the infinite in itself. No finite thing contains the infinite. The idea of God is an immediate knowledge, an experienced perception of God. This, *touching us*, reveals all beings to us. The idea of the infinite is an *effect* of God. Malebranche, then, completes the first cartesian proof with the second, in answering objections. But there is still more.

Malebranche indicates a third proof, which Gratry calls cosmological. Any object seen by us proves God exists, because it can only be seen in and through God. The occasionalist doctrine is well known; according to this teaching, there is no communication between substances, and the human mind sees things in the divine ideas, in God himself, who is spiritual like the mind itself. If we were not to see God, Malebranche says, we should see nothing. But this would pose a very serious problem.

The Two Degrees of the Divine Intelligible—Malebranche inverts the terms of the principle of Saint Paul. The apostle affirms that we see God through creatures; Malebranche believes that we see creatures through God. He does not take into account the word of the Gospel: 'No one has ever seen God' [*Deum nemo vidit unquam*]. Malebranche confuses the two degrees of the divine intelligible; this, Gratry says, is his error. He believes that the natural reason knows God himself; he confuses the vision of God in the mirror of the soul, in image, with the supernatural vision of God in his essence, 'face to face' [*facie ad faciem*]. He realises that imperfection takes us, by way of contrast and eminence, to God; but he does not note that this is still not the direct vision of God, but only a mirror image, absolutely certain, but which does not give us the divine essence such as it is in itself. Gratry points out the agreement with Pascal in going to the limit of reason, but also his profound difference. Pascal believes fully in the supernatural vision alone and depreciates natural reason alone; Malebranche, inversely, takes natural reason, the intermediate, and believes that it gives us the vision of God, believes that it is the end of the procedure. This is the error of Malebranche; but it is an accidental error, notes Gratry, and more than anything, one of exposition within an essential truth: the truth that nothing is visible without the light of God. He errs only in not distinguishing well that light of God in the things illuminated from the sun itself which produces them. Gratry contrasts this accidental error of Malebranche to the fundamental error of the pantheism of Spinoza, whom he considers a sophist who starts with false ideas and proceeds from there.

Gratry considers that both Pascal and Malebranche have supported to the extreme, to the point of falling into error by excess, two truths that achieve their true meaning only when joined. Malebranche shows, with more insistence than anyone else, the presence of God in reason, up to the point of interpreting it as vision of the Divinity and in it. Pascal supports radically the impotence of human reason isolated from God, up to the point of appearing at times to negate reason. Fénelon, then, Gratry says, was charged with reducing this dissonance to a perfect accord.

Fénelon

The Theory of Reason—Gratry has an extraordinary esteem for Fénelon; he knows quite well that many elements of his philosophy have been received from the tradition, remote or proximate, and especially from the Cartesians; but, as I already indicated above, Gratry does not have too acute a sense of originality, such as it is understood in the modern era. What interests him, as I have already said, is rather the truth than the way of obtaining it, and he prefers the rectified thought without errors to the first glimmer, original but affected by error. Fénelon is, he says, the most exact of the philosophers of the seventeenth century. And he attributes this in great part to the precision theology gives; this is the advantage Fénelon has over Descartes and Malebranche, not great theologians, unlike the great archbishop of Cambrai. Gratry believes that Fénelon is the one who raises to maximum clarity the philosophical idea of the century, that of the infinite, and who maintains in all things the equilibrium, the middle point of truth. But, above all, Father Gratry esteems in Fénelon the theory of reason that he expounds in his *Traité de l'existence de Dieu*.

Fénelon sees above all in the human mind a mixture of smallness and greatness, of perfection and imperfection, of infallible rule and constant deceptions, of manifest limits of the finite and visible trace of the infinite. From this he concludes that in reason there is *God and we*. Reason, says Fénelon, is in me, because to encounter it I have to enter into myself; but I am imperfect, changing, I deceive myself, I disabuse myself of every deceit, and at every moment I have recourse to a *superior reason*, perfect, immutable, which does not err nor turn back again to its end, but, without deviating at all, corrects me and is like my master. And this voice makes itself heard by all men and in the whole universe. And Fénelon adds these decisive words: 'Thus, what appears to us to be the greatest and to be the foundation of ourselves, I mean our reason, is what is the least proper to us, and what one must believe to be the most borrowed' [*Ainsi, ce qui paraît le plus à nous et être le fond de nous-même, je veux dire notre raison, est ce qui nous est le moins propre, et qu'on doit croire le plus emprunté*]. 'We receive ceaselessly and at every moment a reason superior to us, as we ceaselessly breathe the air, which is a foreign body, or as we see ceaselessly all the objects near us, in the light of the sun, whose rays are of bodies foreign to our eyes' [*Nous recevons sans cesse et à tous moments une raison supérieure à nous, comme nous respirons sans cesse l'air, qui est un corps étranger, ou comme nous voyons sans cesse tous les objets voisins de nous, à la lumière du soleil, dont les rayons sont des corps étrangers à nos yeux*]. (*Traité de l'existence de Dieu*, Part I, Chapter II, 55.)

Here we have, in the first place, a clear expression of the need for reason to be something transcendent in relation to the subject. Reason puts us into contact with reality; it is not simply something private and personal, but something that, in the measure in which it exists, receives its meaning from what is outside its own subjectivity. This is the point the whole seventeenth century has to defend to be even *rationalist*, justifying the transcendence of reason, problematic from the time when with Ockham it ended up reduced to something purely human and apart from God.

Throughout the seventeenth century it was necessary to regain God once more, by means of the proofs for his existence, in order to affirm the transcendence of reason, and, thus, its character as such. But, on the other hand, we find in this passage of Fénelon a transparent allusion to the *fundamental* truth that in the *depth of our very selves* we discover something that forms our very foundation and by that fact is the most *alien* to us. We shall have to return later on to this important point.

There are, then, two reasons, one which I am and another which is superior to me. The latter is common to all men, perfect, immutable, eternal. And this reason has to be something real, because nothingness cannot be perfect nor perfect others. And so Fénelon asks: 'Where is this perfect reason that is so near me, and so different from me?' [*Où est-elle cette raison parfaite qui est si près de moi, et si différente de moi?*] Where is it? [*Où est-elle?*] 'It must be something real; for nothingness cannot be perfect, nor make imperfect natures perfect' [*Il faut qu'elle soit quelque chose de réel; car le néant ne peut être parfait, ni perfectionner les natures imparfaites*]. Where is this supreme reason? [*Où est-elle cette raison suprême?*] 'Is it not the God whom I seek?' [*N'est-elle pas le Dieu que je cherche?*]

In the will Fénelon encounters something parallel. Here also there is a duality of finite and infinite, essentially complicated. I am at the same time dependent and free. The *dependence* shows the *nothing* from which I come, the finitude that affects me; but the *freedom*, which I cannot doubt, is a greatness that comes from the *infinite*. Fénelon explains here, from the assumptions and concrete problems of the seventeenth century, the ancient Christian definition of man: a 'midpoint between nothingness and God' [*medium quid inter nihilum et Deum*]. In the finite and contingent reality that is man is found his constitutive nothingness, and at the same time this necessarily sends us back to God.

What, then, is reason? God and ourselves, or rather, a relationship between God and us; but we can fail, withdraw, isolate ourselves. Fénelon compares the double meaning of reason with physical sight under the light of the sun. The eye of man is not light, but receives it and is enlightened by it, and at the same time the light passes through the eye making it luminous. Equally, the mind is the sole organ through which the original light of reason passes and which is illuminated by it. Therefore, the soul does not see God directly, but it sees itself, illuminated by God, *in the light of God*. The vision of things and of the soul itself is not possible without God, as the sight of the eyes is not possible without the sun; but yet the sun itself is not seen directly, nor is God, but only by reflected light. Fénelon rectifies the error of Malebranche, retaining his capital truth: 'that if we did not see God in some way, we would not see anything' [*que si nous ne voyions Dieu en quelque manière, nous ne verrions aucune chose*] but one must underline 'in some way'.

This is what Malebranche forgot, when he believed that that vision is 'the direct and immediate sight of God': [*la vue directe et immédiate de Dieu*:] when objections were offered to him, he rectified it momentarily, but again fell into the confusion of the two orders, which Fénelon scrupulously avoided. The human mind is like a *mir-*

ror. The *idea* of God is not God seen directly, but an *image* of God, an image reflected in the mirror of the soul. That there be an image, then, that there be a reflection, there must be a reality that is reflected. From it, from the mirrored image, one conjectures to God himself who will be known directly and immediately in the beatific vision alone. The theory of reason leads Fénelon, then, to the proof of the existence of the Divinity.

The Proof for the Existence of God—The foundation of the demonstrations of the existence of God, which Fénelon expounds in detail and in a fully cartesian spirit, is the theory of reason that has just been indicated. Fénelon raises himself to God from the sight of the human mind, as one arrives at the sun starting from the light. The *point of support* is *reality*; the entire first part of his treatise derives the proof for God from the spectacle of the world and of man. But there is something more: the *divine sense*, that light which is felt immediately and which opens the eyes and gives the desire to be illuminated by it. Unless a moral *obstacle* intervenes; Fénelon speaks of the clouds that veil the divine sun, and these are our passions; he speaks also of the weak eyes that shut before the light; only with a moral force, then, can the clouds be dissipated and can we overcome the resistance of weak eyes that refuse the light and do not wish to see. Finally, the procedure for elevating oneself to God consists, for Fénelon as for the whole tradition we have studied, in the affirmation of all the real, without limits, until one arrives at the infinite. And this infinite is the *infinite in every genus*. The infinite cannot be such in one genus alone, but *in all*. This is, precisely, the fundamental idea of Gratry: the infinite is infinite in every sense; what is finite in any sense is so in every sense; here is found the truth that avoids all pantheism. For Gratry, Fénelon is, then, the philosopher without error, submissive, to the point of intellectual sacrifice, to the truth which is God.

Petavius and Thomassin

Petavius—Gratry occupies himself in *La connaissance de Dieu* with two little known thinkers, authors of two Latin works on Theodicy, that are, in his judgment, the most complete studies of the problem of God in the seventeenth century. Petavius was approximately contemporary with Descartes, and Thomassin lived about a half century later. The first was a Jesuit, the second belonged to the Congregation of the Oratory. Gratry studies them together, because the significance of their works coincides: in both it is a question, above all, of making an original synthesis of the thought of the Fathers about God to arrive at a unitary doctrine; in Gratry's opinion there is no doubt some hint that the works of Petavius and Thomassin anticipate his own in various respects.

Gratry studies in detail only Thomassin, pausing only over one chapter of Petavius' *Dogmatic Theology*, the one that deals with the procedure for elevating oneself to God. Petavius insists especially upon the distinction between *positive* and *negative* attributes of God; God is known through what he is or is not. He is called reason, light, life, spirit, etc.—positive attributes—, or else invisible, incomprehensible, infinite, that is, by negations of attributes known through other things. Petavius compares this to the negative theology of Dionysius the Areopagite, who so greatly influenced the entire Middle Ages. But one must take into account that the negative attributes do not signify *privation*, but *transcendence*, because negation only eliminates all that comes from the accidental and defective, to leave the idea of God more pure, transparent and worthy. Negation alone is capable of elevating one from limited beings to the unlimited being without any finitude. Thus, negation is more efficacious than affirmation for rising to the knowledge of God.

The 'Hidden Sense' of Thomassin—The motto of Thomassin, Gratry says, is this: 'Christ is always at hand' [*Christus venit semper*]. And Christ, the Word, is for Thomassin, at the same time, the Savior and reason; as Savior, he comes for all 'from the beginning of the world'; as reason, he is 'the true light that illuminates everyone coming into this world' [*lux vera quae illuminat omnem hominem venientem in hunc mundum*]. Therefore, Thomassin believes in the fundamental coincidence of all men who have cultivated their reason, and he seeks the truth in all with an open mind. He practices to excess, says Gratry, the principle of Saint Paul: Charity believes all things [*caritas omnia credit*]. The Theodicy of Thomassin, in Gratry's opinion, is 'the work of the Fathers of the Church summed up by a man of genius'.

Thomassin encounters the main point of agreement in the fact that all recognise the natural or innate idea of God, a seed of an implicit knowledge of the Divinity. And about this he puts forth an acute and original theory. Besides the intelligence, he says, there is a certain arcane sense, by means of which one *touches* God rather than sees or understands him: 'Above the power of understanding is a certain arcane sense by which God is touched, rather than seen or understood' [*Supra vim intelligendi est sensus quidem arcanus quo Deus tangitur, magis quam cernitur aut intelligitur*]. There is, then, in the soul a divine sense, distinct from ideas, which are a kind of vision of God. The soul, according to Thomassin, has three distinct senses, an *external sense*, an *internal sense*, and a *divine sense*; by means of the first, one senses bodies; with the second, oneself; with the third, God. This theory will be taken up and utilized amply by Gratry.

Therefore, *one knows God as one knows the world*, says Father Gratry; sensation gives an experiential basis, but obscure and confused, and reason then adds its clarity; the same thing occurs with the divine sense, foundation of the rational knowledge of God. The procedure is the following: the point of departure is the arcane sense which touches God; the moral and affective element of this sense gives the necessary impulse; reason adds its clarity, and proceeds according to the method, which consists in seeking the absolute and infinite in all things, by means of the suppression of limits. In this way one arrives at a rational and experiential demonstration of God's existence, *a priori* and *a posteriori*.

The Two Orders—But of what sort is the knowledge that reason attains of God? The principles and truths, says Thomassin, must be of the divine substance, because they are immutable and eternal; but, on the other hand, they are not simple, and we see that they are multiple; therefore, they are not God himself. They are rather divine rays descended to us [*condescensiones quaedam*] in which the divine light adapts itself to the human mind and lets itself be refracted in it; and this light, abated and tempered, is reason. Therefore, God shows himself in justice, in sanctity, in wisdom, but not as he is in himself, but as they are, and thus souls know him as they are, not as he is, and they know *that he is*, but not *what he is* [*quia Deus est, non vero quid est*]. And apart from this light there is another, not simply natural, but supernatural, in which God shows himself to souls as he is. It is, says Gratry, the distinction of the two grades of the divine intelligible, of the two orders of the light: one, the light of God seen in ourselves; the other, the light of God seen in God.

In Thomassin are found, then, in full consciousness of their great philosophical tradition, the main points that we have encountered throughout this reconstruction of the history of theodicy; and, especially, there appears formulated in him to an unusual extent the doctrine of the *hidden sense* of God in the depth of the soul. This antecedent will have a profound resonance in the thought of Gratry.

Bossuet

The Relation of the Finite to the Infinite—Bossuet, says Gratry, by his works and his polemic with Fénelon, terminating in the condemnation of the latter's book, the *Histoire des maximes des saints*, for its relation with quietism, made clear a point of mystical theology which is at the same time a central metaphysical question: the relation of the finite to the infinite. Translated into practical life, the finite is the soul, the infinite, God, and the relation is love; therefore, the question amounts to that of the union of the soul with God by love. On the other hand, parallel to this, the questions of how the mind arrives at God through the intelligence, the reason, or even through the will, come up. And this has a close connection with the problem of the demonstration of the existence of God.

As we have seen many times, the procedure for this demonstration consists in starting from the finite being as such, that is to say, from *being* and *limits* at the same time, and, by negating the latter, in affirming infinitely all that is positive, all that is true reality. This is what philosophy does; but sophistry, says Gratry, discusses the legitimacy of the procedure: we have being and limits; why affirm the first and deny the second, and not the reverse? If one affirms limits infinitely, one arrives at nothingness. There is, then, a free choice between being and nothingness. Why? asks the sophist. This is the position of the heterodox mystics of the seventeenth century, above all of the quietists who followed Miguel de Molinos, the author of the *Spiritual Guide*. They believed that to arrive at God one must annul everything and annul one's own self, to sink oneself into nothingness. This doctrine of stupefaction is what Bossuet combated, including the error of Fénelon, who let himself stray through inexact texts of orthodox mystics, and that which led him to the central point of his theodicy.

Bossuet believes that the knowledge of ourselves raises us to the knowledge of God. All creation, and especially the body, but above all the soul, proves the existence of the Divinity. It is enough, he says, to reflect upon our own proper operations to understand that we come from a higher principle. The soul knows, comprehends, affirms, but at the same time errs, ignores, and doubts; it therefore has a certain perfection, but it is at the same time imperfect. The imperfect, then, supposes the perfect; if our imperfect wisdom, in spite of being so, exists, with greater reason does the perfect wisdom from which ours derives.

But to elevate ourselves to God we need some special force that starts the dialectic, and that is the presence of God in the soul. This, made in the image of God, *turns itself toward its origin*. That is to say, *it can* do this, although ordinarily it does not do it because it remains enchanted by the senses and the passions, like one who is in his study, says Bossuet, making use of the light, without preoccupying himself with it nor with whence it comes. There is, then, an *obstacle* that must be removed; the will must turn man to God in virtue of the divine sense; in this way, the first love and the first knowledge of truth are given together. The knowledge of God supposes a love that moves us; but without a certain knowledge, even confused, love cannot be given nor move us. It is necessary, then, to start from the primary datum which is the divine sense, that implicit presence of God in the root of the soul. Already Saint Augustine asked himself at the beginning of his *Confessions* whether he had first to praise God or invoke him or know him: 'whether invoking you comes first, or praising you: and if knowing you comes first, or invoking you' [*utrum sit prius, invocare te, an laudare te: et si scire te prius sit, an invocare te*].

This is, then, the procedure of transcendence, by means of which one passes from the finite to the infinite, or from the soul to God.

The Necessary Being—Bossuet does not limit himself to this proof for the existence of God through the spectacle of nature and through its effects on us, says Gratry. He also goes back to the proof of Saint Anselm, to the demonstration of God through the idea of him, but involving in it the *a posteriori* proof, to make it at once rational and experiential. Bossuet tries to prove that there exists a necessary being, which exists by itself and is eternal and immutable. But, if there were a moment in which nothing would exist, nothing would exist eternally, and nothing alone would be true; which, Bossuet adds, is absurd and contradictory. Therefore, there must be a being that exists from all eternity and is necessary, because otherwise there would exist only nothingness, that is, there would be nothing: 'If there were one sole moment in which nothing existed, nothing would be eternally' [*Qu'il y ait un seul moment où rien ne soit, éternellement rien ne sera*]. Thus nothingness will be forever entire truth, and nothing will be true but nothingness: something absurd and contradictory [*Ainsi le néant sera à jamais toute vérité, et rien ne sera vrai que le néant: chose absurde et contradictoire*]. 'There is therefore necessarily something that is before all time, and all eternity' [*Il y a donc nécessairement quelque chose qui est avant tous les temps, et de toute éternité*]. In fact, if in one moment there were nothing, there could be nothing whatever at any time, because nothing could make it be. Bossuet depends upon a fact of experience, namely, that *there is something*; therefore, there must be a necessary being. But Gratry notes that Bossuet says that the hypothesis of nothing is contradictory and absurd, and thus his argument keeps its *a priori* character.

Naturally, this still does not prove the existence *of God*, but only of a necessary being. Gratry realizes this because, in fact, it is a major point that is often forgotten. Once one has demonstrated the existence of a necessary being, it is necessary to prove that that being is God and not, for example, the world. Gratry argues using his idea of the infinite: there is but one infinite, and this is so in every sense; there cannot be anything that would be infinite in only one sense; therefore, the world, which is finite from various points of view, cannot be infinite in duration; and so that necessary and eternal being, which has infinity of duration, must have it in every sense, and it is God. The proof of Bossuet, as Father Gratry interprets it, is founded, then, first, on the fact that something exists; second, on the vision that for it there must be a necessary being; third, on a theory of the infinite, according to which what is infinite in one sense must be so in all senses, and the reverse. To give it its full sense it would be necessary, therefore, to make clear this idea of infinity. On the other hand, God does not strictly speaking have *infinite duration*, but *eternity*; although this, surely, supposes an *endless* life, that is to say, without limits, but possessed in a perfect and simultaneous way.

The Hidden Spring—But there is still something more. We have seen that there is an image of God in us, and that image is we ourselves. The soul sees itself in the light of God, as it sees the world; but it desires further to know the light; and this is, says Bossuet, the most profound likeness of God: God knows himself; his life is to know himself; and as man is made in his image, he seeks also to know him. As we, then, are finite and imperfect, we cannot encounter in ourselves the infinity of God, and when we ask ourselves what it is, a voice from the depth of the soul says to us: *it is not that*. This is the negative theology which raises us to God by eliminating and rebuffing all that we are and think. But whence does the soul draw this energy that makes it deny itself and refute itself and rebuff all it thinks? Bossuet affirms that there is a hidden spring [*un ressort caché*], which is not free in the soul, which has bonds, but which nevertheless has a certain vigor and exceeds matter and is 'as if attached by its point to some higher principle' [*comme attaché par sa pointe à quelque principe plus haut*].

The soul, then, which is bound by one part to matter, touches God by the other part and is united to him at some point, says Bossuet, as Plato said that it is suspended from God by its root, and from this bond it receives a secret power, a *hidden spring* [*oculto resorte*] that allows it to elevate itself beyond itself denying itself in its limitation, in order to elevate itself to what is above it, to the infinite and eternal, in short, to God. But Bossuet notes that this spring immediately relaxes, that the soul turns at once to its phantasms and falls back into matter, if it is not illuminated from without [*si elle n'est pas éclairée d'ailleurs*]. This is the distinction, says Gratry, of the two orders of the intelligible world. The soul, starting from the stimulus of the *divine sense*, from the *hidden spring*, and by means of the moral force of its will, manages to elevate itself to the eternal truths and to know God reflected in its soul and in those truths; and there is even more: that spring can carry the mind still further, to the contemplation of God himself; but for that it is necessary that it should be illuminated from without; that is to say, it requires the help of the supernatural light of God. And Gratry sums up his interpretation of Bossuet's theodicy with these words, whose entire sense will become clear to us only later: 'All that signifies that there are God and the soul; that the soul, which feels itself and the body beneath it, feels also God who is above it, and that the divine sense leads it to know God, as the exterior senses lead us to know bodies' [*Tout cela signifie qu'il y a Dieu et l'âme; que l'âme, qui se sent elle-même et les corps au-dessous d'elle, sent aussi Dieu qui est au-dessus d'elle, et que le sens divin la conduit à connaître Dieu, comme les sens extérieurs nous conduisent à connaître les corps*]. Gratry thus establishes a formal parallelism between the external and the divine sense, between the knowledge of the exterior world and the knowledge of the Divinity.

Leibniz

The Ontological Argument—I prescind here from the problem of the method Leibniz follows in demonstrating the existence of God, as a general procedure of reason, and from its relation to the infinitesimal analysis; in another place I shall aim to occupy myself directly with this theme; in this chapter I shall attend exclusively to the leibnizian proof for the existence of God, and concretely to the interpretation and modification of the argument of Saint Anselm.

According to Leibniz, the argument called 'ontological' is valid and precise, but incomplete. He does not prove that God exists, simply, but only that *if he is possible, he exists*; now it would be necessary, to have the entire proof, to demonstrate the possibility of God. Leibniz does not begin with the idea of God as a being such that no greater could be thought (Saint Anselm) nor as perfect being (Descartes), but as *ens a se*, being from itself. *Aseity* is what makes possible the ontological argument reduced to a modal or conditional proposition, dependent upon possibility. The reasoning of Leibniz to prove the first part is the following:

'The being from whose essence existence follows, if it is possible, that is, if it has an essence, exists (this is an axiom of identity needing no demonstration)' [*Ens ex cujus essentia sequitur existentia, si est possibilis, id est, si habit essentiam, existit (est axioma identicum demonstratione non indigens)*].

'And God is the being from whose essence existence follows (this is a definition)' [*Atqui Deus est ens ex cujus essentia sequitur existentia (est definitio)*]

'Therefore God, if he is possible, exists (by the very conception of necessity)' [*Ergo Deus, si est possibilis, existit (per ipsius conceptus necessitatem)*].

This is the first proposition needed to demonstrate the existence of God, which needs to be completed by the proof of his possibility. As we see, Leibniz moves up to this point in the *a priori*, beginning from the *idea* of the *ens a se*. Now to prove, also *a priori*, the possibility of God, Leibniz appeals to the absence of contradiction in the idea of God: 'Thus God alone, or the necessary being, has this privilege that he must exist, if it is possible. And as nothing can prevent the possibility of what has no limits, no negation, and so no contradiction, that alone suffices to know the existence of God *a priori*' [*Ainsi Dieu seul, ou l'être nécessaire, a ce privilège qu'il faut qu'il existe, s'il est possible. Et comme rien ne peut empêcher la possibilité de ce qui n'enferme aucune borne, aucune négation, et par conséquent aucune contradiction, cela seul suffit pour connaître l'existence de Dieu a priori*]. Here Leibniz utilizes the idea of possibility as simple *absence of contradiction*; all is possible that is not contradictory. But this is what makes the proof vulnerable to the critique of Kant. He notes that the lack of contradiction is the mere *logical* possibility, but not *real*; only this can give us an *essence*, and it consists in the positive conditions that make a thing *really possible*. The pure analysis of the idea of God raises us, then, to see that it is not a contradictory *idea*, but from that alone it does not in any way follow that God should be a *possible being*.

Leibniz however does not limit himself to this. Joined to his *a priori* attempt at proof is an *a posteriori* and experiential proof. If the *ens a se* is impossible, so also are all the *entes ab alio*, the beings from another, given that they exist only through the *ens a se*; therefore, there would be nothing. If the necessary being does not exist, there are no possible beings. But there are possible beings, given that we can see them; and so there exists the *ens a se.* 'This reasoning', [*Ce raisonnement*] Leibniz writes, 'leads us to another modal proposition, equal to the preceding (*if the necessary being is possible, it exists*), and which, joined with it, completes the demonstration' [*nous conduit à une autre proposition modale, égale à la précédente (si l'être nécessaire est possible, il existe), et qui, jointe avec elle, achève la démonstration*]. 'One could state it thus: If the necessary being does not exist, there is no being possible' [*On la pourrait énoncer ainsi: Si l'être nécessaire n'est point, il n'y a point d'être possible*].

These two propositions *together* form, then, the leibnizian demonstration for the existence of God. And if the first is strictly *a priori*, the second is founded upon a truth of experience, namely, the fact that *something exists*. The reasoning is, then, the following: *There is something, so God exists*. But this reasoning, Gratry says, is not a syllogism, but a result of induction, which passes, not by way of identity, but of transcendence, from the finite to the infinite; and this, without intermediary, Gratry adds, *because there is none*.

But Gratry adds something further, to make the argument completely clear. And it is that what is usually taken to be Saint Anselm's proof (that is to say, the reasoning in Chapter II of the *Proslogion*), is only half. Because, in fact, if Saint Anselm indeed *deduces* the existence of God from the notion of him in the *Proslogion*, in the *Mono-*

logion he arrives at that notion by *induction* from created beings. Therefore, in Saint Anselm also there is a point of departure in reality. And, above all, in a sense perhaps even more profound than Gratry thought, the discovery in the depth of the mind of the living idea of God, of the idea that he designates *that itself* which thinks itself, is a contact with reality, which is the point of support for the proof.

The Necessary Being and God—But there remains a capital point for us, the same one we find in Bossuet. The demonstration of God by the contingency of things does not end here. Once it is proved that there is a necessary or *a se* being, there remains the problem of *who* is that being. One could think it were the world, and in this case one would arrive, in one way or another, at pantheism. One would have, then, to prove that the necessary being is God, whom Leibniz was accustomed to take for granted: 'God alone, or the necessary being' [*Dieu seul, ou l'être nécessaire*].

We see how Bossuet noted the idea of the infinite *in every sense*. Leibniz also realizes, although not in a very explicit manner, this difficulty. In his *Monadology* (thesis 36–39), Leibniz seeks the *sufficient reason* for contingent things or truths of fact. But there is, he says, an infinity of elements in the detail of contingencies, and one passes from one to another contingent, which necessitates also a similar analysis. Therefore, however far we go forward in the series of contingent things, we never advance, and it is necessary that the sufficient reason be *outside* the detail of the contingencies: 'It is necessary that the sufficient or last reason be outside the series of the detail of the contingencies, although it be infinite' [*Il faut que la raison suffisante ou dernière soit hors de la série de ce détail des contingences, quelque infini qu'il pourrait être*]. In this way Leibniz intends to prove that the necessary being must be outside the series of contingent beings, even if this be supposed infinite, and, therefore, that it is an ultimate reason extrinsic to the totality of things, transcendent to the world. This would complete the proof for the existence *of God*. But it should be noted that Leibniz slips in a pair of concepts which perhaps it may be necessary to study carefully. In the first place, he insists upon the importance of *contingency*, from which he goes on to seek the sufficient external reason of *anything whatsoever*, without showing concretely in it its contingent being. But, above all, in the second place, he takes the *totality* of contingent things as a *series*, with which he passes from one to another, without really posing for himself the question of that *totality* nor, even less, asking himself if there can be something, for example a *world* as such, which would be *anterior* to each thing and even to *all of them*, that is to say, to the series or the whole. This question, which Gratry does not touch, is of the greatest importance, and it would be necessary to develop it with the greatest rigor in order to broach the problem of the leibnizian metaphysics.

* * *

Here ends the history of theodicy, such as Gratry interprets it in *La connaissance de Dieu*. As we have seen throughout this attempt to reconstruct the traditional ontology, the problem of God is, before all else, the problem of the human being who elevates himself to God making use of the principal procedure of reason, which is induction or dialectic, and this process starts from an ultimate principle, the divine sense or root of the soul, which affects the depth itself of the person. This history of the problem of God sends us back, therefore, necessarily, to three questions, which it will now be necessary to broach: 1) The problem of the person and of its *meaning*; 2) The theory of induction or dialectic; 3) The question of the existence of God and of knowing him. These three topics will complete the present study.

Chapter Four
Ontology of the Person

Man and God

Gratry's point of departure—In posing the problem of man in his book *La connaissance de l'âme* [the knowledge of the soul], Gratry does it from a point of view radically different from what those of his epoch would have done. At a time when psychology, in the mouth of Comte, had been erased from the series of sciences, considered impossible—being reduced, on the one hand, to a purely biological experimental study, and, on the other, to a chapter in sociology—Gratry approached the study of the *soul*, and not only this, but he also posed it from this point on in relation to God. 'To know the soul, we shall not study it altogether isolated. We shall study it in its relation to God and to the body' [*Pour connaître l'âme, nous ne l'étudierons point isolée. Nous étudierons l'âme, dans son rapport avec Dieu et avec le corps*]. These are the first words of his book. The soul, he says, cannot be known isolated, because it does not exist thus; further, the isolated soul is not the whole man, and it is this that interests Gratry. The soul is given bound to a body, and these two can be understood only in their reciprocal light; the soul and the body become like one another, and one must know them through their respective likenesses. Up to this point contemporary positivist science could follow; but: how does one speak of relation with God? What is the presupposition of this idea?

What is the soul? Gratry considers that all possible knowledge about the human soul stands enclosed in the word of Genesis: 'Let us make man to our image and likeness.' Well then, thinks Gratry, and this is characteristic of all his philosophy, one need not take this as a vague pious word, but as a scientific reality. Man is a word of God, conscious of the voice that speaks it; the life of man—something that unfolds in time—is the vibration of the divine voice. For this reason, Gratry says, my life is composed of *waves that follow and push against each other*. God makes us *successive*, like a discourse or a song. Gratry does not think of man, then, as a finished *thing*, but rather as something that unfolds in a temporal succession, as something that flows like a rhythm, something that tells or sings itself, in sum, as *narration, story*.

Indefinite increase of the soul—But it is not enough to say that man is a *word* of God, because all creatures are that; but in mere things the word is brief and ends in itself; things, then, are of one time; on the other hand, a human being, made in the image and likeness of God, is a word that is always growing, that is always being spoken and never finishes being said; it is, he says, a perpetual exhortation. God wishes the soul to have life, and always to have more of it: 'That they may have life, and have it more abundantly' [*Ut vitam habeant, et abundantius habeant* (Jn 10:10)]. Gratry observes that Genesis says, 'let us make man' *faciamus,* 'let us make', not a simple *fiat*, a 'let it be', once for all. Thus, man is not complete and finished, nor will ever be. Why?

Gratry takes most rigorously the affirmation that man is made—or, better, is in a condition of being made—in the image and likeness of God. But God is infinite; what could be the *image of the infinite*? Not actual infinity itself, which belongs to God alone; nor the simple finitude of things, but rather *indefinite growth*. Man continually develops, grows without ceasing; if one should stop, one would cease to live. For this reason man is always search, desire, inquietude, hope. 'Search, desire, inquietude, hope are here below the source of our life. Man is dead from the moment he ceases to hope, to desire, and to seek. Desire is the root of the soul, its source, its primary force' [*La recherche, le désir, l'inquiétude, l'espérance, sont ici-bas le fond de notre vie. L'homme est mort dès qu'il cesse d'espérer, de désirer, et de chercher. Le désir est la racine de l'âme, sa source, sa première force*]. This tendency, this *impetus* or *conatus* which defines the human being, is the image of infinity. The human being can elevate himself and be more and more, without limit. 'The time will never arrive', says Gratry, 'when I will be finished. Light was, from the beginning, what it is today, and what it will be. But I will be that which I am not yet, and even then I will still have an abyss of hopes, and that without end' [*Jamais un temps n'arrivera o je serais fini*—Gratry says—*La lumière fut, dès l'origine, ce qu'elle est aujourd'hui, ce qu'elle sera. Mais je serai ce que je ne suis pas encore, et alors même j'aurai encore un abîme d'espérances, et cela sans fin*].

There is, then, a radical difference between man and things. Things belong to one time, they have a fixed and stable being, the same before and after; not so man; he is not finished, he is in process of being made, and this without any limit; there is no question here, let it be noted well, of any *evolutionism*, in which a first seed, containing already implicitly everything that will unfold, develops, but rather the opposite; man develops forward, attracted by a hope, moved by a desire, a sense of something missing. Man does not believe because of what he *is*, but rather because of what he *is not*, because of what he lacks and misses. And that which he misses, Gratry says, is the infinite perfection of God. The image, to be that and to be able to be it fully, leads back to the inaccessible model. This tendency or tension of the soul toward God is *human life*.

It is a vestige of the Trinity—The soul, Gratry says, is the image of God; the body is the image of the soul. Psychology depends, thus, upon physiology and upon theology, and receives from them much light. Gratry takes these sciences as he finds them; the dominant physiology of his time and the theology as it has been cultivated in the Catholic church, and in them he finds elements for understanding the soul, at the same time that they become clarified by their comparison with the human spirit. I shall prescind from the comparison of the soul with the body, which is more affected in Gratry by the situation of the science of his time and which, on the other hand, would take us far from our principal theme, to pay attention rather, for a moment only, to the comparison of the soul with God. One must realize that Gratry does not claim at all to mix up the sciences, which appear always distinct, but to *compare them*. Comparative science, which studies the three different realities, *distinguishing them*, but *without separating them*, appears to him the fruitful method for arriving at the knowledge of the truth.

We have seen how Gratry finds in the very being of man an image of the infinity of God. Well then, he believes that he can find equally in it a reminiscence, a trace or vestige of the divine Trinity. The soul would be a created Trinity, analogous, image of the Most Holy Trinity. If man is really made in the image of God, one will have to find in him some echo of the trinity of divine Persons. Gratry points to a long series of Fathers of the Church and theologians, from Saint Irenaeus and Clement of Alexandria to Bossuet, passing through the majority of Greek Fathers, Saint Jerome, Saint Augustine, Saint Anselm, Saint Bernard, Saint Thomas, who have sought a trace of the Trinity in the soul. Nevertheless, theology has usually thought that the likeness of man referred to the divine *nature*, and as that is *one*, there would not be found in the soul any trace of the Trinity proceeding from this likeness.

Gratry coincides with a broad Catholic tradition in finding in the soul three terms corresponding, analogously, to the divine Persons. These three terms have usually been designated *being, intelligence, and love*. In St Augustine they are *esse, nosse, velle* [to be, to know, to love]. In Book XIII of his *Confessions* he says, 'For I am, and I know, and I will; *I am knowing* and *willing* and *I know* myself to *be* and *to will*; and *I will to be* and *to know*. In these three how inseparable are life, and one life, and one mind, and one essence! and how inseparable the distinction and nevertheless distinction!' [*Sum enim, et novi, et volo;* ***sum sciens*** *et* ***volens*** *et* ***scio*** *me* ***esse*** *et* ***velle****; et* ***volo esse*** *et* ***scire****. In his igitur tribus quam inseparabilis vita, et una vita, et una mens, et una essentia! quam denique inseparabilis distinctio et tamen distinctio!*]. In other places this *to be* appears identified with *memory*, and love with the *will*, and thus he speaks of a 'sort of vestige of that supreme Trinity which consists of *memory*, *reason*, and *will*'. In St Thomas the same terms appear with the names of *principle, word and love* [*principium, verbum et amor*]. Bossuet says the same: 'These three things . . .: to be, to know and to will, make but one soul . . . Thus, in our imperfect and defective manner we represent an incomprehensible mystery: *A created Trinity which God makes in our souls represents the uncreated Trinity*.' [*Ces tres choses . . . être, connaître et vouloir, font une seule âme . . . Ainsi, à notre manière imparfaite et défectueuse, nous représentons un mystère incompréhensible:* ***Une Trinité, créée que Dieu fait dans nos âmes représente la Trinité incréée***]. Leibniz, finally, speaks of three principles, power, understanding and will [*puissance, entendement et volonté*], which refer respectively to the Father, the eternal Word and to the Holy Spirit. But to Gratry it appears that all this is insufficient and lacking in precision. Why?

There is a fundamental difference between God and the human soul, which distinguishes the sense in which the 'created Trinity' appears from that of the divine: in God all is in act; the three Persons are equally actual and explicit; in man, on the other hand, the first of the terms is implicit, and only the last two are explicit. Man is not totally in act, but rather is essentially in potency, and above all in inmost principle. For this reason Gratry says that as the first Person is called *Father*, the first principle of man can be called *mother*, because it is essentially passive, because the creature is not *first cause* but only second cause. This is the reason for man's usually knowing his intelligence and will, the explicit terms of his soul, and at the same time ignoring the principal term, the foundation from which both emerge. Finally, Gratry observes the impossibility of considering separately the powers of the soul, since these are consubstantial and mutually interpenetrate one another: this mutual penetration corresponds to the *circumincession* of the divine Persons of which theology speaks.

Sense, intelligence and will—The three terms of the soul stand in such a relation that the first is principle of the other two, and the first two of the third. The first, which Gratry calls the *sense*, is the continuous attraction of the desirable or the intelligible, what *drives the soul and life*: 'In the soul, the source or the principle, evidently, is the continual attraction of the desirable or of the intelligible, which never ceases to push our soul to life: it is the source of lights, of desire and of instinct which one calls by the one word *sense*' [*Dans l'âme, la source ou la principe, évidemment, c'est le continuel atraît du désirable et de l'intelligible, qui ne cesse de pousser notre âme à la vie: c'est ce fond de leuers, de désir et d'instincts que l'on nomme d'un seul mot, le sens*].[1] This sense, says Gratry, which drives us to live and to be, implies always two elements, one perceptive and one affective, a *light* and an *instinct*, a seed or root of intelligence and one of will. The sense, then, is principle of these two, and gives them life.

It is in this new sense that Gratry understands the famous principle: Nothing is in the intellect that was not first in the sense. [*Nihil est in intellectu quod non prius fuerit in sensu*]. It does not say, as is usual, in the senses, but *in sensu*, in the sense; that is to say, the *sense* is the root of knowledge and of intelligence. With regard to the will, this proceeds from the instincts and desires, and so also from the sense; but not only from it, because, as Gratry notes, it is necessary to distinguish free will from pure impulse or instinctive desire. The free act is not given without intelligence. Without the two elements, the

1. [A Gratry] *De la Connaissance de l'âme*, 34–35.

impulsive and the intellectual, there is not, properly speaking, will. The third power proceeds from the two. But we have already seen that the first implied in its turn the other two, since it included the moment of light and that of instinct. For this reason, the three powers, clearly distinct, are inseparable.

It is necessary, then, Gratry says, that the three powers of the soul fulfill the formula of the dogma of the Trinity: three are one [*Tres unum sint*]. They must be three distinct but at the same time united. But this is not usually what happens: either the three terms are not distinguished, or else one is not content with distinguishing them, but goes on to separate them, and then to destroy them by assimilating them to one another.

There are *implicit* souls, says Gratry. In them there is neither clear knowledge nor willed love. These are, he says, some of those whom Christ accuses in the Gospel of not developing the talent God confided to them. In them all is dark and instinctive. All thought is dull and confused, all love is passionate and blind. Everything remains in an undistinguished and confused unity and they do not succeed in developing the three powers of life harmoniously.

There are other divided and *isolated* souls, in which intellect and will develop, but while mutually opposing one another and their common principle, and this produces sterility. Either there are not three terms or there is not one soul; this is what happens in the majority of cases, and this *habitual* situation, says Gratry, is a disorder that needs to be understood and pointed out.[2]

Well then, in the soul there cannot be three powers equal, total, and simultaneous, like the divine Persons. For this it would need to be the case that everything potential should become actual, and this, says Gratry, is impossible for this *undefined depth* that is the *root* of the soul. We are infinite, but indefinite; this is the reason why the *sense*, the depth of our soul, cannot ever be completely actual; nor is it possible that man should exist *complete*, like a limited thing which is already what it is, nor is it possible for man to possess all his indefinite possibilities actually, because then one would be the actual infinite, that is to say, God. The destiny of man is *to approximate indefinitely his model*, to grow without limit as the image of God, always to make himself that which he has not yet been.

2. *De la Connaissance de l'âme*, 37–38.

The Sense

The threefold capacity for sensing—I shall concentrate on the study of the first of the powers of the soul, something that has always been badly understood and even ignored, and that is the foundation and principle of all the others. Here we shall encounter, besides, the point of departure of the knowledge of reality, and above all of God, and with it the central nucleus of the ontology of Father Gratry. In the analysis of this power is condensed all the metaphysics of the person, and in it the problem of man is articulated with that of the world and that of God. The philosophical fecundity of this theory can be grasped only from the assumptions of contemporary metaphysics.

Gratry once more has recourse to the philosophy of the past and seeks in it the antecedents of his doctrine, the intuition of that reality which he is going to analyze and describe: 'We have', he says, 'to speak not from the point of view of ourselves alone, but, if it were possible, from the point of view of God, with the voice and spirit of our brothers, in order that the truth reign while man effaces himself' [*Nous tenons*—he says—*à ne point parler à partir de nous seuls, mais s'il se peut, à partir de Dieu, avec la voix et l'esprit de nos frères, afin que la vérité règne pendant que l'homme s'efface*]. And Gratry observes that while the other two powers, intellect and will, have always been so called, the first power has received very diverse names. *Soul* properly so called, and with more precision, as in Bossuet, *depth* or *center of the soul*, and also *treasure of information* or *memory*. Saint Augustine also uses this name, although he nevertheless prefers another, more profound: viscera of the soul [*viscera quaedam animae*]. Thomassin speaks, as we have seen, of a secret sense or arcane sense [*arcanus sensus*]. Plato alludes to a *root* of the soul. All these names point to diverse dimensions of that reality. Gratry prefers to call it the *sense*, or also, at times, the *sensibility*, understood as a general faculty of *feeling*.[3]

Gratry insists that the soul is one; the first power implies the other two, and so the three mutually penetrate one another; therefore, in the sense are found included the other two faculties, and with them all the life of the soul. The impression that the sense receives, says Gratry, is called *sentiment*; this is a seed deposited in the first power, which develops in the other two; in the second, converting itself into

3. *De la Connaissance de l'âme*, I, 186.

clear perception; in the third, as voluntary reaction. The sentiment, then, is at once a muffled intelligence and an instinctive will, which tend to change themselves into clear perception and act of will, under the intimate attraction of the desirable and the intelligible, which raises the soul to knowledge and love.

Gratry discovers a series of qualities in the sense. It is instinctive, obscure, *passive*, (we see already what range this has). Its functions, he says, operate in us without us; they are the functions worked in us by God or by nature. What does this mean? The *sense* is, simply, the primary organ of *reality*. It is not something that comes from ourselves, a product of our subjective activity, but it comes from without, from the *other*, from outdoors, as Aristotle would say. It is, then, the human dimension in which reality gives itself to us: the sense of *transcendence*. This is what Gratry means when he speaks of passivity. The intelligence and the will are something added and *secondary*; before either of them there is a first contact with things, which is still not knowledge nor voluntary act, although it contains the seed of both; put in other words, their ontological possibility. *Because* he has a *sense*, man can *then* know and will. The possibility of these human modes is founded on that immediate feeling which constitutes the ground of the soul, the hidden ground which often remains almost unknown.

'That first power of our soul', says Gratry, 'that profound sphere is then that of the hidden life, that of the functions that God or nature work in us without us; order of functions that the majority of philosophers have noted, without however describing them sufficiently, nor classifying them usefully' [*Cette première puissance de notre âme*—says Gratry—*cette sphère profonde est donc celle de la vie cachée, celle des fonctions que Dieu ou la nature opèrent en nous sans nous; ordre de fonctions que la plupart des philosophes ont remarquées, sans pourtant les décrire assez, ni les classer utilement*].[4] It is therefore necessary to investigate these functions and classify them. The point of view in which Gratry situates himself makes very clear the character of the sense as an organ in which reality gives itself. *The soul feels all there is*; everything can act upon our soul. Gratry invokes the testimony of Bossuet, according to which the soul can make itself conform to everything; and that of Leibniz, for whom the soul is the mirror of

4. *De la Connaissance de l'âme*, I, 187–188.

the universe; he might have remembered also the aristotelian affirmation that the soul is in a certain sense all things. There are, then, as many elements of the sensibility as there are realities, objects that act upon the soul. And these objects are three: things, that is to say, visible nature; our soul and other souls, and finally God. These are the three traditional objects of metaphysics, the world, man, and God, but understood, not now as three beings, but rather as three distinct *modes* of reality. The capacity to feel is, then, triple, according as it refers to bodies, the soul, or God. There is an *external sense*, an *intimate sense*, and a *divine sense*.

The external sense—By means of exterior sensation, the soul senses things, the world and bodies. And it senses things, Gratry says, at the same time as they are and as the soul is. This exterior world does not require demonstration. There are bodies, Gratry affirms, *because I see and touch them*. This proof is good for anyone who is not a sophist or a victim of sophism. The sense of things puts us into evident and immediate contact with their reality, in a primary dimension, anterior to knowledge and, thus, to all possible demonstration. Only that external *sense* makes possible thereafter a knowledge of things.

Sensation, Gratry says, must awaken the entire sensibility. The sense implies the other two faculties, but, above all, each one of the modes of sensing provokes the rest. But as man begins with the predominance of external sensation, many remain always in it, and 'call science the analysis of sensation', taking the details of sensation for the whole. This is materialism, the consequence of the isolation of the external sense, which discovers the world of bodies and remains in it, taking the part for the whole.

The intimate sense—But the soul does not limit itself to sensing the exterior world and its own body. The soul, Gratry says, senses itself, sees itself and loves or desires itself. It applies its three powers, then, to itself. But, above all, to their root, *feeling*. This *intimate sense* [*sens intime*], with which Maine de Biran[5] so largely occupied himself, has generally been unknown. The reason is that the clear and distinct has almost always been sought, in the cartesian manner, forgetting, says Gratry, the word of Seneca, according to which the greater and better part of reason is hidden and occult: 'Reason is not exhausted in the

5. See my study, 'El hombre y Dios en la filosofía de Maine de Biran' (in *San Anselmo y el insensato*).

manifest. Its greater and better part lies hidden' [*Ratio non impletur manifestis. Pars eius major ac melior in occultis est*]. The whole soul is not conscious; the sense is obscure, implicit, and confused, before the development of knowledge and will; the cartesian prejudice, says Gratry, makes psychology impossible, excluding facts that are not clear and distinct; that is to say, precisely the root of the soul.

But Father Gratry adds something extraordinarily important: the intimate sense is the sense of the neighbor, the sense of others [*sens d'autrui*]. Much has been said in recent times about the *perception of others*; Gratry, with greater rigor, speaks of the *sense* of the neighbor. And this sense does not have to do with the exterior. By means of the bodily senses, I know the *body* of my neighbor, as I do my own; but not my neighbor himself, as I do not know myself [in this way]. 'This sense of others', Gratry writes, 'belongs to the intimate sense. It must, in fact, be by the same sense that we sense ourselves and others, our soul and the souls of those like us' [*Ce sens d'autrui*—Gratry writes—*tient au sens intime. C'est, en effet, par le même sens que nous devons sentir nous et les autres, notre âme et l'âme de nos semblables*].[6] And perhaps this is, he adds, the natural foundation of 'that great supernatural reality the Catholic Church calls the *Communion of Saints*'. I immediately feel my neighbor as a *thou*, not as a *body*; and it is not that I infer, from the external likeness of the other's body to my own, the existence in him of an *I* like mine. That would be a process of reasoning, and only probable, and the reality is quite different: I sense immediately and with complete evidence the I of the other, to whom I say *thou*, in as primary, radical, and original a way, at least, as [I do] his body. In the same way as I sense *myself*—not *mine*—in an intimate, direct, and absolute mode. These, says Gratry, are indubitable facts of internal experience. The stubborn blindness toward the intimate sense has totally obscured the problem of the sense of the neighbor, which can be comprehended in its light alone.

But a disturbance can also befall the intimate sense, which is its isolation. Thus as the external sense, taken by itself, apart from the rest, brings us to materialism, the isolated intimate sense leads us to *idealism*. This is the error of almost all modern philosophy, which proceeds, like nearly all great errors, from a great truth *isolated*, that is to say, abstract and taken for the whole. The discovery of the intimate sense, of the I, of the depth of the person, distinct from the body

6. *De la Connaissance de l'âme*, I, 204.

and from the external and visible world, is a capital acquisition of philosophy; but taking that sense in isolation, believing that the intimate reality that it shows us is *the* reality, is an error. Idealism consists in forgetfulness of the reality of the world and of the reality of God, to remain in that of the I.

The divine sense—Still more unknown than the intimate sense is the divine sense. Some thinkers remain in the external sense; others arrive at the internal, but do not recognize the divine. Nevertheless, all philosophers who have raised themselves to the knowledge of God have started from that fundamental fact that God is *sensed* in the depth of the soul. This is the datum whence the rational procedure that raises us to God begins. A sensation or an idea cannot ever lead us, either as principle of deduction, or as point of support for an induction, to the Divinity; for this there is needed, in addition, another datum, which is the divine sense actually awakened. God himself making himself felt in the root of the soul. God is not known without God, says Gratry, one does not rise to God without God.

To speak of the divine sense, Gratry has recourse, as is his custom, to the testimony of the history of philosophy, and most especially to Thomassin. The latter says: 'Beyond intelligence is the apex of the mind, the arcane sense, a kind of obscure contact, one of auguries, the silence of the mind, by which God is more sensed than understood, touched rather than seen' [*Supra intelligentiam est apex mentis, arcanus sensus, contactus quidam obscurus, augurium unum, silentium mentis, quo sentitur magis Deus quam intelligitur, tangitur potius quam videtur*].[7] And Thomassin adds that it is indubitable that there exists, in the center of the soul, a secret sense or touch that feels things and touches them before knowing and conceiving them. And this is, he says, the very unity of the spirit.

The sense is the root of knowledge and of will; it has, then, an implicit intellectual as well as a moral dimension. It is an attraction of the desirable and the intelligible at once, and thus, to be sense of the Divinity, it is that of truth, of goodness, and of beauty. That attraction of the infinite goodness must contend, then, with the attraction of things and with the intimate love of ourselves. These finite attractions can suffocate it; or else it can conquer them and develop in itself the divine sense, which is the spring on which depends the free choice to decide, the very depth of the soul from which the soul can raise itself

7. *Theol. dogm.*, Book I, Ch. 19.

to God, by means of a double force which makes it overcome the sensuality of things created and the pride of itself, sensing its limitation, which enables it to elevate itself, by likeness and contrast, to the knowledge of God. That moral act, that ultimate power of the soul, is what Gratry calls the *sacrifice*, and it has, as we see, a strict *intellectual* significance, as principle of the step from the finite to the infinite, from the creature to God. If freedom, on the other hand, decides for the finite, this is a new departure from God, a fall into egoism, and with that into pride.

But the divine sense, I repeat once more, has been little known and, above all, not explicitly, to the point that, in its speculative dimension, it does not even have a particular name; in the moral order, on the other hand, it is known, although superficially, and it is called *conscience*. Gratry says: 'This power which, in the depth of the soul, draws us to the sovereign good, this sense of the good God, present, living, who touches us and speaks to us, this is conscience' [*Cette force qui, au fond de l'âme, nous attire au souverain bien, ce sens de Dieu bon, présent, vivant, qui nous touche et nous parle, c'est la conscience*]. This force that impels us to the light, that before all things says to us: 'There is something greater!', that leads us, that gives us the power and maintains hope in our hearts, is God present in us, God in whom we live, move, and have our being. And this knowledge, this depth of the soul, is where the sacrifice must support itself: 'Let my conscience be your altar' [*Sit ara tua conscientia mea*], said Saint Augustine. This point of support, says Gratry, is *in us*, but it is not *ourselves alone*. With conscience I lean on someone stronger than I, and thus, *depending upon another*, the soul can escape from *egoism*. Man, then, does not stand alone and isolated, but he *depends upon God*. The role of God in man is that of serving as point of support, of *foundation*, of *root*, and of calling him with the voice of conscience, to attract man to himself, so that the divine sense can develop itself and display the intelligence and the will that it contains implicitly, and convert itself into the knowledge and love of God.

Man, by means of sacrifice, can go out of himself, from egoism, from the pride in which he finds himself, not only from exterior things. But how? Is it a question of annulling the will?. Is it a question of stunning the soul and suppressing it? On the contrary. What must be done is to annul the *limits* of the will, to make it truly free, by making it coincide with the divine will; man is free in obedience to

God, that is to say, when his will is not slave to things nor to his own egoism that shuts him up and oppresses him. And instead of annihilating the soul, it is necessary to overcome the narrowness of haughtiness and pride, which keep the soul isolated, rootless, imprisoned in itself, in order to 'put in God its point of support and its roots'. This is the sacrifice, capital point of *philosophy*, which is the contrary of the annihilation that false mysticism claims.

Because, in fact, mysticism in this sense is the error corresponding to the divine sense, parallel to materialism and idealism: it is the result of taking in isolation the divine sense, forgetting the external and the intimate, annulling the world of corporeal things and the reality of one's own self. This is the meaning of pantheism, which in saying that all is God, ends by denying the world and man.

Reason and Liberty

Rationalism—The sense we have just finished considering is the point of departure of knowledge and free will, which holds in itself their common root. This is what the ancient maxim: Nothing is in the intellect that was not previously in the sense [*Nihil est in intellectu quod non prius fuerit in sensu*] means for Gratry; not a declaration of *sensualism* or *empiricism*, but that the sense in general—that is to say, not only the external, but also the intimate and the divine—is the root of knowledge. All that is in the intelligence, save itself, (except the intellect itself [*nisi ipse intellectus*], according to Leibniz), which is another faculty, comes from the sense.

The ignoring of this truth is the cause of sterility in thought; Gratry notes that if the science of nature has made enormous progress in the modern period, it is because it has adhered to what concerns it, that is to say, in respect to the external sense, to that principle: modern physics consists in knowing that one must *receive* in order to *know*, in that observation and reasoning must be united. Natural science is not constituted in a purely *a priori* manner, by means of abstract reasonings, but by listening to nature and looking at it, receiving from it its data and turning them into science by using reason. Instead, says Gratry, philosophy has fallen into a grave error in reference to intelligence, called *rationalism*.

Rationalism consists in the belief that pure thought suffices for itself, that reason can know God, the soul and the world without data external to itself. It is, then, an intellectual egoism. Reason, then, isolated from its origin in sense, exhausts itself and withers. 'Deprived of root and sap, it exhausts itself and withers. It becomes empty and vain' [*Privée de racine et de sève, elle s'épuise et s'évanouit. Elle devient vide et vaine*].[8] Thus is fulfilled, says Gratry, the word of Saint Paul: 'They fade away in their thoughts.'

Naturally, where rationalism results in the greater error is in the science of God. The rationalist spirit isolates itself, becomes dry, makes only a *separated philosophy*. In separating itself from the divine sense it alienates itself from God and snuffs out that point in which God touches us and reveals himself to us. Man then loses the idea of God. Why? Precisely because he has mutilated his soul, because he has destroyed in it the fount through which God develops in us his idea. In separating himself from the depth of the soul, man loses something in which he could meet the *image* of God: himself, the center of his being. For this reason the Scripture says, with absolute rigor: 'The fool has said in his heart: there is no God' [*Dixit insipiens in corde suo: non est Deus*]. The *fool* [*insensate*], who does not have *sense*, he who is deprived of the root, does not know God with reason, because ideas come from the sense. Gratry speaks of the *separated souls* who do not live, by the heart, with the fecund heat of the common sun, and who cannot arrive through the spirit at the contemplation of the light. 'These unhappy souls', he adds, 'doubly cut off, doubly separated, both from the universal faith and from the common reason, unhappily are immense in number in this century' [*Ces tristes âmes*—he adds—*doublement sectaires, doublement séparées, et de la foi universelle et de la raison commune, malheureusement sont en nombre immense dans ce siècle*]. And he cites the profound word of Saint Jude: 'Uprooted, twice dead [v 12].'

Reason—The danger that threatens the separated reason, rationalism, is forgetfulness of God, atheism. And this is at the same time the falsification of reason. What is this? What is an idea? Gratry says that his book on the knowledge of God [*La connaissance de Dieu*] is, except for the name, a treatise on the origin of ideas. In explaining how one knows God he makes one see in Him what an idea is in general. And it is, he says, 'a certain vision of God, indirect and mediated'. In the first place, a vision of God. Those who believe that the soul is its

8. *De la Connaissance de l'âme*, I, 224.

own light and do not in any way see God in seeing the truth, deceive themselves by defect. Man is not the light, but only its witness. But, on the other hand, other thinkers, for example Malebranche, err by excess, and believe that the idea is a direct vision of God himself. But no one has seen God, according to Scripture; (No one has ever seen God; [*Deum nemo vidit umquam*;]) it is not a question of a direct face to face vision, but of a vision in the mirror of things, a mediated and reflected vision. And this is reason, according to the definition of Saint Thomas, which Gratry makes his own: a reflection in the soul of the divine clarity: 'The natural reason of man is nothing else than the refulgence of divine clarity in the soul' [*Nihil aliud est ratio naturalis hominis, nisi refulgentia divinae claritatis in anima*].[9]

What is reason? God, says Gratry, knows his essence and sees it partially imitable by finite beings. This knowledge in God constitutes the divine ideas, which are God and are the principles which create things and illuminate minds. Beings and ideas in man are his effects and are like him; they are like God, then, partially, and thus are his *images*. But thus as beings only begin to be when God creates them, in the same way minds, which are in potency, know God only when God makes them pass into act, when he awakens them. And how does God awaken them? First, by inculcating in them the image of the uncreated truth, that is to say, the soul itself, and then, so that they may pass into act, God presents them with his ideas exteriorly, realized in creation. In knowing things, then, the mind knows them illuminated by the divine light, and at the same time they are an image of God. The idea is, then, an indirect and mediated vision of God, and reason is a reflection of the divine light in the soul of man.

Freedom—I shall not enter into the theory of free will that Gratry expounds, and that offers notable analogies with his doctrine of reason. One point alone interests me, that which refers to the very existence of liberty. Gratry compares freedom with the existence of the exterior world, and thus as he has said that the existence of things requires no proof, because it is evident and immediate through the sense, anterior to all knowledge and rational demonstration, he says that there is freedom, given that one feels it and exercises it: 'There is moral freedom, for I sense it, and touch it, and exercise it at each instant of the day' [*Il y a liberté morale, puisque je la sens, et la tou-*

9. *Expos. in David, 36.*

che, et l'exerce à chaque instant du jour].[10] Man *is* free, because he feels himself free and lives exercising his freedom. Gratry, therefore, appeals to immediate evidence; all demonstration or negation of freedom would tend to support itself first with this irrefutable fact that I feel myself to be free, that for me, to be is to be free, self-determining, to exercise my freedom continually. The method of Gratry is, then, the appeal to the ultimate and irreducible evidence that stands at the base of reason. As the *sense* is the very depth of man, the root of the person, and so of the rest of his faculties, all the reality of human life must derive from this sense, and consequently from God, given that the divine sense is the presence of God, obscure and implicit, in the depth of the soul. It is a matter, then, of understanding man in his integrity, such as he is: a creature with a free and personal *I* linked to a body and with it to an exterior *world*, and rooted in God.

This is, reduced to its minimum expression, the ontology of the person in the system of Gratry.

10. *De la Connaissance de l'âme*, I, 330.

Chapter Five
Logic

The Two Procedures of Reason

Gratry's Point of View—Logic, according to Father Gratry, is a development of psychology. At first sight, this would be a declaration of psychologism; but nothing could be farther from it. We have seen how psychology, the science of the soul, is not for Gratry a positive science, but strictly metaphysical: an ontology of man in his integrity, referred to the world and rooted in God. And logic, which studies the soul in its *intelligence*, is, above all, the metaphysical theory of the reason. Logic is nothing other than ontology; thus Gratry in his *Logic* attacks the problem of pantheism, to expose it to the light of a theory of reason and of reality which is known by means of reason.

But, on the other hand, the intelligence, the second power of the soul, cannot be taken separately. It must be understood in its origin and foundation, which is the *sense*, and as the sense is the organ of reality, logic appears as the mode of apprehending rationally this same reality which it touches in the sense in an immediate and obscure way; far, then, from being a science of abstractions, of concepts with no more existence than that which they have in thought or as ideal objects, logic is for Gratry a science of transcendence, the science of the faculty of apprehending intellectually all reality, corporeal, psychic, or divine. And, further, as intelligence is not separable from the will, from which it must receive a moral impulse to be set in motion, the logic of Gratry has a close connection with ethics, on which it depends in a decisive dimension. The theme of logic is, thus, *the problem of philosophy*, taken from a peculiar point of view: that of the intelligence and of knowledge.

The Two Roots of Reason—Gratry's *Logic* is a dense work, original and full of philosophic content; a surprising book, that departs from the usual paths in books about this matter, precisely because it goes back to the depth itself of the logical problem, trivialized in the mechanics of the so-called 'formal logic'. But here I cannot enter into detail, nor even allude to ample parts of his work. This ascetic renunciation is obligatory, because this study cannot hope to replace the direct reading of Gratry, still less to expound his philosophy in an integral fashion, but only to recollect the most living and essential part of it in order to display it in the present situation and so allow it to be incorporated in philosophy. It is not a question, then, of an exhaustive exposition, but of a hermeneutic of the capital point of the metaphysics of Gratry.

The point of departure is the sense, as we have seen at length. This sense is the root of the intelligence and of the will and it implies two ideas, implicit and obscure in it, which are the roots of reason: the idea of *being* and the idea of *cause*. Being, finite and infinite; cause, first and last. The soul senses God, who is infinite, and also senses the soul and the world, which are finite, and as it senses God, who is the first and last cause, this two-fold idea is equally in the sense. From these two roots proceed, Gratry says, the two rational principles: the principle of *identity*, relative to the idea of *being*, and the principle of *transcendence*, relative to the idea of *cause*. Thus, the two irreducible procedures of reason, *induction* and *deduction*, have their foundation in the two roots of that whose origin is found in the sense.

Deduction draws consequences by way of identity. The consequent is included in the principle from which it proceeds; there is, then, identity between the being of the consequent and the content of the principle. Induction, on the other hand, raises itself to those principles, which are not contained in its consequences, but transcend them. The major premises from which consequences derive are not obtained by way of syllogism, by deduction, but by way of transcendence or induction. The principles are given implicitly, says Gratry, in the form of sentiment or necessity or tendency. They are not, then, principles of deduction, but rather *powers*; that is to say, they are the spring of reason, which impels it to launch out toward the idea whose presentiment it has, toward the light it seeks and guesses at.

Syllogism and Induction—Deduction, we have seen, passes from one identity to another; but it does not treat usually of a total and immediately visible identity, but only of a partial and mediate one. The form of this deductive thought is the syllogism, which consists in passing from one term to another making use of a third term as middle, which shows the partial identity of the two first, something not immediately evident. The syllogism, then, does not make us know anything that was not already implicit in the major, because the conclusion is contained in it; but that this identity appear in an actual and explicit way, it is necessary to establish a new relation, also of the same identical type, that will serve as a bridge between the two extreme terms. There is not, then, *invention* in the syllogism, but only *explication* or demonstration of something already known implicitly. The syllogism functions, then, in a necessary way in so far as immediate connections are established. Its evidence is automatic, and one is compelled to recognize the identity of the two extreme terms if the middle term is introduced, whose partial identity with both is directly visible. This is what gives the syllogism its demonstrative force and its appearance of rigor, and, on the other hand, what makes it accessible to all: the syllogism, once formulated, is understood by all and must be assented to.

In induction, on the other hand, things occur otherwise. The consequence is not included in the point of departure; there is no middle term that can make known the identity, because there is no identity. Our knowledge grows, effectively, because the truth found is new and exceeds that first possessed: it is an *inventive* procedure. But as it is necessary to elevate oneself to something not contained in the point of support, the process is not completed in an automatic way, but requires a spring and a force. Even to *comprehend* inductive reasoning it is necessary to posit this spring, that is to say, to elevate oneself really to the result attained by induction. But not all have this spring, not all are capable at all times of this force. Not only can all men not *discover* the truths that the procedure of transcendence gives us, but they can scarcely even *follow* and reproduce them if they do not have in themselves the point of support and the necessary impulse. This explains in great part the strange destiny induction has had in philosophy along with the great good fortune of the syllogistic method. While the theory of the syllogism was already worked out by Aristotle, and with such perfection that it remains essentially unaltered, that of induction is, says Gratry, still to be worked out, and one finds only hints as to the essence of that principal procedure of reason, always used by philosophy.

Pantheistic Logic

Sophistic—We have seen that for Father Gratry philosophy consists in the knowledge of God and of oneself, which implies that of the world; more concretely, in the elevation of the mind, from finite things to the infinite, or God. Sophistic, then, is just the *reverse*: the path of the mind toward non-being, toward nothing. Plato and Aristotle already said that sophistic deals with non-being and that it is an apparent wisdom, but that it really is not; therefore, it consists in an inversion of philosophy. For Gratry, sophistic culminates in pantheism, and this signifies in the end atheism. It is in every case a matter of negation of infinite being, or at least of that distinction between the infinite and the finite that is the root of philosophic thought, as Gratry understands it. Either one denies God or one denies the world; in the end, it is the same thing to rob the world of its reality, to reduce it to a pure non-being, and to affirm it as the unique reality, to which one gives the name of *divine*. In any case the distinction between God and creature, in which the two preserve their being, infinite in the one, finite in the other, disappears.

The inversion of philosophy, then, cannot be realised more than by inverting its procedure, its method, thus inverting the use of reason and its principles. Gratry considers that pantheism has taken refuge in logic, and that only by destroying reason can it prosper. But at the same time, he adds, only in logic can the pantheist error be destroyed. How? By making it apparent that it consists in the inversion of the rational procedure, that its necessary condition is the corruption of reason itself. Thus it is made plain that pantheism is manifestly *absurd*, a contradiction in terms. Therefore, there results an indirect demonstration of God *by absurdity*. Strictly speaking, then, there is no *refutation* of sophistic; for this to be possible, there would have to be a possibility of arguing from a common supposition; but this supposition could not be other than reason, and it is just this that the sophist denies and inverts; there remains no other possibility than to *expose* the sophistic attitude and *show* that it is the inversion of the rational procedure, that it is a contradiction *in terms*.

The Principle of Identity—Reason, as we have seen, has two procedures: sophistic inverts both, and in so doing destroys the two principles on which they are founded and in whose application they consist: the principle of identity, for the syllogism or deduction, and that of transcendence, for dialectic or induction.

The principle of identity is expressed, in negative form, as the principle of contradiction. Of a subject there is affirmed what is identical—in whole or part—with it, and what is contradictory is denied. In this consists, says Gratry, the essence of the syllogism and of all deductive reasoning. Sophistic, however, denies this principle of identity in both its forms and suppresses the distinction between the identical and the contradictory. With this is annulled all possibility of reasoning by way of identity. Things are and are not, each of them is its contrary, being is non-being, God is nothing. From Protagoras and Gorgias to Hegel, this is the content of sophistic.

For Gratry, in fact, the foremost representative of the sophistic of all time is Hegel. He signifies the brilliant culmination of that process which destroys reason and moves toward nothingness. Hegel, he says, has a powerful and systematic, but *inverted* logic. 'The time has come to transform logic', said Hegel. Gratry recalls this sentence and understands it as a radical alteration of the only true logic, as an inversion of all its meaning. And, in fact, Hegel affirms textually that the absolute is the identity of the identical and the non identical. And the *Logic* of Hegel—which is his metaphysics—affirms as fundamental principle that being and nothing are the same. Gratry gathers in his *Logic*[1] the hegelian texts in which the identity of contraries is affirmed: that of the good and the bad, that of the finite and the infinite, that of the continuous and the discontinuous . . . The principle, says Hegel, is the unity of identity and of difference. Because—and this is the most serious—Hegel affirms that contraries are identical, not in another aspect, but precisely *in as much as they are contraries*. Each of the contraries is *other* with respect to its contrary; but this is, in turn, *other* with respect to the first; thus, the two are *other*, and so identical. The opposition of the finite and the infinite must be overcome; the finite is infinite; therefore this is equivalent, Gratry says, to the formula of *pantheism*. But since Hegel understands this in the sense that the finite in its continuous transformations is the truly infinite, in the end it results that the finite is affirmed as the true reality and this, says Gratry, is *atheism*. The hegelian system would be, then, atheism at bottom, with a pantheistic form.

1. *Logique* (1864) I, 267–330, 327–365; *Logic*, translated by Helen and Milton Singer (La Salle, Illinois: The Open Court Publishing Company, 1944), 175–265.

Finally, Hegel affirms that truth must reconcile itself with error, and that the latter, which is the *other* of truth, is its necessary moment, inasmuch as it is *absorbed*. (Gratry already translates thus the hegelian term *aufgehoben* with a penetrating sense of its meaning). As a consequence of this, Hegel denies the validity of the principle of the *excluded third*, according to which one and only one of contradictories is true; Hegel replaces it by the *principle of the intervening third*, according to which there is a term that embraces and unites the two contradictories: *A is, at the same time, A and not A*. And to show this he appeals to the principle that the two terms are identical, since each is *other* than *the other*: '*Etwas* und *Anderes* sind beide erstens Daseinende oder *Etwas. Zweitens* ist eben so jedes ein *Anderes*. Es ist gleichgultig, welches zuerst und bloss darum *Etwas* genannt wird. . . . Beide sind auf gleiche Weise auch Andere. Beide sint sowohl als Etwas als auch als *Anderes* bestimmt, heirmit *dasselbe*' [*Something* and *other* are both first being or *something*. Secondly, each is also an *other*. It is unimportant, which of them is first and simply called *something* . . . Both are in the same way also *other*. Both are thus determined as *something* and also as *other*, and so as *the same*]. In this way Gratry sees that Hegel annihilates the principle of identity in its three forms, and, with it, the syllogistic or deductive form of reason, to end with an identity of all, and so, of the finite and the infinite, of the world and man with God, and of being with nothing; that is to say, with a pantheism that at bottom is no more than atheism.

The Principle of Transcendence—The principal procedure of reason is for Gratry dialectic, the passing, by way of transcendence, from a point of departure to a result that is not included in it, but exceeds and surpasses it. In what direction, then, does that rational process move? The point of departure is the finite thing, in which is found reality and limitation, being and limit. The legitimate dialectic affirms being and denies the limit, and thus elevates itself to the infinite being, which no limitation or negation encloses, and who is God. Sophistic also uses the dialectic procedure, but *by inverting it*. The distinction of positivity and negation appear to it to be *abstraction*. It must include the contradictories, non-being, nothing; thus nothing remains included in the absolute; negation is taken, then, infinitely; it limits, instead of affirming being to the infinite. Hegel says that the absolute as *being* and the absolute as *nothing* are two abstract definitions; the concrete and true is that which contains being and nothing at once as two *moments* of the absolute.

For pure reason being and nothing result indifferently; but, says Gratry, when this happens to it, it is no longer indifferent in reality, but it is the prey of the doctrine of nothing; it prefers nothing, and understands the infinite as the indeterminate and indefinite; thus, for it the infinite does not exist, but nothing. Gratry calls this, even more than the *spirit of sophism*, the *spirit of darkness*. The mind, deprived of the interest of the practical reason of which Kant spoke, of that interest in love for justice and for truth, which is the very spring of the dialectical procedure, inverts the progress of the dialectic and turns to nothingness. As Plato already said, sophism takes refuge in the darkness of nothing, while philosophy, which seeks being, remains enveloped in the divine splendor. The hegelian dialectic, according to Gratry, is inverted dialectic, which instead of elevating itself from the finite to the infinite, descends from the infinite to the finite and from the finite to nothingness.

But, says Gratry, Hegel inverts not only the movement of the dialectical procedure, but its very principle, its theory. Dialectic consists, as we have seen since Plato, in eliminating the limits of the finite and conceiving its perfections in an infinite degree. Hegel takes the contrary position, following the principle of Spinoza: Every determination is a negation. [*Omnis determinatio negatio est*]. Being is pure indetermination: *Being is the indefinitely immediate*, he says at the beginning of his *Logic*. Determination, then, is a particular circumscription in indeterminate being: this is what creatures are, and there Gratry sees the hegelian pantheism. Thus, dialectic must obliterate all indetermination, and so it falls again into the identity of the determinate and the indeterminate, which is God himself. This is, says Gratry, the principal procedure of reason applied *backwards*.

Understanding and Reason—For Gratry, Hegel is the *sophist*, as Cicero is the orator or Aristotle the philosopher: he is the sophist par excellence. But this interpretation is very problematic. I cannot enter here into the discussion of this, because this would oblige one to set up the problem of hegelianism, which would require a volume to itself and would take us further from our purpose. It suffices to indicate the point that should be studied to clarify this question sufficiently.

Gratry notes that Hegel is one of the men who have distinguished with the most energy and rigor the two procedures of reason; only, he says, he destroys the first when he introduces the *principle of the inter-*

vening third, and he inverts the second. The two procedures are called in Hegel *Verstand* and *Vernunft*, understanding and reason. The first is discursive thought, and above all the syllogism; the second, dialectic. Gratry recognises that Hegel describes the dialectic process perfectly as a movement of reason which departs from an object distinct from God, taking it only as point of departure, to pass beyond it and arrive at God. But then it turns out that that point of departure, taken as a *middle* [*medium; means*] is enclosed and included in God, and the speculative moment grasps the unity of the contraries. With this, Gratry says, Hegel destroys the dialectic he has just described.

But Gratry, even while alluding explicitly to it, does not seriously discuss the distinction between *Verstand* and *Vernunft*. What is usually called *reason*, the reason to which traditional logic refers, is the *Verstand*, the hegelian *understanding*, and for it the principle of contradiction, like that of identity, is valid, and the contraries are mutually exclusive: Hegel would never think of denying this. Things considered *abstractly*, that is to say, separated and in themselves, are thus subject to the admitted logical principles. The identity of contraries makes sense only from the point of view of the *Vernunft*, of the *reason* in the sense of Hegel. What is this sense?

It is a question of *absolute knowledge* [*das absolute Wissen*]. It is a total knowledge that apprehends things in a *concrete* mode that is to say, as moments of the absolute. For this, in each thing all the rest are present, including its contraries; this has a close relation with the structure of the *system* in Hegel. In the dialectical movement, which is not a movement of thought, but of the absolute itself, there are conserved, suppressed and separated, that is to say, *absorbed* (*aufgehoben* [sublated]), all the anterior moments, which find their *truth* only in the later state. Even error remains conserved and absorbed in the truth of absolute knowledge. Thus, the critique of Gratry misses the real problem; with which I do not say, it is clear, that he does not touch upon it, but that he only borders on it, avoiding it in its ultimate gravity. The identity of the contraries that Hegel affirms does not move on the plane of the usual logic; the good as such is not evil; Hegel does not think this; the identity exists only in the dialectical movement, in absolute knowledge. This absolute knowledge is, then, in the last instance, *the point of view of God*. The absolute knows itself—it is not a question of knowledge *about* the absolute—and this is philosophy, according to Hegel: the explicit form of the absolute, which happens in man. But is this admissible? Can man possess that absolute knowledge? Can he put himself in the point of view of God? This is precisely the problem.

Pantheism—Hegel, then, is not a sophist, as Gratry believed. But there is, nevertheless, in him a dimension of error, and perhaps of *radical* error, such as corresponds to the radical significance of his brilliant philosophic thought. This was no doubt what Gratry suspected, even though his critique missed the point of view which would have proved more fruitful: the interpretation of hegelian absolute knowledge. But Hegel, if not a sophist, is a pantheist, although in a peculiar sense. He resolutely denied he was a pantheist and considered that his principle of the identity of being and nothing excluded it, while the principle *from nothing, nothing comes* [*ex nihilo, nihil fit*], which denies the passage from nothing to being, and thus creation, seemed to him the very formula of pantheism. Hegel does not say of the reality of the world that it is divine; he does not believe that *all* is *God*; in this sense he is not pantheist, and his denial makes sense. But, from another point of view, the God of Hegel, the absolute, exists only in becoming; he is a God who makes himself, 'God in becoming' [*Gott im Werden*]. Finite beings are not distinct from God, but are *moments* of that absolute being, stages in its dialectical movement. And if Hegel indeed speaks of *creation*, he does not mean by that the Christian creation, the putting into existence of a being distinct from God by an act of the divine free will, but a necessary production, and the world and every finite being are, I repeat again, moments of the absolute. Thus, if Hegel's system seen from within is not pantheist, as my master Zubiri once said, seen from without, for example from the Christian idea of God, it undoubtedly is.

Gratry, in his extraordinarily profound critique of Hegel, (although I feel compelled to make essential criticisms of it), already noted the relation of pantheism with this pretension of the intelligence to arrive at the divine point of view, that is to say, at absolute knowledge. 'Pantheism' he says, 'is the intellectual root of sin. To believe oneself God, that is the evil of the intelligence, and pantheism, as Aristotle himself shows, comes from this, that the human mind claims to think as God alone thinks'. This is, in fact, the proximate danger that always menaces philosophy: to claim to think as God does. Vanity, pride, which is a *sin*, is also an *error*, and it consists, in both senses, in separating oneself from God.

The Theory of Induction or Dialectic

The theory of induction is the central point of Gratry's logic and even of his entire philosophy, in the measure in which the results of his theory of the person and the springs that allow him to arrive at the rational knowledge of God converge in it. In his book, *La connaissance de Dieu*, Gratry insists especially upon the importance and the range of the dialectical or inductive method; and faithful to his habitual procedure, he shows in detail how all the philosophers 'of the first rank' from Plato to Leibniz, have made use of it—in greater or lesser measure and in distinct forms—to prove the existence of the Divinity and know its attributes. But it is in the *Logic*, as was to be expected, that Gratry expounds his doctrine in detail. All of Book IV[2] is dedicated to 'Induction or the dialectical procedure'; but in addition he treats of the same theme in the preface and in the introduction he added to the fifth edition of his *Logic*,[3] and also a polemical appendix against the criticism of Saisset;[4] thus, about 400 pages. It is surprising that, despite this, Gratry does not appear nor is he even mentioned in a book like that of Lachelier[5] on induction, published in 1871, three years after that fifth edition of the *Logic*, or in the great historical works of Brunschvicg,[6] etc.

Not everything is equally interesting in those 400 pages of Gratry. Beginning with certain polemical developments that are not to the point, the posing of the problem of induction in Gratry is affected by three factors that at times serve to confuse it: the first is the imprecision of the logic of the mid-nineteenth century, to which Gratry has to refer to find support for his point of view;[7] the second, the excessive importance that the model of mathematical knowledge has for him, and that leads him to subordinate his exposition to the connections with the infinitesimal calculus, even though he has a clear

2. *Logique* (1855; fifth edition, 1868) II, 1–198.
3. *Logique*, I: 1–145.
4. *Logique*, II: 431–472.
5. Jules Lachelier, *Du fondement de l'induction* (1871).
6. Léon Brunschvicg, *Le progrès de la conscience dans la philosophie occidentale* (1927); *Les étapes de la philosophie mathématique* (1930).
7. Gratry refers to the works of Whewell: *History of the Inductive Sciences* (1837) and *Philosophy of the Inductive Sciences Founded upon their History* (1840); to Hamilton: *Fragments de philosophie* (translated by L Peisse); to Royer-Collard: *Oeuvres de Reid*, t IV; and, above all, to Apelt: *Die Theorie der Induction* (1854).

understanding of the fact that the theory of induction is something autonomous and superior to its possible applications or mathematical derivations; the third, which is initially a virtue, the tendency of Gratry to seek antecedents of his thought in the history of philosophy; this leads him to certain approximations and even somewhat violent identifications of doctrines which, although they possess a common nucleus, are disparate, and all this robs of clarity and rigor the most lively and efficacious line of his thought. Here I shall limit myself to gathering what is most important of the historical foundation Gratry gives to his theory of induction, in order then to expound in its most precise and original traits that same theory of inductive or dialectical procedure.

Platonic Dialectic—According to the testimony of Xenophon[8] and of Aristotle,[9] induction comes from Socrates; he first uses the word ἐπαναγεῖν [*induction*]; Aristotle affirms that we owe to Socrates two things: inductive reasonings and the universal definition; and he adds that both things belong to the beginning of science. These first Socratic glimpses appear mature in Plato. Gratry gives a dense and penetrating exposition[10] of the essence of the process of which Platonic dialectic consists.

Gratry bases himself principally upon the last pages of Book VI of the *Republic* and the first pages of VII, above all the commentaries and explications of the myth of the cave; and he bolsters his thesis with testimonies of other Platonic dialogues. 'There is', says Gratry,[11] 'a page of Plato, which seems to us never to have been understood, and from which, in any case, no one has ever drawn out what it contains. It is the one where he describes what he calls the dialectic procedure, and the law of this procedure and the term of this procedure.' I am going to cite that page, as Gratry does, keeping the decisive expressions in Greek.[12]

8. *Memorabilia*, IV, 6, 13.
9. *Metaphysics*, XIII, 4.
10. *Logique*, II, 1–16.
11. *Logique*, 3–4.
12. *República*, 510b–511d. . . . the word *hypothesis* must be understood in the Greek sense of 'supposition' or 'point of departure' . . . Gratry notes (*Logic*, II, 8): 'It is well understood that the Greek word ὑπόθεσις means *point of departure*. If one translates this word by the French word *hypothèse*, one makes a contradiction, and one does not at all understand that fundamental page. Plato and Aristotle

'Consider then again the way in which we are to make the division of the intelligible section.'

'In what way?'

'By the distinction that there is one section of it which the soul is compelled to investigate by treating as images the things imitated in the former division, and by means of assumptions [ἐξ ὑποθέσεων] from which it proceeds not up to a first principle [οὐκ ἐπ' ἀρχὴν πορευομένη] but down to a conclusion [ἀλλ' ἐπὶ τελευτήν], while there is another section in which it advances from its assumption to a beginning or principle that transcends assumption [ἐπ' ἀρχὴν ἀνυπόθετον ἐξ ὑποθέσεως ἰοῦσα], and in which it makes no use of the images employed by the other section, relying on ideas only and progressing systematically through ideas.'

'I don't fully understand what you mean by this', he said.

'Well, I will try again', said I, 'for you will better understand after this preamble. For I think you are aware that students of geometry and reckoning and such subjects first postulate the odd and the even and the various figures and three kinds of angles and other things akin to these in each branch of science, regard them as known, and, treating them as absolute assumptions [ὑποθέσεις], do not deign to render any further account of them to themselves or others, taking it for granted that they are obvious to everybody. They take their start from these [ἐκ τούτων δ' ἀρχόμενοι], and, pursuing the inquiry from

---

understand by *hypothesis* a positive point of departure, the existence of which is given' [*Il est bien entendu que le mot grec ὑπόθεσις signifie point de départ. Si l'on traduit ce mot par le mot français hypothèse, on fait un contre-sens, et l'on ne comprend point cette page fondamental. Platon et Aristote entendent par hypothèse un point de depart positif, dont l'existence est donnée*]. And he invokes the text of Aristotle, (*Posterior Analytics*, I, 2): 'The thesis that establishes either of the two parts of the enunciation, take for example, that something is or that something is not, is a hypothesis, and that which does not meet these conditions is a definition' [72a19–22]. Trendelenburg (*Elementa logices Aristoteleae*, sixth edition, 1868, at section 66, comments on this passage saying: 'For it is *thesis* or definition that poses what a thing is, or *hypothesis*, which poses that a thing exists or not, as for example motion is, a vacuum does not exist . . . Whatever therefore Aristotle wishes to postulate as existing or not, for him is a *hypothesis*' [*Est enim θέσις vel definitio, quae ponit quid res sit, vel ὑπόθεσις, quae aliquam rem esse vel non esse*]. And finally GRG. Mure comments on his translation of the passage of the *Posterior Analytics* (Oxford, 1928) with this note: '*Hypothesis* to Aristotle and Plato means an assumption not calling for proof within the sphere of the special science in which it operates, not a *working hypothesis*.'

this point on consistently [διεξιόντες τελευτῶσιν ὁμολογουμένως], conclude with that for the investigation of which they set out.'

'Certainly', he said, 'I know that.'

'And do you not also know that they further make use of the visible forms [τοῖς ὁρωμένοις εἴδεσι] and talk about them, although they are not thinking of them but of those things of which they are a likeness, pursuing their inquiry for the sake of the square as such and the diagonal as such, and not for the sake of the image of it which they draw? And so in all cases. The very things which they mold and draw, which have shadows and images of themselves in water, these things they treat in their turn as only images [ὡς εἰκόσιν], but what they really seek is to get sight of those realities which can be seen only by the mind [τῇ διανοίᾳ].'

'True', he said.

'This then is the class that I described as intelligible, it is true, but with the reservation first that the soul is compelled to employ assumptions [ὑποθέσεσι δ' ἀναγκαζομέη χρῆσθαι] in the investigation of it, not proceeding to a first principle [οὐκ ἐπ' ἀρχήν ἰοῦσαν] because of its inability to extricate itself from and rise above its assumptions [οὐ δυναμένη τῶν ὑποθέσεων ἀνωτέρω ἐκβαίνειν], and second, that it uses as images or likenesses the very objects that are themselves copied and adumbrated by the class before them, and that in comparison with these latter are esteemed as clear and held in honor.'

'I understand', said he, 'that you are speaking of what falls under geometry and the kindred arts.'

'Understand then', said I, 'that by the other section of the intelligible I mean that which reason itself [αὐτός ὁ λόγος] lays hold of by the power of dialectic [τῇ τοῦ διαλέγεσθαι δυνάμει] treating its assumptions not as absolute beginnings but literally as hypotheses [ὑποθέσεις ποιούμενος οὐκ ἀρχάς, ἀλλά τῷ ὄντι ὑποθέσεις], underpinnings, footings, and springboards so to speak [οἷον ἐπιβάσεις τε καὶ ὁρμάς], to enable it to rise to that which requires no assumption and is the starting point of all [μέχρι τοῦ ἀνυποθέτου ἐπὶ τὴν τοῦ παντὸς ἀρχὴν ἴων], and after attaining to that again taking hold of the first dependencies from it, so to proceed downward to the conclusion, making no use whatever of any object of sense but only of pure ideas moving on through ideas to ideas and ending with ideas.'

'I understand', he said, 'not fully, for it is no slight task that you appear to have in mind, but I do understand that you mean to distinguish the aspect of reality and the intelligible, which is contemplated by the power of dialectic, as something truer and more exact than the object of the so-called arts and sciences whose assumptions [αἷς αἱ ὑποθέσεις ἀρχαί] are arbitrary starting points. And though it is true that those who contemplate them are compelled to use their understanding and not their senses, yet because they do not go back to the beginning in the study of them but start from assumptions you do not think they possess true intelligence [νοῦν] about them although the things themselves are intelligibles when apprehended in conjunction with a first principle. And I think you call the mental habit of geometers, and their like, mind or understanding and not reason because you regard understanding as something intermediate between opinion and reason.'

'Your interpretation is quite sufficient', I said. [510B–511D; Translated by Paul Shorey]

This is the platonic text that serves as a basis for Gratry, something he confirms by appealing to a whole series of texts coming from other dialogues.[13] What follows from these passages of Plato, in fact little utilized, and not always—even today—well understood?[14]

---

13. For the assistance of the reader, I give here his references, since to transcribe them would be too extensive: *Sophist*, 253e; *Republic*, 534e, 533c; *Phaedo*, 101c; *Parmenides*, 136e; *Euthydemus*, 290c; *Phaedo*, 176; *Republic*, 522, 523, 515b, 518c, 532.

14. Interesting precisions can be seen in the book of Victor Goldschmidt: *Les dialogues de Platon: structure et méthode dialectique* (1947), which acutely brings into relation with the cited passages from the *Republic*, Letter VII—whether or not it is authentic. Despite his considerable and most minute work, Goldschmidt is not free of a certain confusion on the decisive point. Of course he uses the equivocal expression 'hypothesis'; in the second place—and this is more serious—he takes the hypothesis to be a definition, despite everything we have seen in the earlier note, to the point of speaking of the 'hypothesis-definition'; but above all he formally annuls the peculiarity of the dialectic, which consists in surpassing the *hypothéseis* in order to elevate oneself to a principle not contained in them [*arkhè anhypóthetos*]. Goldschmidt in fact writes (10): 'This initial hypothesis, of which the geometrician takes no further notice, is the *definition*. Once the *definition is supposed true*, [*la définition supposée vraie*] he deduces from it the qualities of the circle—not the essence!—thus carrying on this obscure science which is found at the fourth rung of the modes of knowledge. The geometric procedure would then be the following: image, definition, science (in the sense of the fourth mode). The dialectician, for his part, proceeds like the geometrician up to the point at which he arrives at the *hypothesis-definition*. But instead of

passing immediately and without return to the consequences, he raises himself *progressively from hypothesis to hypothesis* to end up at the "principle of all", "the most luminous part of being", the essence; from there alone he redescends to conclusions ("perfect" science) ["science *parfait*"].' [My emphasis]. And the curious thing is that he cites in support of his phrase 'progressively from hypothesis to hypothesis' the text of Plato (511b6), in which the latter describes the use of the *hypotheses* as 'rungs and springboards'.

On the other hand, Joseph Moreau, in *La construction de l'idéalisme platonicien* (1939), has seen perfectly the meaning of the dialectic, and concretely of this passage of the *Republic*. He writes: 'The text of *Republic* VI, 511bc, distinguishes clearly two moments of the dialectic and characterise metaphorically the intellectual nature of each of them; the first is an ascension; it consists of elevating oneself *by a leap*, the hypotheses serving as springboard, high enough to seize the unconditioned principle; the second consists, after having touched the summit, in redescending while supporting oneself by the successive conditions which depend upon it [ἐχόμενος τῶν ἐκείνης ἐχομένων]. In this *leap on high followed by a descent along a knotted rope*, it is easy to recognises the *intuitive* character of the ascending dialectic, the discursive character of the descending dialectic' [*Le texte de Rep. VI, 511bc, distingue nettement deux moments de la dialectique et caractérise métaphoriquement la nature intellectuelle de chacun d'eux; le premier est une ascension; il consiste à s'élever* ***d'un bond****, les hypothèses servent de tremplin, assez haut pour saisir le principe unconditionné; le second consiste, après avoir touché le sommet, à redescendre en se soutenant aux conditions successives qui y sont suspendues . . . Dans ce* ***saut en hauteur suivi d'une descente le long d'une corde à noeuds****, il est aisé de reconnaître le caractère* ***intuitif*** *de la dialectique ascendante, le caractère discursif de la dialectique descendante*] (346, note; my emphasis; for the rest, read all of chapter VII). Certainly, neither Goldschmidt nor Moreau seems to know Gratry.

One may also read Goldschmidt's book, *Le paradigme dans la dialectique platonicienne* (1947), above all the section on 'Paradigm and Induction' (92–97).

For his part, León Robin: *Platon* (1938), 84–86, observes accurately: 'While the method of the sciences and, in particular, that of mathematics, consists in taking as point of departure a "given" or a "supposed" [*hypothesis*], of which one does not give account to oneself or others, and observes whether 'what results from it" [*symbaïnonta*] agrees with or destroys this point of departure, the dialectic method for its part does not see in it any "principle": for the dialectic it is simply "a point of support from which to launch oneself forward", up to a point Plato calls "anhypothetic", that is to say, one that does not suppose anything further, but which imposes itself inasmuch as it is unconditional and self-sufficient . . . Thus the capital step of the dialectician will be that which, precisely because one is never satisfied, consists in raising oneself "on high," "still higher" (VI, 511a; *Phaedo*, 101d), until one will have attained, if one can, the unconditional and perfectly assured foundation to which one aspires. This is then the *ascending* [*épanodos*] procedure which is specific to the dialectic' [*Tandis que la méthode*

Plato distinguishes two procedures of reason. In the first, as in the second, one starts from certain data, from those that are called *hypothéseis*,[15] and which are, as Gratry translates well, 'points of departure', or better, *suppositions*. These suppositions have a real character, they are not 'hypotheses', provisional guesses of a merely methodical value, 'working hypotheses'. Thus these are not definitions, in which precisely there is lacking the character of real positing; and the fact that, in a certain type of objects, the definition is already the positing of its type of 'reality' can only lead to this confusion. So far what is common to both procedures; but now the differences begin.

The function of those suppositions or *hypothéseis* is not the same. In the first case they are principles [*arkhaí*], and thought advances toward the consequences or conclusions of those principles; that is to say, it *deduces* from them, by way of identity, what was already contained implicitly in them. In the second case, which is dialectic *in the strict sense*, reason begins equally from suppositions—which in the final instance are sensible—but it uses them in a different way: not as principles, but as mere points of support, springboards to launch itself toward something that altogether exceeds them, which is not contained in them. Instead of proceeding by way of identity, it advances by way of transcendence; and instead of seeking consequences included in the suppositions, it raises itself to an unconditioned *principle*, not contained in them, and which, thus, transcends them. Only then, from this principle, does reason descend, by way of

des sciences et, en particulier, celle des mathématiques, consiste à prendre pour point de départ un 'posé', ou un 'supposé' [hypothesis], dont on ne rend raison ni à autrui ni à soi-même, et à observer si 'ce qui en résulte'. . . s'accord avec ce point de départ ou bien le ruine, de son côté la méthode de la dialectique n'y voit nullement un 'principe': pour elle il y a là seulement 'un point d'appui pour s'élancer en avant', jusqu'à un terme que Platon appelle 'anhypothètique', c'est-à-dire qui ne se supposse {sic} plus, mais qui s'impose en tant que qu'il est inconditionnel et se suffit à lui-même . . . . Ainsi, la démarche capitale du dialecticien sera celle qui consiste, justement parce qu'on n'est pas satisfait, à s'élever 'vers le haute', 'encore plus haut' (VI, 511 a; Phédon, 101 d), et jusqu'a ce qu'on ait atteint, si on le peut, le fondemont inconditionnel et parfaitement assuré auquel on aspire. C'est donc la marche ascendante . . . qui est spécifique de la dialectique].

These notes taken from the recent French bibliography on Plato, and brought forward in reverse chronological order, give significant results with reference to the actual state of ideas on this point, as difficult as it is important.

15. [Where Greek transliteration is used by Marías, it is used in this translation—Translator].

consequence, from idea to idea; and this function of making things comprehensible and justified *from the* first *principle* is what Plato calls *to give reason* [*lógon didónai*].[16]

In Book VII of the *Republic* Plato adds new precisions about dialectic, at the same time as he underlines its difficulties and the task required to understand in what it consists.[17] Plato says that when one 'makes use of dialectic in order to attempt to turn his attention, with the help of reason and without the intervention of any sense, toward that which makes each thing what it is in itself, and when one refuses to stop until he reaches, with the help of intelligence alone, that which is good in itself, then he finally arrives at the very essence of the intelligible'.[18] And he affirms energetically that there is no other means than dialectic for arriving at those true realities: 'The dialectic faculty is the only one that can demonstrate it . . . and it is not possible to arrive at it by any other means.'[19] The other sciences, geometry and the rest, have only the dream of being, but are not capable of contemplating it wide awake, because they make use of *suppositions* leaving them intact and cannot *give a reason* for them.[20] 'The dialectical method', he concludes, 'is the only one that, leaving behind the hypothesis (more exactly, annulling the suppositions or points of support), sets out toward the principle itself to set foot there on terra firma; and the eye of the soul, which is truly sunk in a barbarous quagmire, it attracts with gentleness and lifts it up to the heights'.[21]

In these terms, as Gratry saw with perspicacity, Plato formulates his theory of the dialectic method, in which sensible things and the objects accessible to the *diánoia* are what *induce* us to elevate ourselves, transcending them, to the true reality of the ideas, and, above all, of the good.

Aristotelian Induction—'Everyone knows well enough', says Gratry, 'that Aristotle is the author of the syllogistic laws; but people usually fail to realize how much he has spoken of induction'.[22] Even the more recent books pass over almost completely the aristotelian theory of

16. *República*, 510c; 533c.
17. *Cf* 531b–533e.
18. 532ab [Translator C McNamee].
19. 533a.
20. 533c.
21. 533cd.
22. *Logique*, II, 16.

induction. Copleston, for example, says: 'The analysis of deductive processes he carried to a very high level and very completely; but he cannot be said to have done the same for induction.'[23] Rivaud, for his part, affirms that: 'The *Prior Analytics* represent induction [ἐπαγωγή] as a form of imperfect syllogism, dialectic, or rhetoric.'[24] And each disposes of the question with a few imprecise lines.

Gratry gives a minute exposition, supported by the original texts, of the ideas of Aristotle on induction. Reason has two procedures: syllogism and induction. Some reasonings are syllogistic and others inductive; both procedures are the origins of all we learn, the founts of all belief or conviction [*pístis*], and from these two proceed all science and all demonstration.[25]

What is induction? The inverse of the syllogism: the syllogism leads to conclusions for which it furnishes a middle term [*méson*]; induction leads to those in which there is no middle term. The syllogism starts from the universal; induction, from the particular, but that universal can only be obtained by induction. Induction is the passage from the particular to the universal, and shows the latter in the light of the particular; it gives, then, the principle [*arkhé*] and the universal [*kathólou*], while the syllogism begins from universals. The principles of the syllogism are the majors; but these are not obtained by means of the syllogism, but by induction, which is the way that leads to the principles, the procedure that finds the primitive proposition, that to which no intermediary leads. Deduction, then, is not enough; induction is needed to discover the primitive propositions, when there is no intermediary, despite the fact that all science comes from some anterior knowledge.[26]

Starting from these elements, Gratry cites and analyses the last chapter of the *Posterior Analytics*, 'summary of the logic of Aristotle'. After expounding the theory of the syllogism and demonstration, and, thus, of demonstrative science [*epistéme apodeiktiké*], Aristotle

23. FC Copleston, SJ: *A History of Philosophy*, I (1947), 282.

24. A Rivaud: *Histoire de la Philosophie*, I, (1948), 254.

25. *Logique*, II, 16–17. The aristotelian texts cited by Gratry are: *Prior Analytics*, II, 23; *Posterior Analytics*, I, 1; I, 18; *Topics*, I, 8; I, 12; *Nicomachean Ethics*, VI, 3; *Rhetoric*, I, 2.

26. *Logique*, II, 17–19. The texts cited are: *Prior Analytics*, II, 23; *Posterior Analytics*, I, 18; *Topics*, I, 12; *Posterior Analytics*, I, 1; *Nicomachean Ethics*, VI, 3; *Posterior Analytics*, I, 23; *Prior Analytics*, II, 23; *Posterior Analytics*, I, 3; II, 19.

must *inquire* about the principles, how they are known and what is the habit that makes them known. It is not possible to know by means of demonstration if the first immediate principles are not known; the grasp of those is the problem; it is necessary to see in what measure it is a matter of *epistéme* in either case. Aristotle encounters the double difficulty of whether that knowledge is innate or acquired and comes from outside; if it is innate, how do we possess it without knowing something more precise and rigorous than demonstration? And if we do not possess it, how can we learn without a previous knowledge? The principles are neither innate, nor do they come from without, but rather we have a certain faculty or power [*tina dynamin*], which all animals possess, and which is what in them is called sensibility or *aísthesis*. In some a persistence of perception is produced, and from it, memory, and this engenders experience or *empeiría*, as Aristotle also indicates in the first chapter of the *Metaphysics*; and from this derive art or *tékhne* and science or *epistéme*, according to whether it is a question of production or of what is. 'Thus, then', Aristotle adds,

> these habits neither exist already determined in the soul, nor do they proceed from other habits more capable of knowing, but from sensation [*aísthesis*], as in a battle, where, when flight is indicated, once one stops, then another one stops, and then another, until authority is re-established: the soul is constituted in such a way that it can experience this. Indeed, when an individual focuses on this, first it is universal in the soul (it also perceives the particular, but the sensation is of the universal, for example of man, and not of the particular man Callias); and, in the second place, one focuses on this until one sees clearly the universal without any particular, for example on this concrete animal until one sees the essence of 'animal', and so on with other things as well. It is evident then that for us it is necessary to know the first by induction and in fact it is only thus that sensation produces 'the universal' in the soul. And given the fact that of the habits of thought by which we arrive at the truth, some are always true and others sometimes false, like opinion and reflection, while science and intellect [*noûs*] are always true, and no other kind of science is more exact than intellect, and principles are more knowable than demonstrations, and all science is accompanied by reason, there cannot be a 'science' [*epistéme*] of principles. And given

> the fact that nothing can be truer than science unless it is intellect, intellect will be of principles, if we pay attention to these reasons, and, at the same time, because the principle of the demonstration is not itself a demonstration, neither will the principle of science be itself a science. Therefore if we do not have, outside science itself, any true foundation, intellect itself will be the other principle of science.[27]

Induction, says Gratry, makes us know principles, because only through it does the *aísthesis* [sense] put into our mind the universal. There are, then, two classes of principles for Aristotle: the common principles or rules of demonstration and the principles proper to each science;[28] these latter principles, which are not innate, which are not possessed beforehand, although they have no intermediate that leads to them, can be called, says Gratry, *tesis.* They are the proper principles or majors of syllogisms, which are neither possessed beforehand, nor deduced, nor arrived at by any intermediate, but by induction applied to the data of experience or *empeiría.*[29] Such is the form in which Gratry understands the presence of the inductive method in Aristotle, that is to say, the form in which he acquires the 'principal procedure of reason'.[30]

The Infinitesimal Method—Gratry, dominated by the forces of his time and by his education at the Polytechnical Institute, gives great attention to the mathematical applications of the inductive and dialectical procedure, to such a point that for some his logic was nothing but a derivative from the infinitesimal calculus; thus Saisset, who—let it be said in passing—misunderstood both the *Logic* of Gratry and the mathematical meaning of the operation of passing to the limit.[31] But in the mind of Gratry, the things are distinct: the infinitesimal method in mathematics is nothing but a consequence or application,

27. *Posterior Analytics*, II, 19. The translation cited is that of M Araújo in my Anthology *La filosofía en sus textos*, I, 102 (1950).
28. *Posterior Analytics*, I, 10.
29. *Posterior Analytics*, II, 19.
30. On recent interpretations of aristotelian induction, the book of Hamelin, *Le systéme d' Aristote* (1920), 253–259, can be consulted, as well as that of L Robin, *Aristotle* (1944), 52–59. The interpretation of Ross, which is very close to that of Gratry, represents a step forward; see *Aristotle's Prior and Posterior Analytics*, revised text with an introduction and commentary by WD Ross (Oxford, 1949).
31. See the appendix to the *Logic* (1868), II, 431–472.

especially brilliant, of the 'principal procedure of reason', of induction or dialectic, which is applied in all sciences. The differential and integral calculus is for him the confirmation of the efficacy and the rigor of induction in the sense that he gives to the term, connected, as we have seen, with Plato and Aristotle, quite distinct from the baconian 'incomplete induction', which yields at best only a probable conclusion, and from the 'complete induction', with its strictly limited scope, usually connected with Aristotle, and whose range is strictly limited. It is not necessary to enter here into the minute details Gratry gives about the infinitesimal procedure in mathematics; it is enough to indicate the most concise formula he uses to express his thought on this point.[32]

Gratry takes account above all of Kepler and Leibniz, with frequent reference to Wallis, to Newton, and also—by contrast—to Lagrange, who tried to construct mathematics while avoiding the idea of the infinite; and of the contemporary mathematicians: his masters Poinsot and Ampère, his friend Cauchy, and Cournot. The general problem the differential calculus poses, says Gratry, is this: 'Given a difference, a variation between two data, two magnitudes, two velocities, two positions, two forces, which depend upon one and the same law, to find beneath that difference, that variation and that plurality the unity of the law that associates them.'[33] Given, for example, points on a curve, it is a matter of finding in its various positions, in the particular relations dependent on them, 'the essential relationship that characterizes them all as points on a unique and definite curve.'[34] In these relations, the analysis discovers two parts: one dependent upon the relative position of the different points on the curve, the other dependent upon the fact of their all belonging to the same curve. The analysis breaks down the complete data into its two components: one indefinitely variable and the other fixed. The formula that the infinitesimal analysis finds is this: $f'x + X\Delta x$,[35] calling X a function of x which, in general, does not become infinite when Δx becomes zero, and Δx has the finite difference. 'Of the two terms of this binomial',

32. The developments alluded to are to be found especially in Vol. II of the *Logique*, 36–168, and also in other places and in *La connaissance de Dieu*, Ch. 9.

33. *Logique*, I, 102.

34. *Logique*, I, 103.

35. The author noted a misprint of the equation in the Spanish edition. It is here corrected—Translator.

adds Gratry, 'the first term is invariable for a given curve, the second varies dependent on the choice of points; it suffices to eliminate the second and keep only the first; in this does induction consist'.[36]

In a different form, Gratry reproduces his argumentation: Given points randomly designated on a curve, the analysis takes any one as basis of comparison, and refers to it the rest that are distinct from it, each one according to its particular position. The variable and total relation of each point with the point of comparison is called the *difference*; and the essential part of that relation, which comes from the fact that all those points are points on the same curve, is called the *differential*. The admirable secret of the analysis consists, then, in finding always, by means of a very simple operation, the *differential* in the *difference*. And this operation consists precisely in eliminating the differences of the individual positions, to obtain in this way the unity of the essential point. But how does the analysis eliminate these differences, variable for each point, so as to keep only the constant and permanent relation that links all the points of the curve? By going out from a finite quantity, being raised above the quantity to that limit of the quantity that Leibniz says is exterior to the quantity[37] *in order to analyse*, he says, *the indivisible and the infinite*. And how go beyond quantity, when quantity is composed of points in space? Precisely by supposing and establishing that those points stop being dispersed and coalesce. Then the differences are eliminated and there is no longer anything but the differential. Then the curve is studied, outside of space, dissemination, and quantity, in that ideal simplicity in which, according to the expression of a great geometrician,[38] *the entire curve*, to the eyes of the mind, *is as it were united in a point. All the characteristices of changeability found in the curve are concentrated at that point*. And, in fact, the simple differential implies and gives all the properties of the curve. This is truly the type of the entire inductive procedure.[39]

The infinitesimal calculus proves, says Gratry, the *legitimacy* of the procedure. What is important in this mathematical example is to see

36. *Logique*, I, 103–104.

37. Gratry always cites the expression of Leibniz, according to which the infinite and the infinitesimal are *extremitates quantitatis* [bounds of quantity], *non inclusae sed seclusae* [not included but secluded].

38. Cauchy.

39. *Logique*, I, 104–105.

how one goes from the finite to the infinite, not by way of identity, by intermediaries, but by means of a unique and direct operation, which is called *passing to the limit*. In the same way, when we affirm in all rigor that the sum of the *infinite* terms of the series:

$$1/2 + 1/4 + 1/8 + 1/16 + 1/32 + \ldots + 1/2n$$

is equal to 1, we do not arrive at this conclusion by adding infinite terms, which is neither possible nor has any sense, but by means of passing to the limit, basing ourselves upon the *law* of the series and upon its general term, that is to say, upon a finite number of terms, in which we seek and find, without intermediaries, their relation to the infinite.

Induction or dialectic, as general procedure of reason, can be applied in mathematics, as Leibniz, Newton, and their successors have done, and, in a less perfect form, the most ancient mathematicians; in physics, as the works of Kepler, and above all the *Philosophiae naturalis principia mathematica* of Newton,[40] prove, and principally in philosophy, in particular as a way to the knowledge of God. What is, finally, the idea of the inductive method of Gratry?

The Theory of Induction in Gratry—I have insisted various times upon the general ignorance of Gratry's philosophy, even more upon the lack of 'currency' of his thought, which has brought it about that even some books[41] dedicated to his thought have turned out to be useless and have not succeeded in impeding the persistent neglect of his work. A propos of induction, the matter is even more strange, because not only can the great treatises on Logic ignore Gratry, but the monographs dedicated to induction, including those in French, completely ignore him. Already I have recalled the case of Lachelier, in 1871, during the lifetime of Gratry, after five editions of his *Logic*; only social reasons or those relating to university politics can explain the absence of any mention in the thesis of Lachelier. In recent books,

40. On the method of Newton, see my study, 'Physics and Metaphysics in Newton,' (in *San Anselmo y el insensato*, *Obras*, IV).
41. Especially those of B Pointud-Guillemont: *Essai sur la philosophie de Gratry*, and EJ Scheller: *Grundlagen der Erkenntnislehre bei Gratry*, very detailed, but insufficient theoretically.

like that of Lalande,[42] and that of Dorolle,[43] the very name of Gratry is altogether missing, despite the fact that the first is, in greater part, of a historical character.

Gratry utilises the works of some contemporaries on the problem of induction: Hamilton, Whewell, Apelt, Remusat, Waddington.[44] They are all agreed that the theory of induction remains to be worked out. Gratry cites the statement of Whewell, according to which 'the logic of induction has not yet been constructed';[45] Apelt picks up that position and makes it his own.[46] It is necessary to note that the position of Gratry does not derive from his contemporaries, but rather from the sources studied in the earlier works: Plato, Aristotle, and the mathematicians of the seventeenth century; for the rest, the general thesis of Gratry is that induction or dialectic has been used by all philosophers, at least as regards the knowledge of the Divinity, of the divine nature and attributes; and the greater part of *La connaissance de Dieu* is dedicated to showing this and to expounding his own theory. The explanations of the *Logic* although essential, are only refinements, and enrichments of a theory Gratry already possessed, actually before the publication of Apelt's book, which is the most serious attempt of those made to formulate the problem.

The attitude of Apelt coincides with that of Gratry in some respects. Induction is for the German philosopher the junction in which empirical and metaphysical knowledge come together: 'der Knotenpunkt in welchem Empirie und Metaphisik zusammenhängen.'[47] Apelt distinguishes between empirical and rational induction: the first consists in the conjoined enumeration of similar cases, and from it there follows only a mathematical probability that analogous cases are founded in a *regularity*, whose *rule* is not discovered. Rational induction, on the other hand, permits one to infer more from what is contained in the reunited perceptions: '*Die rationelle Induction dage-*

42. *Les théories de l'induction et de l'experimentation* (1929, edition of class notes at the Sorbonne, 1921–1922).
43. *Les problèmes de l'induction* (1926). I have not been able to consult the work of J Nicod, *Le problème logique de l'induction* (1924), but it is not likely that he utilises Gratry.
44. See *Logique*, I, 91.
45. [William Whewell,] *Philosophy of Inductive Sciences* II, 616.
46. EF Apelt: *Die Theorie der Induction* (1854), 6.
47. Apelt: *Die Theorie der Induction*, 6.

gen lässt auf ein Mehreres schliessen, als was in der blossen Zusammenstellung der Wahrnehmungen liegt.'[48] The most ancient original sin [*der uralte Erbfehler*] of the theory of induction, for Apelt, is to have separated it totally from all *a priori* knowledge and to have taken as its principle the anticipation or expectation of similar cases, which has led to its being confused with arguments of probability.[49] Apelt carries the history of induction back to Socrates, Plato, and Aristotle, and comments on some texts of the last two, although with less penetration and care than Gratry; he concerns himself more with the moderns: Tycho-Brahe, Galileo, Kepler and Newton, and the English philosophers of the seventeenth and eighteenth centuries, ending with Whewell, historian and philosopher of inductions (Geschichtschreiber und Philosoph de Inductionen). He also pays attention to Stuart Mill, one whose absence from the work of Gratry is surprising. And in the last chapter he studies the relation of induction with mathematics, and takes as the prime example—as Gratry did—Kepler.[50]

Despite these analogies, the sense of the book of Apelt is quite distinct, much more oriented toward the sciences of nature and the coordination of English inductive philosophy with German speculative thought. Now we have to ask ourselves what is the most personal and proper nucleus of the theory of induction of Gratry.

For Gratry, logic is, above all, inventive, a logic of discovery of the truth. He makes his own the position of Leibniz when he wrote to a correspondent, Wagner, that the existing logics are barely a shadow [*kaum ein Schatten*] of what he desired and guessed at; but that, despite that, they are useful, and one cannot arrive at a satisfactory logic without the help of the innermost part of mathematics [*ohne Hülfe der inneren Mathematik*], that is to say, the infinitesimal calculus.[51]

This reform of logic is what Gratry intends in giving all its value to the principal procedure of reason, despite its being less well known, which he calls *transcendence* in the unique and strict sense that it *does not concern identity*, and whose historical antecedents have been called *dialectic* or, with greater frequency, *induction*. Let us see, in the first place, the metaphysical foundations of this inventive logic.

48. Apelt: *Die Theorie der Induction*, 44.

49. Apelt: *Die Theorie der Induction*, 45.

50. Apelt: *Die Theorie der Induction*, 189ff.

51. *Logique*, I, 149–151.

a) *Certainty and its Sources*—When questions are posed, says Gratry, the first is this: Can we be certain of something? Well then, he adds, certainty is the ultimate proof of truth, and, thus, cannot be proved except by itself. It is necessary, consequently, to renounce—not to content oneself with less, but in a scientific spirit—'absolute demonstration'; rationalism is an error that consists in seeking not certainty, but demonstration; in wanting to demonstrate what is already certain. Skepticism, which denies the truth of all that is not demonstrated to it, takes it one step further: 'The vision of the world does not prove the existence of the world. This means, you cannot prove the existence of the world, and you must doubt it.'[52] Gratry denies this formally and in the most systematic way: 'The sight of the world being nothing other than the world itself, in presence of man, and seen by him, it implies necessarily, or rather manifests directly, its existence.'[53]

Data, irrational in themselves and as such, are the bases of rational propositions. Philosophy is full of problems badly posed and insoluble: 'Philosophy must demonstrate directly the insolubility of insoluble questions.'[54] The pretension of absolute demonstration is absurd and comes from a profound vice of the mind, from a radical immorality: instinctive egoism, in which the mind makes itself center, author, point of departure, first cause of truth; that pretension applies to everything the procedure of identity, of the syllogism. 'One regards', Gratry concludes, 'as unknown what is well known, as doubtful, what is seen . . . Philosophy would do well to ask humankind to grant to her, without previous demonstration, that there exists something, of which we are certain, and that the legitimate and rigorously scientific way to arrive at that certitude is simply to open one's eyes.' [*On regard*—Gratry concludes—*comme inconnu ce qui est très-connu, comme douteux ce qui est vu . . . La philosophie ferait bien de prier le genre humaine de lui accorder, sans démonstration préalable, qu'il existe quelque chose, que nous en sommes certains, et que le moyen légitime et rigoureusement scientifique d'arriver à cette certitude est simplement d'ouvrir les yeux*].[55] It is easy to see in this attitude an anticipation of what has led the philosophy of our century to resolve

52. *Logique*, I, 167–170.
53. *Logique*, I, 171.
54. *Logique*, I, 175.
55. *Logique*, I, 218.

with a strange simplicity decisive questions that modern thought dragged from various centuries, and most especially to overcome idealism, without falling again into the limitation and the error of the realist thesis.

A second source of philosophical errors is that which Gratry calls the exclusive methods. When a man has thought a little, he takes his particular point of view, his way of looking at things, as the only possible one, and he believes that reality exhausts itself in what he has seen. For some, the method is, simply, the analysis of sensation; for others, the spontaneous development of pure reason, which draws all from itself; or the practice of the good; or the authority of human kind, common sense and language; or the authority of the sound part of humanity; or the comparison of all doctrines by means of the history of philosophy; or, finally, the heart and the inspiration of God in each soul. 'It is evident', concludes Gratry, 'that each of these points of view has its truth, but that all are false in as much as exclusive . . . the true method consists in the uniting of all the sources and all the means' [*Il est éviden—Gratry concludes—que chacun de ces points de vue a sa vérité, mais que tous sont faux en tant qu'exclusifs . . . la vraie méthode consiste dans la réunion de toutes les sources et tous les moyens*].[56]

b) *The Foundation of Induction*—Gratry sums up the constitutive parts of the dialectical procedure in this enumeration, to which we shall return later: *perception, abstraction, generalization, analogy, induction.*[57] To perceive, Gratry affirms, is to reach *outside myself*, by means of thought, to the object whose impression is in me; in it there is something that can cross the famous abyss from the *I* to the *not-I.* And he adds these decisive words: 'For all living connection with what is not we, there is needed a kind of going out of ourselves. There must be an *élan*, there must be something altogether different from the syllogistic immanence; there must be a dialectic *élan* that passes from the same to the different' [*Pour tout rapport vivant à ce qui n'est pas nous, il faut cette espèce de sortie de nous-même. Il faut un élan, il faute toute autre chose que l'immanence syllogistique; il faut l'élan dialectique qui passe du même au différent*].[58] In other words, *all vital*

56. *Logique*, I, 239–240.
57. *Logique*, II, 43.
58. *Logique*, II, 45.

relation is transcendence. In every vital action, in simple perception, there is included the *germ* [*germen*]—the expression is Gratry's—of the dialectical procedure.

Gratry further affirms what will later be an important thesis of the psychology of Brentano: that perception is a judgment: 'The act of simple perception crosses the abyss of a sensation to an implicit judgment.'[59] There is, he says in another place, a step of the mind toward the object that solicits it, and that is *epagogé*; on the other hand, the concrete data of all perception are innumerable, and the mind must execute an operation that consists in abstracting, if it wishes to know, that is to say, to know what something is, to go back to the essence, or, at least, to the essential character of each thing.[60]

There is, consequently, in the mere perception a tendency and as it were an abbreviated induction: abstraction accompanies the transcendence of the I toward the distinct thing, eliminating and obliterating the individual characters of the sensible data; generalization passes from an individual or a few to all possible, and, in a certain sense, from the finite to the infinite; analogy shows, 'in the image seen, the characters of the invisible model'; the data, then, *lead us* to elevate ourselves to an essential knowledge. But for that there is needed a spring, which is concretely a *belief*, and it is this, that there *are laws*, that is to say, that reality has a structure or consistency; that the eternal ideas of God—Gratry says—govern the world; that it, in some sense, becomes like God.[61] This belief or faith, he adds, is *more than half of science*.[62] 'Reason believes in advance in laws; but it wishes to know their precise character'.[63] That is to say, knowledge mobilizes itself by beginning from a faith in its possibility; because it believes that there is a structure, a lawfulness of the real, it sets out to discover it: 'There is', Gratry concludes, 'at the basis of the dialectic procedure, fundamental act of the life of reason, an act of will, a free act, a choice, an act of faith which the mind makes its own or refuses, following which the mind goes toward being and rises toward the infinite, or falls toward nothingness' [*Il y a—*Gratry concludes*—aun {sic} fond du procédé dialectique, acte fondamental de la vie raisonnable, un acte*

59. *Logique*, II, 171.
60. *Logique*, II, 60.
61. *Logique*, II, 170–173.
62. *Logique*, II, 173.
63. *Logique*, II, 177.

de volonté, un acte libre, un choix, un acte de foi que l'esprit exécute ou réfuse, par suite duquel l'esprit va vers l'être et monte vers l'infini, ou baisse vers le néant].[64]

c) *The Dialectic Process—In the syllogistic procedure*, reason passes by way of identity from one truth to another implied in the first; *the inductive procedure*, on the other hand, adds new clarities, passes from one truth to another that exceeds it, 'crossing an abyss with its wings', according to the platonic expression. This procedure has three steps: 'perception, induction, the infinitesimal procedure, or dialectic pushed to the limit' [*la perception, l'induction, le procédé infinitésimal, ou la dialectique poussée à bout*].[65] Perception implies an act of faith that affirms being; induction implies faith in laws: the total movement of reason leads to the infinite, but to the abstract infinite; the direct vision of the concrete and real infinite, that is, of God, corresponds to the supernatural order.[66]

Induction depends upon *sense*, which puts us into pre-intellectual, pre-cognitive, contact with reality, with all reality: bodies, myself and my neighbors, God. 'Induction does not then lack data', says Gratry, 'as people ordinarily say. Far from lacking, it has too much of it . . . It is then evidently a procedure of elimination that is needed here. *Efface the accidental, cut away the limit and the boundaries*' [*L'induction ne manque donc pas de donnée*—Gratry says—*comme on le dit ordinairemente. Loin d'en manquer, elle en a trop . . . C'est donc évidentement un procédé d'élimination qu'il faut ici.* ***Effacez l'accident, retranchez la limite et les bornes***].[67]

For this, the supreme form is the *via eminentiae* [way of eminence], a method for knowing the attributes of the Divinity. And its moral correlate is a human attitude, in which man unites himself to 'the supernatural gift which the Incarnation of God introduced into the world' [*la donnée surnaturelle qu'introduit dans le monde l'incarnation de Dieu*], 'by cutting back and renouncing, by suppressing obstacles, the accidents of error and of evil, by the subordination of the individual, by that *philosophic death* already seen by Plato, by Christian *mortification*, by sacrifice, by the cross, which, far from being the *perverse annihilation* of the false mystics, renews, transfig-

64. *Logique*, II, 194.
65. *Logique*, II, 195.
66. *Logique*, II, 195–198.
67. *Logique*, I, 100.

ures, glorifies the individual in uniting him to his infinite source' [*par le retranchement et le renoncement, par la suppresion des obstacles, des accidents de l'erreur et du mal, par la subordination de l'individuel, par cette* **mort philosophique** *déjà entrevue par Platon, par la* ***mortification*** *chrétienne, par le sacrifice, par la croix, qui, loin d'être* ***l'anéantissement pervers*** *des faux mystiques, renouvelle, transfigure, glorifie l'individu en l'unissant à sa source infinie*].[68] The uprooted soul, which by pride or sensuality is poured out upon things or enclosed in itself and forgets its rootedness in God, cannot elevate itself dialectically to the Divinity, nor even *comprehend* the process of induction. This is the profound root of atheism.

On the other hand, the point of departure of dialectic could be of very diverse natures: a reality, a fiction or even a contradiction. And the result depends upon its foundation: it will arrive at a real principle, or an abstract and fictional one, or at absurdity. The first occurs when I start from the finite reality of creatures to elevate myself to God; the last explains that strange and alarming possibility of *inverting* the dialectical procedure and arriving at the total absurdity of sophistic.

Induction is not, then, a vague procedure of guessing, with a merely statistical certainty, that leads us to truths that are only probable, as the methodology of the positive sciences believed, taking as their only model the induction of Bacon. The sensible and finite, point of departure of the procedure, leads us to elevate ourselves to the principle not contained in that point of support; this is the originating sense of induction, magical enchantment [*illicium magicum*], *epagogé*. 'Taken in this sense, induction goes forward without guesses and proceeds with security. Dependent on one single particular case, it affirms the universal with complete certitude.'[69]

But Gratry does not pause over the schematic idea of the particular and the universal; he has a supremely perspicacious vision of the 'functional' character of universal and abstract knowledge: 'Algebra', he writes, 'can represent all possible ellipses by one sole very short proposition which is this:

$$a^2 x^2 + b^2 y^2 = a^2 b^2.$$

68. *Logique*, I, 112.
69. *Logique*, II, 51.

In this algebraic statement, all the individual conditions are blank, are indeterminate and abstract; there remains only the pure and universal idea of the ellipse, although the sentence indicates also *the inevitable existence of the individual characters*' [*L'algèbre*—he writes—*peut représenter toutes les ellipses possibles par une seule proposition très courte que voici: . . . Dans cette phrase de la langue algébric, toutes les conditions individuelles sont en blanc, sont indéterminées et abstraites; il ne reste que l'idée pure et universelle de l'ellipse quoique la phrase indique aussi l'existence inévitable des caractères individuels*].[70]

Gratry said already, at the beginning of his investigation of the problem of God, that the procedure that takes us to him must be an elementary and everyday operation, accessible in principle to everyone, given that the divine light illuminates everyone who comes into this world. This is what happens with induction, the foundation of which is an immediate operation which the mind, and even every vital act, always realises, and which consists in transcending toward the other, toward reality, and at the same time doing away with the accidental, with limitation and imperfection, so as to affirm it in its perfect infinity. It is the fundamental attitude of man, eternally discontent before everything created, whom each thing, by its reality and its limitation at the same time, sends back to the absolute reality. The theory of induction or dialectic, nucleus of the metaphysics of knowledge in Gratry, is the scientific justification of this radical human dimension.

70. *Logique*, II, 47.

Chapter Six
Five Interior Adventures

The Journey to God

The forces tending toward the metaphysical knowledge of the Divinity were not mobilised in Gratry in an abstract or merely theoretical manner. For him the appeal to the effective history of philosophy is essential in his attempts to reach the divine reality rationally; that is to say, intrinsic reference to the history, to 'the real story' of the intellectual path of a human being to the Divinity, of the itinerary of the mind toward God, understood as a historical process. But another aspect of the question must also be kept in mind: the roots of Gratry's inquiry in his own life, the personal experiences that carried him forward, by means of the steps he recounted, the steps that are fitting to recall here, to the philosophical posing of the problem of God. Only from this point of view do the logical theory and the metaphysics of the knowledge of God acquire the fullness of their meaning, which Gratry formulates in his principal book.[1]

Gratry's World

In Paris, on November 1, 1854, All Saints' Day, Gratry began a journal of intimate annotations[2] which opened with these words: 'What is this writing? [*Qu'est-ce que cet écrit?*] Is it my testament? [*Est-ce mon testament?*] Is it my general confession? [*Est-ce ma confession*

1. *La connaissance de Dieu*, 1853. (Spanish translation by Julián Marías, Madrid 1941).
2. Published after his death under the title, *Souvenirs de ma jeunesse*, 1874. Cited according to the twelfth edition, Paris 1925.

générale?] Is it the story of my soul?' [*Est-ce l'histoire de mon âme?*] Gratry makes it clear, in short order, that his first serious recollection, at the age of five years, in 1810, was a powerful and profound impression of God. This is the first adventure, whose meaning, it seems clear, became evident to him only when he recorded it as an adult.

He narrated it, with full consciousness of its significance, in *La connaissance de Dieu*: 'I remember, in my earliest childhood, having felt that impression of Being in its liveliness' [*Je me souviens, dans ma première enfance, d'avoir un jour senti cette impression de l'Etre dans sa vivacité*]. A great effort expended against an exterior mass distinct from me, the inflexible resistance of which astonished me, made me articulate these words: I am! [*Un gran effort contre une masse exteriéure, distincte de moi, dont l'inflexible résistance m'étonnait, me fit articuler ces mots: Je suis!*] I was thinking for the first time. [*J'y pensais pour la première fois*]. The surprise was elevated soon to the most profound astonishment and then to the most vivid admiration [*La surprise s'éleva bientôt jusqu'au plus profond étonnement et jusqu'à la plus vive admiration*]. I repeated, transported: I am! . . . Being! . . . To be! [*Je répétais avec transport: Je suis! . . . être! . . . être!*] The entire religious, poetic, intelligent depth of the soul was, at that moment, aroused, moved [*Tout le fond religieux, poétique, intelligent de l'âme était, en ce moment, éveillé, remué*]. A penetrating light, which I believe I can still see, enveloped me: I saw that Being is beautiful, happy, lovable, full of mystery! [*Une lumière pénétrante, que je crois voir encore, m'enveloppait: je voyais que l'Etre est beau, bienheureux, aimable, plein de mystère!*] I still see, after forty years, all these interior facts, and the physical details that surrounded me [*Je vois encore, après quarante années, tous ces faits intérieurs, et le détails physiques qui m'entouraient*].[3]

These details Gratry notes carefully in his journal:

> In fact, I still see clearly the place in which I received that grace, forty-five years ago [*En effet, je vois encore clairement le lieu où j'ai reçu cette grâce, il y a quarante-cinq ans*]. I still see that little courtyard full of sunlight [*Je vois encore cette petite cour tout éclairée par le soliel*]. I see the door I was trying to open and before which I remained immobile with surprise and

3. *Souvenirs de ma jeunesse*, 3.

> admiration, for a time which was very long for a young child [*Je vois la porte que j'essayais d'ouvrir, et devant laquelle je suis resté immobile de surprise et d'admiration, pendant un temps fort long pour un enfant*]. I see the little staircase I ran up, with transports of the heart, to go to embrace my mother: for from that moment I felt a redoubling of my love for her [*Je vois le petit escalier sur lequel je m'elançai, avec des transports de coeur, pour aller embrasser ma mère: car depuis ce moment je sentis un redoublement d'amour pour elle*]. God came to inundate me with light and with love [*Dieu venait de m'inonder de lumière et d'amour*]. I felt I do not know what triumphant certitude which raised me up and fortified me [*J'avais senti je ne sais quelle certitude triomphante qui m'élevait et me fortifiait*]. I had seen with enthusiasm the beauty of Being and of life [*J'avais vu avec enthousiasme le beauté de l'Etre et de la vie*]. My mind plunged into an undefined, unreflected light, and my heart overflowed [*Mon esprit plongeait dans une lumière indéfinie, irréfléchie, et mon coeur débordait*].[4]

It is clearly a question of a strong impression of reality, revealed in the fact of resistance. (During the same years, another Frenchman, this one already a grown man and a philosopher, Maine de Biran, was intent upon founding a new metaphysics upon the experience of resistance and force, and with it he was going deep into that unknown territory [*terra incognita*] which today we call human life). The child Gratry—at least thus he interprets it in his maturity—becomes aware for the first time of a reality that is both alien and irreducible, and at the same time becomes truly aware of himself. The awareness of his own self as reality is the immediate result of his experience. But something else must be added: the 'positive' character of it, the fruition and complacency in the real, which as a result manifests itself under the aspect of the good [*sub specie boni*]. It is important to underline this, because it conditions the later thought of Gratry, and because it shows at the same time how open to diverse possibilities is the radical encounter with reality, and not only to the negative mood from which some recent philosophical attitudes set out without further ado, as if it were at the same time obvious and inevitable.

Nevertheless, one should not think of a religious predisposition proceeding from his upbringing: just the contrary. The parents of

4. *Souvenirs de ma jeunesse*, 20–21.

Gratry were not religious, and they exercised great influence over him, above all his mother, only seventeen years older than he, and whom he admired and loved deeply. Besides, the social situation of the world in which Gratry grew up was in reality irreligious; the lack of esteem for the clergy went as far as disdain:

> I had been brought up, apart from the time of my first communion [*J'avais été élevé, sauf l'époque de ma première communion*], writes Gratry, in the contempt and horror of churches and priests [*dans le mépris et dans l'horreur des églises et des prêtres*]. I shall never forget that at ten years of age, the sight of a priest in his clerical robes was for me the most hateful and frightening object [*Je n'oublierai jamais qu'à dix ans, la vue d'un prêtre dans ses habits sacerdotaux était pour moi l'objet le plus odieux et le plus effrayant*]. This disposition was not entirely destroyed by my first communion, and I can never explain the impression produced in me, a short time later, by the sight of a procession [*Cette disposition ne fut pas entièrement détruite par ma première communion, et je ne puis rendre l'impression que produisit sur moi, peu de temps après, la vue d'une procession*]. The choir, whom I took to be priests; their appearance, their bearing, their tone, their voice, their heavy chant, stripped of all meaning, of all heart, of all spirit, of all beauty; the devout and hypocritical air of several faces, the copes, the serpent [a musical instrument—Translator], the birettas, this whole spectacle should have made me lose my faith in one hour [*Les chantres que je regardais comme des prêtres; leur figure, leur tenue, leur ton, leur voix, leur chant lourd, dénué de tout sens, de tout coeur, de tout esprit, de toute beauté; l'air dévot et hypocrite de plusieurs visages, les chapes, le serpent, les bonnets pointus, tout ce spectacle faillit, en une heure, me faire perdre la foi*]. Is that, I said to myself, the costume of truth, the worship of God? [*Est-ce là, me disais-je, le costume de la vérité, le culte de Dieu?*].[5]

To that lamentable impression, scandalous in the most literal sense of the term, there was joined a social pressure. During the entire first half of the century, says Gratry, the majority of men in France, in the upper and middle classes, lost their faith during their secondary

5. *Souvenirs de ma jeunesse*, 20–21.

school years. Furthermore, the young people and the romantic adolescents of the time of Louis XVIII and Charles X, in a reactionary time in officialdom, were, for that very reason, revolutionaries; and that double situation brought them to hostility toward the Church, which appeared to their eyes linked to the State and put at its service.

> Like nearly all the young people of that time, we cursed the Constitution of 1814 and the Bourbons, we admired the *carbonari* and the secret societies; [*Comme presque tous les jeunes gens de cette époque, nous maudissions la Charte et les Bourbons, nous admirions les carbonari et les sociétés secrètes;*] the Church was in our eyes only a hotbed of lies in league with the tyranny of princes to brutalize the peoples [*l'Église n'était à nos yeux qu'une officine de mensonge se liguant avec la tyrannie des princes pour abrutir les peuples*]. We were mad [*Nous étions fous*] comments the Gratry of fifty years, after having taken part in two revolutions and the founding of the Second Empire.[6]

At seventeen years of age he had not only alienated himself from religion, but his sincerity and passion had brought him to a 'great zeal for irreligious propaganda'.[7] He adds some time later that from the age of five years he had still not spoken even once to a priest or a Christian; the priests continued to inspire the greatest disdain, the habitual devotional language produced in him an insuperable repulsion; as a consequence of that, he never set foot in a church.[8] In this situation, some experiences happened to the young Gratry, certain intimate adventures, we might say, which became connected with that of his childhood—this came to be like a background or supposition of all the rest—and provoked in his life a profound crisis: the rediscovery of the faith and his later decision to dedicate himself to the Catholic religion. The story of this process is of the greatest interest, but here I wish only to pause over the *methodical* character—so to speak—of those experiences, vital correlate of the philosophical doctrine of his maturity.

6. *Souvenirs de ma jeunesse*, 24.
7. *Souvenirs de ma jeunesse*, 24.
8. *Souvenirs de ma jeunesse*, 50–51.

The Horizon of Life

In the autumn of 1822, Gratry, recently returned to the Lycée Henri IV in Paris abandoned himself one night to imagining his future. It was a moment of youthful plenitude—we must not forget the precociousness of Gratry, multiplied by the historical precocity which characterised him as a romantic—: health, strength, intellectual vigor, friends, happy parents, academic success and 'an artificial rose, fragment of a hair-clasp from a dance', which one day was given him and from then on he always kept with him. Gratry anticipated the future in imagination: the prize of honor in philosophy in the coming year, study of law, fame as a lawyer, literary successes, the French Academy, perhaps glory, a house in the country near Paris, love, marriage. 'In that moment' [*En ce moment*], he adds, 'God gave me an imagination of astonishing lucidity, of fruitfulness, of movement, and of beauty' [*Dieu me donna une imagination étonnante de lucidité, de fécondité, de mouvement et de beauté*]. I saw my life unfold from year to year in a growing happiness; [*Je voyais se dérouler ma vie d'année en année dans un bonheur croissant;*] I saw the persons, the things, the events, the places [*je voyais les personnes, les choses, les événements, les lieux*] . . . All the possible happiness of the earth was concentrated there. [*Tout le bonheur possible de la terre était concentré là*]. But that contemplation advanced progressively [*Mais cette contemplation avait son progrès*]. Everything went from good to better: and I kept saying: Again! Again! More! [*Tout allait toujours de mieux en mieux: et je disais toujours: Encore! encore! après!*] . . . The sparkling sun that an instant before, gilded my imagination, began to give another light altogether [*L'étincelant soleil qui, un instant avant, dorait mon imagination, commençait à donner une tout autre lumière*]. A big black cloud passed before the sun [*Un large et noir nuage passait devant le soleil*]. Everything turned pale, and it became inevitable to say: [*Tout pâlissait, et il fut inévitable de dire*:] 'After all that, I, I too will die! [*Après tout cela, moi aussi je mourrai!*] There will come a moment when I shall be lying on a bed, and I shall struggle to die, and I shall die and all will be over [*Il viendra un moment où je serai couché sur un lit, et je m'y débattrai pour mourir, et je mourrai et tout sera fini*]. God always gives my imagination the same force [*Dieu donnait toujours à mon imagination la même force*]. He made me see, and sense and taste death, as he comes to make me see, feel, and taste life [*Il me fit voir, et sentir et goûter la mort, comme il venait de me faire voir, sentir et *goûter la vie*]. It is impossible to express with what truth I saw death, I felt it all together [*Il est impossible d'exprimer avec quelle vérité je vis la mort, je la sentis toute entière*]. It was shown, given, unveiled for me [*Elle me fut montrée, donnée, dévoilée*].[9]

Imagination, abandoned to the real experiences of life, led Gratry to the consideration of the last things. What in another place[10] I have called 'the imaginative anticipation of death', not the 'simple realisation of its inevitability', is what gives its efficacy to the knowledge—otherwise trivial and inconsequential—that 'we must die'; it will be well to keep this in mind, because only the concrete character of that vision, which exceeds enormously the simple 'knowledge', explains its meaning and its effects.

This consideration brought Gratry to the experience of the nothingness of things: 'I am no longer [*Je ne suis plus*] . . . no more sun, no more men, no more world! [*plus de soleil, plus d'hommes, plus de monde!*] Nothing more!' [*Plus rien!*][11] And the reflection upon the universality of that situation, the evidence that it happens thus to all generations, one after the other, put him finally into the presence of the *absurd*: "No one worries about one, one passes without knowing anything! [Personne ne s'en inquiète, on passe sans s'informer de rien!] . . . for what, then, do those apparitions of an instant in the midst of this flowing river, serve? [à quoi servent donc des apparitions d'un instant au milieu de ce fleuve qui passe?] Why does one pass? [Pourquoi passe-t-on?] Why has one come? [Pourquoi est-on venu?] For what good? [A quoi bon?] I was desperate. [J'étais désespéré.] I always regarded the abominable and insoluble enigma with terror. [Je regardais toujours avec terreur l'abominable et insoluble énigme.] Despair then brought me to reassemble my forces, to search somewhere some resource. [*Le désespoir alors me porta à rassembler mes forces, à chercher quelque part quelque ressource*]. Could it be that this is all? [*Se peut-il que ce soit là tout?*] Could it be that all is absurd, useless, and deprived of sense? [*Se peut-il que tout soit absurde, inutile et dénué de sens?*] Do things have a meaning, and what is it? [*Les choses ont-elles un sens, et quel est-il?*] If this is not *all*, where is the rest

9. *Souvenirs de ma jeunesse*, 32–37.
10. *Miguel de Unamuno*, 1943, chapter III (*Obras*, V).
11. *Souvenirs de ma jeunesse*, 37.

and what purpose does what I see serve? [*Si ce n'est pas là tout, où est le reste et à quoi sert ce que je vois?*][12]

This is the concrete root of the intellectual activity of Gratry. For this reason his philosophy is not abstract nor merely an interior intellectual question, but it is conditioned and mobilised by an authentic vital necessity, at feeling itself lost and needing to search for something to hang onto. In this situation, Gratry found two solutions inauthentic; one, to abandon himself to that absurdity and nothingness; the other, the automatic appeal to a Divinity, which would eliminate mechanically the decisive problem. The reaction of Gratry is neither the one nor the other, and it consists in taking into account the two terms of the question, but precisely in so far as they are problematic: 'I did not see any answer to these questions, but I began to think of God'. [*Je ne voyais aucune réponse à ces questions mais je commençais à penser à Dieu*][13] Gratry tells us that he entered into himself, entered into what Unamuno would later call 'the depths of his soul', and that from that depth there came forth a sharp cry, repeated, heartbreaking, penetrating, capable, he says, of reaching the ultimate limits of the universe and resonating further in the vacuum, or in God, he adds, if the universe is enclosed by God. 'O God! [*O Dieu!*] O God! [*ô Dieu!*] I cried, and I did not cry alone' [*Criais-je, et je ne criais pas seul*][14] Gratry felt that he had not cried in vain, that he had or would have a response; he glimpsed that the solution *should be* religion, but this appeared to him 'soso' (*insipid*) and did not interest him. 'Only', [*Seulement*] he concludes, 'I had emerged from despair, I felt that truth existed, that I could know it, that I would consecrate my entire life to it' [*j'étais sorti de désespoir, je sentais que la vérité existait, que je la connaîtrais, que j'y consacrerais ma vie entière*].[15]

This is the first intimate adventure of Gratry's adolescence. We can now ask: what precipitated it? In my judgment, four moments can be distinguished: 1) The realisation—in the sense of the phenomenologists—of his own life, which ceased to be lived in a hollow and mechanical way, to be captured in the concrete and in its *movement.* 2) Grasp of that life in its *totality,* and, thus, presence of its 'final moments' or *last things.* 3) Comprehension of the radical *deficiency,*

12. *Souvenirs de ma jeunesse,* 38–39.
13. *Souvenirs de ma jeunesse,* 39.
14. *Souvenirs de ma jeunesse,* 40.
15. *Souvenirs de ma jeunesse,* 40.

inanity, and nothingness of that human reality, and so, of the world as such. 4) A *problematic* turn—I wish to say it now without addressing its results here—toward *the* real as such, to seek a certitude—from one or the other sign—of an intellectual order, founded in the experience that *the truth exists.* It is easy to see the connections between this point of departure and the whole body of Gratry's philosophy; and this is what allows one to consider it as an effective point of departure.

The Threat of Annihilation

The second of these experiences has a more restricted application, but it is significant. It represents, with singular plasticity and energy, in a tangible form, the experience of the lack of reality, what we could call the beginning of annihilation. At that very time, Gratry says, a dream produced in him a vivid impression:

> I saw myself lying on my bed, in my room; [*Je me voyais étendu sur mon lit, dans ma chambre*;] and I, who at that time so loved energy, physical and moral force, I saw my body softened and my flesh cooked, in some way, by I don't know what evil fire [*et moi, qui alors aimais tant l'énergie, la force physique et morale, je voyais mon corps tout ramolli et mes chairs cuites, en quelque sorte, par je ne sais quel feu mauvais*]. An interior voice told me that it was the fire of sin [*Une voix intérieure me disait que c'était le feu du péché*]. My hands, still in this dream, were carried here and there on my body, and everything gave way; [*Mes mains, toujours dans ce rêve, se portèrent ça et là sur mon corps, et tout fléchissait;*] I lifted pieces of flesh, without pain! [*j'enlevais des morceaux de chair, sans douleur!*] I felt my bones, still without pain! [*Je découvrais les os, toujours sans douleur!*]. That absence of pain was something frightful! [*Cette absence de douleur était quelque chose d'effroyable!*]. Horror awakened me; [*Je me réveillai d'horreur;*] I found myself once again alive, whole, sensible, but I understood the truth of the dream, and I keep a profound and salutary impression of it [*Je me retrouvai vivant, entier, sensible, mais je compris la vérité du rêve, et j'en conservai une profonde et salutaire impression*].[16]

16. *Souvenirs de ma jeunesse*, 49.

That flabby body, which gives way and is taken apart—unresisting—so touchingly described by Gratry, passive and inert, is a kind of antithesis of the glorified body; and the progressive destruction, not only without physical resistance, but even without pain, like something horribly stupid and absurd, translates with insuperable force the imagined 'atmosphere' of the degradation of his own reality and the overwhelming threat of annihilation.

The Free Will

The following year, 1823, Gratry met a boy of his own age, in the same school in which he was studying. It was his first contact with a serious and sincere Christian, of living faith and clear mind, and a short time later, under his influence, Gratry decided to seek a confessor. Some time later, having revived his Catholic faith, he received communion. And here he underwent the third experience, something that would leave its mark more forcefully upon the theodicy of Gratry.

After communion Gratry did *not* experience any of the effect he had hoped for:

> But, after a silence, and as it were a dull calm of about an hour, I returned to myself; [*Mais, après un silence, et comme un calme plat d'une heure environ, rentré chez moi;*] I felt arise in my soul the most furious tempest, and the most terrible combat between complete faith and radical incredulity, between pure light and absolute darkness [*je sentis s'élever dans mon âme la plus furieuse tempête, et le plus terrible combat entre la foi pleine et l'incrédulité radicale, entre la lumière pure et les ténèbres absolues*]. This was so strong that it became almost a vision [*Ce fut si fort que ce devint presque une vision*]. I still see, in the corner of my room toward which my eyes were turned, a sort of double column, brilliant light from one side, deep darkness from the other: [*Je vois encore dans le coin de ma chambre que regardaient mes yeux, une sorte de colonne double, lumière éclatante d'un côté, ténèbres épaises de l'autre*:] and, in the first moment, no love of the light, no horror of the darkness, but complete indifference [*et, dans le premier moment, nul amour de la lumière, nulle horreur des ténèbres, mais pleine indifférence*]. I was held in perfect equilibrium for a quarter of a minute [*Je fus tenu en équilibre parfait pendant un quart de minute*]. That was perhaps the most solemn moment

> of my life! [*Ce fut peut-être le moment le plus solennel de ma vie!*] I had to choose by my liberty alone [*Je dus choisir par ma liberté seule*]. I felt the moment when I was about to lean toward the side of absolute incredulity . . . [*Je sentis le moment où j'allais pencher du côté de l'absolue incrédulité . . .*] Happily, a very weak but very difficult movement of my free will, which no grace, no force seemed to push, which God seemed to have abandoned to its nothingness, an imperceptible movement, entirely free, of mind and heart, inclined me lightly toward the other side, and from there I sprang transported into the light, stretching out my arms to God, and saying to him: [*Heureusement, un très faible mais très difficile mouvement de ma volonté libre, qu'aucune grâce, aucune force ne semblait appuyer, que Dieu semblait avoir abandonnée à son néant, un imperceptible mouvement tout libre, d'esprit et de coeur, m'inclina légèrement de l'autre côté, et de là je m'élançai avec transport dans la lumière, tendant les bras à Dieu, et lui disant:*] 'It is you whom I desire!' [*'C'est vous que je veux!'*][17]

It was, says Gratry, his last serious temptation against faith.

This essential freedom of choice, this free movement which confronts all reality to say yes or no, is a constant theme of the thought of Gratry and in this autobiographical confession we find the root of his decisive idea about that spring which sets in motion the knowledge of God and whose radical inversion is the concrete origin of effective atheism.

The Reality of the Good

Finally, I want to record a little detail, recalled by Gratry in the memoirs of his youth, and which appears to me to complete the vital elements that serve as a basis for his theory of the knowledge of God. After a crisis of aridity and profound sufferings, of sterility and almost desperation, one day he had, he says, a moment of consolation, when he discovered something perfect and complete. The anecdote is very short, and, by that very fact, revealing:

> It was a poor drummer who beat the retreat in the streets of Paris; [*C'était un pauvre tambour qui battait la retraite dans*

17. *Souvenirs de ma jeunesse*, 69–70.

> *les rues de Paris*;] I followed him on returning to school, the evening of a day out [*je le suivais en rentrant à l'école, le soir d'un jour de sortie*]. That drum beat the retreat in such a way, at least at that moment, that, however depressed and sad I was, there was absolutely nothing to criticize [*Cette caisse battait la retraite de telle manière, du moins en ce moment, que, si difficile et chagrin que je fusse, il n'y avait absolument rien à reprendre*]. One could not have conceived of greater spirit, more *élan*, better beat and clarity; [*On n'eût pu concevoir plus de nerf, plus d'élan, plus de mesure et de netteté*;] more richness in the roll; [*plus de richesse dans le roulement*;] the ideal desire could not go further [le désir idéal n'allait pas au-delà]. I was surprised and consoled [*J'en fus surpris et consolé*]. The perfection in that wretchedness did me good; [*La perfection dans cette misère me fit du bien;*] I followed it for a long time [*je le suivis longtemps*]. Goodness is possible, then, I said to myself, and the ideal can sometimes take flesh! [*Le bien est donc possible, me disais-je, et l'idéal parfois peut prendre corps!*][18]

This scene of the drum that rolls insistently on the streets of Paris and realizes perfection within its extreme limitations, this little exemplification of the good and of perfection in the most humble reality, simple street music with the crudest of instruments, signifies precisely the point of support of the whole intellectual process that will lead Gratry to the knowledge of the Divinity itself: the point of departure which induction, as he explains at length in all his work, uses as a basis to arrive at other realities, the real basis, with its certainly finite perfection, but real nevertheless, which allows one to elevate oneself to the total and absolute perfection of the divine infinity. And it all appears a lived reality, not simply thought, and therefore the words of Gratry transmit to us the enchantment of the scene into which he felt himself drawn, absorbed by the magical drum roll, through the dark streets of romantic old Paris.

But all this is but the documentation that allows us to trace the genesis, in Gratry's mind, of his metaphysical theory of the knowledge of God and root it thus in a historical situation and in a personal life.

---

18. *Souvenirs de ma jeunesse*, 100–101.

Chapter Seven
The Problem of God

The Radical Relation of Man with God

The Presuppositions of the Demonstration of God—We have seen how Gratry interprets the history of theodicy, how he pursues in the philosophic past the practice of induction as procedure to elevate oneself to God. As a consequence and summary of this history, there appears his personal contribution to the problem of God. Gratry appeals constantly to the testimony of the philosophers; but it is not a question of adducing *authorities*, simply, to substitute for the evidence; rather, the profound meaning of this permanent reference is to show the lack of *novelty* in his doctrine; and in this consists, precisely, his *superior originality*. Father Gratry wishes, as has been noted in a passage already cited, that it be said that his affirmations contain nothing new and have been known from antiquity; with this he will show his *radical* and *original* character. Gratry believes, in fact, that the demonstration of God's existence, and in general the knowledge of the Divinity, cannot be a *happening*, something obtained in virtue of a new and ingenious formula. If a proof for the existence of God is possible, he says, this will have to be within the reach of all, because the divine light illumines *everyone* who comes into this world. What does this mean?

Naturally, not that all men arrive at the demonstration of God, but that in all of them are to be found the *presuppositions* of the demonstration. If there is a knowledge of God, this possibility responds to an *essential* dimension of man, in the same way that the knowledge of things is founded upon the fact that in man there is something which makes him be with them, have contact with their reality. The *knowledge* of God, as, in general, all knowledge, is something *derived* from another prior ontological dimension, in which is founded its *possibility*. It is necessary, then, to seek in man that which makes possible the knowledge and the demonstration of God's existence and his attributes. Thus, this problem, which is that of theodicy, is not reduced to God alone, but also involves man. To seek the suppositions of theodicy is to investigate the ontological structure of the human being; and as this human being appears endowed with a body—and not, Gratry notes, in an accidental manner, but essentially—and exists in a visible and corporeal world, the ontology of man draws us inexorably back to that of the world in which he is found. In the problem of theodicy, taken in its radicality, that is to say, from its real suppositions, is summarized all metaphysics. The *knowledge* of God supposes, in sum, a previous *relation* of man with him, not intellectual, but anterior to intelligence and *constitutive* of the human being.

Prayer—The ordinary and everyday operation of the human mind in which it is referred explicitly to God is *prayer*. Prayer is an *integral* act of man: not only, nor primarily, intellectual, but at the same time a matter of the will, of love, of the very depth of the person; and, on the other hand, including the body, as the Catholic church has always indicated, although Gratry does not allude to this. But prayer is not only the beginning; it is already an *explicit* reference to God, and it has in its turn deeper suppositions: it is only possible *from* a previous situation. Gratry means by prayer, in the philosophical sense, what Descartes did when he affirmed: 'I sense that I am a limited being, who tend and aspire unceasingly to something better and greater than I am' [*Je sens que je suis un être borné, qui tends et qui aspire sans cesse à quelque chose de meilleur et de plus grand que je ne suis*].[1] This is the movement of the soul that is raised from the finite to the infinite, and which starts from a twofold sense. It is necessary, then, that man find himself imperfect and needy, in an act of humility. Already Nicole determined as a condition of prayer the 'poverty or humbling of the heart that comes from the sense of one's needs' [*pauvreté ou abaissement du coeur qui vient du sentiment de ses misères*].[2] And Saint Augustine notes the difference between the prayer of Adam innocent and Adam blameworthy; in the first case, he is not deprived of God nor does he reach out to attain him, but he already enjoys him; in the second, in the knowledge of imperfection, he cries to God, and

1. *Meditation III*, end.
2. *Traité de la prière*, Book III, chapter II.

thus overcomes the pride of sin: 'In paradise you did not cry out, you praised; you did not weep, you enjoyed the fruit. The one placed outside cries. The tribulation which the proud deserves comes close to him' [*In paradiso non clamabas, sed laudabas; non gemebas, sed fruebaris. Foris positus clama. Propinquat tribulatio qui deseruit superbientem*]. The meaning of the starting point for the demonstration of the existence of God in the *Proslogion* of Saint Anselm is no different. But the mere sense of need and one's own limitations is not enough; the aspiration to something greater, as Descartes says, is needed. The root of prayer, for Saint Augustine, is charity: 'Charity itself weeps and prays' [*Caritas ipsa gemit, ipsa orat*]. And in another place: 'It is asked by love, it is sought by love, it is impelled by love, it is revealed by love, in a word, what is revealed, let it perdure by love' [*Amore petitur, amore quaeritur, amore pulsatur, amore revelatur, amore denique, in eo quod revelatum est, permanetur*]. It is necessary, then, for there to be prayer in the *strict sense*, that there be a *sense* of finitude and perfection and a *desire* for the infinite and perfect. Without this twofold element the elevation of the human soul to God in the everyday act of prayer is not possible, nor, thus, any communication or demonstration of the Divinity. Already Saint Augustine said: 'One does not enter truth except through charity;' [*Non entratur in veritatem nisi per caritatem;*] although here there appears, joined to the simple desire and tendency toward the better, a reference to the supernatural order.

The Rooting of Man in God—This is possible because in man there is found a divine sense. It is what defines the primary relation of man to God, a relation that I have called *radical* in a strict sense, because, in fact, it consists, as we saw, in the fact that the human being has his foundation and his *root* in God. The soul finds in its own depth a divine contact, and there resides its *energy*, what makes it be. Gratry had to show that whenever a man knows himself in his depth he has encountered that intimate presence of God. This is what defines, as we have seen in detail, the *being* of the human being. Gratry sums up this doctrine concisely in some lines of *La connaissance de Dieu*, which it is important to cite:

> All the philosophers have spoken of this sanctuary of the soul, where God is, and where he is necessarily, as *cause of my being and of my life*. They have spoken of this point where God touches the soul in order to *suspend* it from him, by which

> he *makes it live* in *holding it.* Whoever does not know that is on this side of all philosophy. The world touches us on the surface, God in the center, and we, we are between the two, and three worlds live in us: God, nature, and ourselves [*Tous les philosophes ont parlé de ce sanctuaire de l'âme, où est Dieu, et où il est nécessairement, comme* ***cause de mon être et de ma vie****. Ils ont parlé de ce point où Dieu touche l'âme pour la* ***suspendere*** *à lui, par où il la fait vivre en la tenant. Qui ne sait pas cela est en deçà de toute philosophie. Le monde nous touche par la surface, Dieu par le centre, et nous, nous sommes entre les deux, et trois mondes vivent en nous: Dieu, la nature et nous*].[3] [Emphasis mine]

God is the root of man, and man depends upon him; thus God appears as cause of being, and in a more precise way, as cause of life; but it should not be thought that it is simply a matter of creation, in the sense that God would be the cause of the *living being*, but of the fact that God *makes* man *live*, that God is the principle whence man receives the impulse and the force for *living*. It is not only that God has made man—we already saw that man is never, according to Gratry, *made* in the strict sense—but that he *makes* him—in the present, and thus *actually—live*. But to live is not merely to be, but something active, which the man himself does, in virtue of the force he receives from contact with God, because the concrete way in which God makes man live is *by sustaining him*. God is, thus, the point of support, the *foundation* of human life. Man is and lives from his center or root, which is the *divine sense*, *resting himself* upon God. And this fundamental rooting is the effective situation of man, in relation to God, and the necessary supposition of all later knowledge, still more of demonstration, of the Divinity; in the same way as contact with the world on our *surface*, by means of external sense makes possible knowledge about things, and the intimate sense allows us to know our own person and that of our neighbor. In this ontological structure of the human being is founded all possible theodicy.

Atheism

The Existence of the Atheist—There is a fundamental fact that must be reckoned with: not all men possess faith in God; there are those who

3. *La connaissance de Dieu*, I, 270.

deny the existence of the Divinity, and they are the atheists. How is this possible? If the very root of man is dependent upon God, if man is and lives by him, how can there be men who deny this capital fact and say in their heart: 'There is no God'? Gratry says that the explanation of atheism lies in this, that man is *free* and that there are *evil* men. Let us look at this.

In the first place, what precisely is it to be an atheist? Above all, to lack the divine sense, or, better, to be *deprived* of it, because the divine sense is not something that one can simply be without, but what is *possessed* or *wanting*, given that it is the very foundation of the person, the root of the soul. One who is deprived, then, of the fundamental *sense* is *insensate*, a man not in possession of his mind, but is rather afflicted with *dementia*; he is not *in himself*, but *alienated*. The entering into ourself puts us in touch with God in the depth of the soul; on the other hand, madness takes us from him; in the words of Saint Augustine, 'To cast out one's inmost parts is what it is to put oneself far from God' [*Intima projicere id est longe a se facere Deum*].

What is wanting to the man deprived of the divine sense, says Gratry, is the real point of support for the knowledge and the proof for God. Nor is he able to understand this if one explains it to him. His intelligence cannot arrive at the knowledge of God, although it functions normally, because there is lacking the *spring* which puts it in motion to elevate itself to the divine being. One who lacks the divine sense does not understand the significance of the name 'God' and does not comprehend that he is the one who necessarily is; thus, as we saw earlier, the argument of Saint Anselm, based on the fool, consists principally in depending upon the senseless statement of the atheist and showing that one cannot deny the existence of God if one holds the true idea of him; in other words, if one is speaking, in fact, *of him*.

The Uprooted Soul—But how does one arrive at this situation of the insensate? How can man deny God? Finite and created things, as we have seen many times, are the way to raise ourselves to the Divinity: the perfections of God are seen through the things he has made [*per ea quae facta sunt*], according to the word of Saint Paul.[4] The finite being, then, shows us at once reality and limitation; being, life, goodness, and, at the same time, finitude. The soul raises itself

4. Rom 1:20.

to God by affirming *being* infinitely and denying limits; this is the dialectical procedure which is familiar to us. But men, says Gratry, separate from one another at this point, and while some go to God, others depart from him. Some, by the contact with God in the depth of the soul, affirm, in effect, the infinite; the others, by contrast, at the sight of disorder and evil, and above all of death, abandon the ideal toward which they tend and choose negation. These are, says Gratry, the two moral and intellectual races who divide the world between them. 'There are minds and hearts that affirm; there are those who deny. There is the whole question: God or not, yes or no' [*Il y a des esprits et des coeurs qui affirment; il y en a qui nient. Là est toute la question: Dieu ou non, oui ou non*].[5]

But the cause of this choice in the depth of the person comes from the moral nature. The root of atheism is, according to Saint Paul, *iniquity*, by which truth is held captive. And, as Plato already knew and Saint John says, the causes of the departure from God are sensuality and pride, the double concupiscence of the flesh and the eyes. By sensuality, man puts his center in external things and departs from God; it is an aversion from God [*aversio Dei*], an inversion of the truth; but, above all, pride makes one put the foundation in man himself, and then the divine sense is extinguished and the heart is darkened, at the same time as the mind becomes vain according to the splendid expressions of Saint Paul (Romans 1:20): 'They became futile in their thinking and their senseless minds were darkened. Claiming to be wise, they became fools' [RSV]. [*Evanuerunt in cogitationibus suis, et obscuratum est insipiens cor eorum. Dicentes enim se esse sapientes, stulti facti sunt*].

These souls, deified—here is, says Gratry, the root of pantheism, in which man makes himself God—are doubly separated, from universal faith and common reason. They have quenched the divine sense and, as this is the *root*, they turn into *rootless and dead* [*Eradicatae, bis mortuae*] souls, as Gratry says, citing Saint Jude.[6] And the Epistle of Saint Jude adds other expressions, which Gratry does not cite, but which put even more clearly the meaning of atheism: 'Waterless clouds, carried along by winds, wandering stars . . .' [*Nubes sine aqua,*

5. *La connaissance de Dieu*, II, 154. Recall the 'third' adventure of Gratry, cited above.

6. Jude, 12.

quae a ventis circumferentur, sidera errantia . . .]. And he says finally: 'loudmouthed boasters' [*Et os illorum loquitur superbiam*][7] Atheism is, thus, an essential human possibility, and a risk that always threatens man. The soul, even though it has a root in God, can uproot itself, and then it becomes vain and empty, it is changed into a wandering star, into a cloud blown by the wind, without any substance. For this reason Gratry says that the human mind can escape *vanity* only by depending upon God.[8]

The Two Kinds of Atheism—But there are two quite distinct ways of being atheist. Gratry uses a felicitous comparison to explain them: that of the two modes of faith, living and dead faith. There is, equally, he says, a living atheism and a dead atheism; an atheism as doctrine, as intellectual conviction, and an atheism as real principle of life. Naturally, this is the more serious, as the living faith is what truly matters.[9]

Atheism as a doctrine results from a moral or intellectual infirmity, says Gratry; or rather, he adds acutely, the atheist is at times a lost spirit through 'a fragment of science suddenly hardened and which converts itself into an obstacle against all new light'. And Gratry adds these words, of dramatic profundity, that distinguish the superficial atheism of the intellect, that atheism that does not go beyond being stupidity [*stultitia*], although that is a sin [*peccatum*], as Saint Thomas says,[10] from the profound and radical atheism that resides in the *heart* of the insensate, not only in his words or ideas:

> But this is not yet the *atheist in the soul*. The latter says in his heart: 'There is no God'. Every man who remains moral, even while declaring himself an atheist, is not an atheist in his soul. He is inconsistent, he is absurd, it is evident; but he is not a monstrosity. The atheist in the soul is the one who denies, not with the mouth alone, but with the heart and in fact, the distinction between justice and injustice, and who comes from that to the complete despising of man, living image of God.

---

7. Jude, 16.
8. See on these problems the extraordinary essay of Zubiri, *En torno al problema de Dios*, whose importance will take time to become known. In it he approaches the problem of God and of atheism in an original and seminal way, and precisely from the perspective of contemporary philosophy.
9. *La connaissance de Dieu*, II, 156.
10. *Summa Theologiae*, II-II, q 46, art 2.

> The latter is a monster; they exist, but God alone knows them [*Mais ce n'est pas encore* ***l'athée dans l'âme****. Celui-ci dit dans son coeur: 'Il n'y a point de Dieu'. Tout homme qui maintient la morale, lors même qu'il se déclare athée, n'est pas athée dans l'âme. Il est inconséquent, il est absurde, c'est évident; mais ce n'est pas un monstre. L'athée dans l'âme est celui qui nie, non pas de bouche seulement, mais de coeur, et de fait, la distinction du juste et de l'injuste, et qui en vient au plein mépris de l'homme, vivente image de Dieu. Celui-là est un monstre; il en existe, mais Dieu seul les connaît*][11]

The Knowledge of God

The Elevation to God—We have seen the ontological structure of the human being which makes possible a knowledge of the Divinity. Theodicy is founded upon the ontology of the person, but it in turn is incomprehensible without God. Thus, in one unique question the three traditional themes of metaphysics are united: that of *man*, that of the *world* in which he is found, and that of *God* in whom he is rooted. The source of movement of the soul toward God is, then, the divine sense, the mysterious and obscure contact with the Divinity in the depth of the person. But there is a double obstacle, that of sensuality and that of pride; man can ignore his rootedness and take the world or his own life absolutely; then man becomes empty, he is *less* and tends toward nothingness, toward that which, nevertheless, he cannot reach but, having it nearby, he believes in it and affirms it; this is atheism. It is necessary, before an effective elevation of the soul to God is attained, to overcome that obstacle; and its removal is executed by a *moral* act, which is at the base of the later logical process. This moral act is a voluntary and free act; the will, which is the interior zone of the person, close to the sense, succeeds in freely overcoming the obstacle, by means of an operation of *pruning* the sensual impulses and of recognition of one's own finitude and imperfection. Thus man recognizes his insufficiency and need, and can raise himself to God, by *likeness*, and above all by *contrast*. This is what Gratry calls, in a very precise sense, *sacrifice* as philosophic method, and also *philosophical death*, recalling the socratic principle: To philosophize is to learn to die.

11. [A Gratry], *La morale et la loi de l'histoire*, I, chapter XV.

Thus the demonstration of God's existence has, in addition to its general ontological suppositions, other moral conditions; without them, it is not realisable nor even comprehensible. This explains the strange fortune this problem of the demonstration of God, perhaps the most important—and most disquieting—of metaphysics, has had. This theme would require a mature and thorough investigation, and through it the thought of Gratry would have its greatest fruitfulness.

Dialectic as Elevation of Reason—This need for an *effort*, which has very ancient antecedents—recall the Platonic *gymnasia*—is reproduced within the logical process. The demonstration of God, including the knowledge of his attributes, cannot be accomplished, as we have seen, by way of identity, by syllogistic deduction, which is the procedure of reason functioning in a mechanical and necessary mode. The intellectual way of arriving at God is induction or dialectic. And, as we have seen at length, this supposes an impulse, a spring, an *élan*—the word is repeated many times by Gratry's pen—which some minds lack, and which is needed to comprehend the dialectical process, which is of an *inventive* nature. Since the result of induction is not contained in the point of departure, we cannot obtain it simply by considering the latter; nor is it enough to proceed by way of likeness, given that dialectic uses by preference contrast; the data given send us back to *another*, which is not included in any way in the point of support, but which transcends it; and an inventive impulse to elevate oneself to it is indispensable. One can find an analogy with this process in mathematics, in the infinitesimal calculus; compare the nature of the mental operation which is the resolution of an equation of the second order, for example, with the integration of a function; in this case it is not enough that the function be capable of integration and, besides, to know how to integrate, but there is also required in the third place an *event*, an *invention*, in the literal sense, which is or is not produced in each case. It is necessary to keep this in mind in order to understand Gratry. Thus, when he says that the intellectual procedure that arrives at God is *mathematical*, one must be careful not to take this as an affirmation that it is algebraic or *mechanical*; he refers simply to the rigor of mathematics, which appears as much in the resolution of an equation as in the integral calculus, although the integration does not follow necessarily and unconditionally from the positing of the data.

Things, then, *lead* us to raise ourselves to God; this is the radical meaning of induction, to which it is necessary to restore its primary value. Anything, says Gratry, can serve as point of support, if we know how to consider it with that gaze that contemplates it soberly and questioningly, sufficiently to see its reality and its imperfection, briefly enough so that it does not absorb us and hide from us the other term of the comparison: the perfect and infinite being to whom it sends us back. In the dialectical process it is already *reason* that elevates itself to the Divinity; but, as we have seen, not reason *alone*; there must be a movement of the whole soul, intellectual and moral, moved by the deeper and more radical spring of the *divine sense*, also called, since Aristotle, with an expression whose profundity of content now becomes transparent, *the attraction of the desirable and the intelligible*. It is a question, in fact, of a double attraction, for the intellect and the will, by the *sense*; God appears as the highest good, as the first desirable, and at the same time as the first intelligible, given that he is himself intelligence and the true light.

The Proofs for the Existence of God—Gratry has expounded in his capital book all the proofs for the existence of God, which seem to him, in general terms, certain, although perhaps not in isolation, but rather all joined, as we have seen. These proofs have usually been distinguished into cosmological, psychological, and ontological, according to whether the point of departure is nature, the soul, or the idea of God taken in itself. Gratry observes, then, that the first two can be reduced to one: God known through his effects; with which, he says, we return to the schema of the double cartesian proof: God demonstrated through his effects and through the simple idea we have of him. But this is not enough, because the idea of God is only obtained through his effects: 'The invisible things of God are known through those that are made', according to Saint Paul. Thus, says Gratry, every proof of the existence of God is through his effects and is, therefore, at once *a priori* and *a posteriori*. Its formula should be: *There is something, therefore there is God.*

This, as we have seen, will be the ultimate meaning of the proof of Bossuet and of Leibniz. In this it became effective in resting upon a real datum, namely, there are contingent beings; from this it is inferred that the necessary being must exist. This still does not prove, however, with absolute rigor, the existence of God, and it is what has been too often forgotten when the intention is to demonstrate the existence of the divine being *from the contingency of the world*, because one starts from the contingency *of things*, and one arrives at proof that there must be a *necessary being*. But now it would be necessary to prove the divine character of this being, that is to say, that it is concretely *God*. Because the contingency of things is not the same as that of the *world* as such. The world is not a thing, nor even the sum of them, but something anterior to all, *in which they are*. The contingency of each thing does not prove, of itself, that of the world. And this is now the problem.

We have already seen how Leibniz considered contingent things as a *series*, from which one must go out to encounter the necessary being, which would thus be extramundane, and so God. But this does not remain sufficiently justified in the leibnizian system. Gratry insists especially, as will be recalled, upon the idea of the *infinite*: what is infinite in one sense is infinite in every respect; and the inverse, what is finite in some sense is also finite in all. In this way, as finitude corresponds in many senses to the world, it must also be finite in the rest of its dimensions; for example, in duration, in its widest sense; thus, it is not the necessary being, whose essence implies its existence. But this appeal to the *idea of the infinite* turns out to be not sufficiently evident either, and the proof of the existence of *God* remains affected by an ultimate imperfection. The traditional proofs *of themselves* demonstrate the existence of a necessary being, and so exclude the absolute contingency of reality; but they leave open a door to pantheism, into which, as is clear, philosophy at one time or another has relapsed. What profound intuition is pulsating beneath the idea of the infinite in Gratry?

The Nothingness of Creation—In the first place, Gratry must eliminate sensuality and pride; that is to say, he must recognise the radical insufficiency of *things* and of *himself*. But Gratry conjectures also that this insufficiency, from the moment in which I encounter it, affects the whole of created being; thus, that the constitutive nothingness of each thing and of my own 'I' involves the entire creation, the *ens creatum* as such. But since this *ens* [being] exists and is *nothing* only by comparison with the infinite being—'my substance is as nothing before you'—[*substantia mea tanquam nihil ante te*—], the existence of *something* sends us back necessarily to an *other*, infinite in every sense, which is *a se* [from or by itself] and which we call *God*: a transcendent being distinct from man and from the world in its totality. Thus we must exclude definitively all pantheism, which Gratry opposed with an energy and an intelligence lacked by those who, with incredible ignorance, have tried to attribute it to him.

How can Gratry arrive at this idea that the discovery of contingency itself, in *sacrifice*, implies the radical contingency of the world in its integrity? I repeat that this idea is not sufficiently justified in Gratry, at least in an explicit way, nor perhaps was it possible from the philosophical suppositions of his time. But Gratry, as we have seen, in his analysis of the person has discovered as its ultimate root a triple *sense*; the external sense of things, the intimate sense of myself, and the divine or radical sense of the Divinity; thus, Gratry has the intuition that the exterior world remains involved in the profound reality of man, on the one hand, and on the other, that man, who is not self sufficient and is needy, even with the world turns out to be *radically* insufficient, given that he always lacks his *foundation*, which is found only in contact with God. Upon entering into his own depth, man finds, joined to contingency, the point of support that makes him be and live, *sustaining him*; and this foundation is not the *world*, which touches us at the *surface*, but *God*, on whom depends our *root*.

Now we can get some idea of how the metaphysics of Father Gratry is inserted into contemporary philosophy. To establish with ultimate rigor the proof for the existence of *God*, it is not enough to begin from *any* contingent *being*: it would have to be one of such a nature that it involves ontologically the whole of intramundane being, and so sends us back to its *transcendent* foundation. This being has been discovered by contemporary philosophy—although we have seen already that Gratry at least suspected it—with the name of *existence* or *human life*. This being is characterised by a *being in the world*, it is defined as *I and things*, *I and circumstances*. The intentionality of man makes his life involve, not only his *I*, but at the same time the world. Thus, the contingency of *existence* or of *human life* as such—not simply of "man" as a being among the rest of them, or of 'things'—would show that the necessary being is *other* than life: precisely its *foundation* or *root*; and so, that it is transcendent. But for this it would be necessary to arrive first at a comprehension of existence or life as something *rooted* or founded; it would be necessary to descend as far as the *depth of the person*. This is what I have meant to show at length in Gratry, whose philosophical power is beginning to be clear. Zubiri, in the essay cited earlier, above all in its French version,[12] has shown the fact of the constitutive *linking back* of human existence, hidden by the *pride of life*, and which is manifest in the *ruin* of existence itself, in its *uncoupling* or *uprooting*. This is decisive. Man finds himself in God, constitutively bound back, and by this fact he is *implanted* in existence. There is something that *binds* me to life, that *makes* me live and at the same time *gives* me *powers* for it. By the binding, at the same time, *I have to* live and *I can* live. But with all this, says Zubiri, I have not given a *demonstration* of the existence of God, nor a *concept* of God. It is a question only of 'discovering' the point in which the problem arises and the *dimension* in which it is already posed: the constitutive and ontological *binding back* of existence. 'Now', he adds, 'the flood of questions would begin to surge'.[13] Including, above all, that of the proof for God's existence.

This proof Zubiri does not attain, but he indicates its *sense* and the way by which it could be reached. Now there appears the problem of *being*, in relation to God. Man knows what *is*, as *being*, and he moves in being. As man is open to things, being is applied to them first, and to know himself he must *turn* from things, and there is a big difference between the *being* of things and human existence. The ontology of the latter turns out to be problematic, and then it is necessary to return to the being of things to modify it in its turn and give its *being* a new meaning, which then allows the new *being* to be lodged in it. There is then discovered not only a new being, but a new *ratio entis* [reason for being], which reabsorbs the *concept* preserved.

The understanding finds that there are things and there is existence; but now, it further finds that there is what *makes* be, God. And this obliges it to pose the *intellectual* problem of God. To resolve it would be to lodge it—if possible—in being, in a new *ratio entis*, and this would make problematical the sense of being in things, in men and in the person, to discover an *analogy* in a sense much more radical than that of Aristotle. This is what Zubiri calls *regressive metaphysics*, because it consists in a *turn or regression* to those beings already known, to see them in the light of a new *ratio entis*. Only from this point could a 'discursive' proof for the existence of God be attempted, which would signify that God and the world are linked 'because of being'.

12. 'Autour du problème de Dieu', in *Recherches philosophiques*, 1935–36. (Complete text in *Naturaleza, Historia, Dios*, 1944).
13. In *Naturaleza, Historia, Dios*, 467.

In order not to fall into pantheism, it is necessary to appeal to a *radical* contingency, to the nothingness constitutive of existence, which involves that of the *I* and *things* and sends one back to a fundamental *other*, transcendent to it, which makes it be. And from this foundation we can indeed speak properly of *God*. In this dimension the metaphysical problem of *being* referred to the Divinity will and should be able to attain its greatest efficacy.[14]

The Double Mode of the Vision of God—But it is well to touch also, although it be only allusively, upon one last question, which has the greatest importance for the philosophy of Gratry: that of the two orders of the divine intelligible, that of the two possible modes of seeing God.

For Gratry, reason can be used in three ways, and to that use three modes of philosophy correspond: the abuse of reason, its radical inversion, leads to sophistic, which is not properly philosophy, but its negation; the purely human use of reason is philosophy before faith, or 'separated philosophy'; the use of reason illuminated by faith is divine and human philosophy at once, the philosophy of Christians as such, *grafted philosophy*, or also, as Gratry says, 'the spirit of God grafted upon the spirit of man'. This is complete wisdom.

The first, sophistic, leads us to nothingness and to darkness; its double form is pantheism and atheism, two modes of arriving at nothingness, by means of an absolute annulling of the world or of God. The second leads us to a vision of God, certain and true, but only reflected, indirect, mediate, mirrored: the *reflection in a mirror* of which scholasticism speaks. It is the vision of God through his effects, the vision of creatures, which are the image of God, above all of man himself. The third is the only one that can raise us to a direct, immediate vision of God: to a vision of *God himself*, face to face.

Gratry uses an image to explain this. Let us think of an eagle before a lake, in the waters of which the solar disk is reflected. The eagle contemplates the lake and in it the radiance of the sun. And there are three possibilities. The first is that the eagle believes that what he sees shining in the water is the sun itself, and he plunges into it; then he sinks into the abyss and the darkness, loses himself and loses at the

14. More precise information on this point will be found in my study, 'The problem of God in the philosophy of our time', published in Number 11 of the review *Escorial*. (In *San Anselmo y el insensato*).

same time the sun and its reflected image; this is what sophists do; but Gratry recalls that eagles never do this. In the second case, the eagle contemplates the reflection and infers from it the existence of the sun that produces it; he understands the disk visible in the water as image of a real sun distinct from it, and in this sense he knows it, seeing it in its effect. But he can also, and this is the third possibility, lift his gaze to the real sun and fly toward it to know it in itself; only, as Saint John Chrysostom says, the eagle has better sight than flight; but man, adds Gratry, has flight equal to sight, and he can arrive at the direct vision of God.

But not by himself alone, nor by his natural powers, but with a supernatural help from God. Joined to the natural divine sense, there is a supernatural divine sense. The intuitive vision of God is only given in the other life, in the supernatural fatherland; in this life, and by the natural light of reason, one can only arrive at an indirect and mediate vision of God, a vision *in a mirror*, through creatures, not of God in himself: No one has ever seen God [*Deum nemo vidit unquam*]. There is possible in this life only an obscure and confused vision of *God himself* in faith, which is only a beginning of vision, an anticipation of the beatific vision; and faith is a gift of God, and supposes, thus, a divine intervention in human reason. This is what Gratry calls, following Saint Augustine, reason attaining to its end [*ratio perveniens ad finem suum*]; and of this he says that it is called virtue [*virtus vocatur*]. The natural reason, by itself alone, can know only its limits and *miss* what it needs; in this way it is raised inductively to God, but it knows him only in an image, and the natural desire to see God, says Gratry, is absolutely insufficient and ineffective, and requires the supernatural intervention of divine grace. To confuse Gratry with the followers of 'ontologism', as has at times been done, including in a history of the Church, reveals only a profound ignorance of the terms confused. The capital proposition of 'ontologism', condemned by the decree of the Holy Office of 18 September 1861, says, as is well known, in the official formula of its condemnation: 'The *immediate* knowledge of God, at least habitual, *is essential* to the human intellect, in such a way that without it, nothing could be known: since indeed it is itself the intellectual light' [***Immediata** Dei cognitio, habitualis saltem intellectui humano **essentialis est**, ita ut sine ea nihil cognoscere possit: siquidem est ipsum lumen intellectuale*] [Emphasis mine]. And, for greater clarity, if it were needed, the two principal propositions condemned by the decree of 14 December 1887 as errors of the Italian philosopher Antonio Rosmini-Serbati say this: 'In the order of created things there is *immediately* manifested to the human intellect *something divine in itself* in such a way namely that it pertains to the *divine nature*' [*In ordini rerum creatarum* ***immediate*** *manifestatur humano intellectui* ***aliquid divini in se ipso*** *hujusmodi nempe quod* ***ad divinam naturam*** *pertineat*]. And the second: 'When we say "divine" in nature, we do not use this word 'divine' to mean a *non-divine effect of a divine cause*; nor is it our intention to speak of the *divine* in such a way that it be such by participation' [*Cum divinum dicimus in natura vocabulum istud* ***divinum*** *non usurpamus ad significandum* ***effectum non divinum causae divinae****; neque mens nobis loqui de divino quodam, quod tale sit per participationem*].[15] There is no need for greater clarity; Gratry stands a hundred leagues from this error, which, precisely, he pursues up to its ultimate manifestations, not only in the pantheists, Plotinus, Spinoza, or Hegel, but also in Malebranche, as we have seen. To assimilate him to the followers of ontologism is, literally, to take the radish for the leaves: to confuse the proximity of Gratry to Rosmini and Gioberti in so far as they tried to reestablish metaphysics, with the error of ontologism, which Gratry, far from falling into it, formally opposed in all its aspects.[16]

But God, as Saint Augustine and Saint Thomas said, does not fail to speak to the rational creature, Gratry affirms. This brings it about that a supernatural germ can be inserted into human reason, by means of which it is possible to pass from *reason* to *faith*. In this way, human reason, after having arrived at the end of the lower order of knowledge of God, can, *with the help of God*, penetrate in some way into the other order and arrive at the other light, the supernatural light of reason, which does not annul the purely human, but enlightens it. But the developments of this question, principally theological, go beyond our theme.

* * *

15. Denzinger-Bannwart, 1659, 1891, 1892.
16. *Cf* EJ Scheller, *Grundlagen der Erkenntnislehre bei Gratry* (1929), 178–210, where he studies very minutely the question of ontologism and shows that it is altogether distinct from the thought of Gratry.

I have intended to show throughout this study the philosophical substance of the thought of Gratry. His work has appeared to us as a reconstruction—and at the same time a restoration—of metaphysics, in the midst of the nineteenth century, anticipating Brentano by thirty years and doing so in a much more thematic and explicit way, at the same time as it is more clearly inserted into the history of philosophy, understood as philosophy itself. We have found also an *inductive* method, in which one appeals to a concrete and real datum, to raise oneself in an immediate and certain manner to an absolute result, of metaphysical value, whose relationship to the 'empiricism' of Brentano, starting point of phenomenology, is quite clear. But, above all, Gratry elaborates an ontology of the person, the philosophical timeliness of which does not need to be underlined; and in its root arises, in a radically ancient manner, and so *originally*—which is a higher form of being original—the great question of God. In the moment in which existential philosophy has discovered the adequate method for apprehending the reality of being that is human life, and, having arrived at its depth, sees itself obliged to pose the problem of the root of the person, and with it of his relation to God, the metaphysics of Gratry comes to show all the fullness of its meaning and to cast an extraordinary light upon the central problem of ontology.

It has been said of a famous thinker that he had been 'kept in reserve in the heaven of the Church'. Of Gratry it could be said with greater reason. It appears, in fact, that the philosophy of Gratry, so long unknown, has been kept in reserve to be inserted into history in the moment when it is *needed*: when it can save time and prevent wasted effort, and perhaps grave errors, in the philosophy of our time, and make it advance in the direction that its internal problematic demands. This, and not the satisfaction of any vain erudite curiosity, is what I resolved to accomplish in the present study.

Bibliographic Appendix

The doctoral thesis of B Pointud-Guillemot, *Essai sur la philosophie de Gratry* (Paris: 1917), includes a bibliographic essay on Gratry. The book—already cited many times in the text—of Emil J Scheller, *Grundlagen del Erkenntnislehre bei Gratry* (Halle: 1929), amplified this bibliography enormously, claiming to be exhaustive, since it included not only studies dealing more or less directly with Gratry, but also the mere mention of his name in books, essays, and articles of every kind. The very fact that a list of this nature would be possible arouses in the informed reader an impression opposite to that which its length (264–76) might suggest: that the author is generally unknown. Imagine what it would be like if one were able to make a list of the occasions on which a contemporary author, effectively known throughout the intellectual world, was named.

The bibliography of Scheller, despite his best efforts, is not exhaustive; furthermore, it ends in 1928. Although his interest is limited—and from the point of view of the present investigation is eminently insufficient—I wish to include here some studies and references, especially recent Spanish ones, that can be added to those collected by Scheller.

Julián Sanz del Rio, *Discurso pronunciado en la Universidad Central en la inauguración del año académico de 1857 a 1858* (Madrid: 1857).

Fernando de Castro. *Discurso acerca de los caracteres históricos de la Iglesia española* (Madrid: 1866):148.

Urbano González Serrano, *Elementos de Lógica* (Madrid: 1847), 153, 219–223, 258.

W [Gumersindo de Azcarate], *Minuta de un testimento* (Madrid: 1876), 54.

Marcelino Menéndez Pelayo, *Historia de las idéas estéticas en España* (1940 edition) V: 89.

Zeferino González, *Historia de la Filosofía*, second edition (Madrid: 1886) IV: 435–38.

Miguel de Unamuno, *Del sentimiento trágico de la vida* (Madrid: 1913), chapter 10.

B Brunhes, *La dégradation de l'energie* (part IV, chapter 18).

Anselmo Herranz, *Compendio de Historia de la Filosofía*, fourth edition (Barcelona: 1933), 223–34.

F Mourret y J. Carreyre, *Précis d'Histoire de l'Eglise* (Paris: 1924) III: 179, 180, 235, 267.

Thomas Greenwood, *Les fondaments de la logique symbolique* (Paris: 1938) I: 65.

J Tredici, *Breve curso de Historia de la Filosofía* (Barcelona: 1944), 238–78.

F Klinke, *Historia de la Filosofía* (Barcelona: 1947), 765, 768.

JA Maravall, *Los fundamentos del derecho y del Estado* (Madrid: 1947), 79, 86.

Victorino Capánaga, Introduction to the *Obras de San Augustín* (Madrid: 1946) I: 223, 263, 266, 298.

José Ferrater Mora, *Diccionario de Filosofía.*, fourth edition (Buenos Aires: 1958), 600.

Enciclopedia Espasa, art. Gratry.

Encyclopedia of Religion, edited by Vergilius Ferm (New York: 1945), 310.

Juan Zaragüeta, 'Acerca del problema de Dios', *Escorial.* 36 (Madrid: 1943): 27–53.

Pensamiento, volume 1 (Madrid: 1945), 106, 108, 136, 236, 265, 396; volume 6 (Madrid 1950), 386.

Eugenio Frutos Cortés, *Historia de la Filosofía* (Saragossa: 1943), 167.

W Grabmann, *Die Geschichte der katholischen Theologie seit dem Ausgang der Väterzeit* (Freiburg: 1933), 260, 263, 343.

Azorín, *El Enfermo* (Madrid: 1943), 133–134.

J Rogerio Sánchez, *Principales sistemas filosóficos.*

P Vila Creus, *Historia de la Filosofía.*

Studies and various references to Gratry will be found in some works of Julián Marías: *La filosofía del Padre Gratry* (first edition 1941); *Historia de la Filosofía* (first edition 1941); *Miguel de Unamuno* (1943); *San Anselmo y el insensato* (1944); *El tema del hombre* (1943); *La filosofía en sus textos* (1950); *Teoría de las concepciones del mundo*, by Dilthey [translation and introduction by Marías] (1944); *Biografía de la Filosofía* (1954).

Mme J Sauvage has prepared a thesis at the Sorbonne on Gratry, under the direction of Professor H Gouhier, suggested by the first of the books cited in the preceding paragraph.

The Interpretation of Aristotelian Induction by WD Ross

I am interested in retrieving the most recent interpretation of aristotelian induction—which is also one of the most authoritative—because it approaches rather closely that of Gratry as I have expounded it in Chapter V of this work. Ross was concerned with induction, naturally, in his book on Aristotle;[1] now a work has just been published that marks an important stage in aristotelian studies: on the one hundred fifth anniversary of the publication of Theodore Waltz's critical edition of Aristotle's *Organon* (1844–1846), Ross has added to his admirable critical editions of the *Metaphysics* and the *Physics* an analogous edition of the *Prior and Posterior Analytics*, with Introduction and Commentary.[2] In both works Ross gives certain precisions about induction that are worth keeping in mind.

According to Ross, Aristotle applies the word 'induction', in different places, to completely different things: 'He means by induction, in different places, quite different things.'[3] Induction, in the sense in which it can be reduced to a form of syllogism, that is to say, complete induction, such as he explains it in *Prior Analytics* II, 23, is for Ross—as for Gratry—the least important: 'the least important kind of induction.'[4] More often Aristotle calls 'induction' something that cannot be reduced to syllogistic form; for example, in mathematics; and Ross adds that this is *not* an inference, because if one took the first proposition for the premiss, the second *does not follow* from it;

1. *Aristotle* (1923), Chapter II.
2. *Aristotle's Prior and Posterior Analytics*, a revised text with introduction and commentary by WD Ross (Oxford: 1949).
3. Ross, *Aristotle's Prior and Posterior Analytics*, 37.
4. Ross, *Aristotle's Prior and Posterior Analytics*, 37.

induction is an original act of intuition: 'This cannot be regarded as an inference; if you regard the first proposition as a premiss you find that the second does not follow from [it]; the "induction" is a fresh act of insight.'[5]

Ross observes that *epagogé*, like the verb *epágein*, is not, strictly speaking, a technical term; 'the root idea' contained in these words is that of arriving at some sort of truth or other, and more concretely the step from certain 'cases' to a universal conclusion.[6] In another place he has enumerated at length the nuances of both words in the aristotelian texts and their relations to some platonic words.[7] What is the fundamental sense?

Aristotle says that the first principles of science, or some of them, are known by induction; in every discipline the *ultimate* premises are not demonstrated; thus, says Ross, Aristotle thinks about a mental process which is not proof, but upon which knowledge supervenes. Ross chooses the most fundamental premiss of all, the basis of all possible demonstration: the principle of contradiction. How do we arrive at a knowledge of it? Seeing that a particular subject B cannot both have and not have at the same time the attribute A, and so on successively; and the same thing occurs with the principles proper to each science; we do not know the principle by reasoning nor by demonstration, but by induction, as a *direct intuition*, what modern logicians call intuitive induction, says Ross; and he adds that this is by far the most important kind of aristotelian induction:

> Take the most fundamental proposition of all, that on which all proof depends, the law of contradiction. How do we come to know it? By seeing, Aristotle would say, that some particular subject B cannot both have and not have the attribute A, that some particular subject D cannot both have and not have the attribute C, and so on, until the truth of the corresponding general proposition dawns upon us. And so, too, with the ἀρχαί proper to a particular science. The induction here is not proof of the principle, but the psychological preparation upon which the knowledge of the principle supervenes. The knowledge of the principle is not produced by reasoning but

5. Ross, *Aristotle's Prior and Posterior Analytics*, 37.
6. Ross, *Aristotle's Prior and Posterior Analytics*, 47.
7. Ross, *Aristotle's Prior and Posterior Analytics*, 481–483.

> achieved by direct insight—νοῦς ἂν εἴη τῶν ἀρχῶν. This is in fact what modern logicians call intuitive induction. And this is by far the most important of the types of induction which Aristotle considers.[8]

And in another passage Ross recalls the character of sudden illumination that belongs to the inductive process, which he calls a 'flash of insight'.[9]

The reason Aristotle treats especially as induction its least important and precious form is, according to Ross, the enthusiasm for his recent discovery of the syllogism, which led him to try to reduce every sort of reasoning to the syllogistic form.[10] Chapter 23 of Book II of the *Prior Analytics* is for Ross a *tour de force*, in which Aristotle tries at all costs to reduce induction to the form of the syllogism.[11] Perception, by which induction makes us arrive at first principles, implants the universal in us: 'Clearly, then, it is by induction that we come to know the first principles; for that is how perception, also, implants the universal in us.'[12]

Such is the understanding of the *epagogé* in the most recent interpretation of the aristotelian logic, by the man who probably knows best today the results of historical investigation about this question; in substance, it coincides exactly with the pages Gratry wrote at the beginning of the second volume of his *Logic*, in 1855.

---

8. Ross, *Aristotle's Prior and Posterior Analytics*, 49.
9. Ross, *Aristotle's Prior and Posterior Analytics*, 50.
10. Ross, *Aristotle's Prior and Posterior Analytics*, 50.
11. Ross, *Aristotle's Prior and Posterior Analytics*, 486.
12. Ross, *Aristotle's Prior and Posterior Analytics*, 674.

Appendices to the English Edition

Appendix 1

Peter Maurin

Peter (Pierre) Maurin was born into a large French peasant family on 9 May 1877. As a young man he lived in a community of Christian Brothers and taught in their schools. Later, having left this group, he became part of the Sillon movement in Paris, a movement that traced its spiritual ancestry in great part to Father Gratry. Coming to America, first to Canada and then, after further travels, to New York, he met Dorothy Day and eventually became the mentor of the Catholic Worker movement she had founded. His *Easy Essays* appeared in *The Catholic Worker*. In them he commented upon all aspects of social life, suggesting common sense solutions, generally based upon Christian principles.

See: Arthur Sheehan, *Peter Maurin: Gay Believer* (New York: Hanover House, 1959).

The key role of Peter Maurin in conceiving of the Catholic Worker and in guiding Dorothy Day is told in detail in: Dorothy Day, *Loaves and Fishes* (San Francisco: Harper & Row, 1963).

A sample of the *Easy Essays* follows. Reprinted with permission from the *Catholic Worker*, published by The Catholic Worker Movement, August–September 2002, page 8.

EASY ESSAYS
by Peter Maurin

BOURGEOIS COLLEGES
Catholic Bourgeois

. . . .
And Catholic colleges
as well as non-Catholic colleges
turned out stock promoters,
stock brokers
and stock salesmen
who stocked people with stocks
till they got stuck.

College Graduates

Sociology is not a science,
it is an art.
The art of sociology
is the art
of creating order
out of chaos.
Bourgeois colleges
turn out college graduates
into a changing world
without ever telling them
how to keep it from changing
or how to change it
so as to make it fit
for college graduates.
College graduates
think in terms of jobs,
not in terms of work.
Since the world is upside down,
taking the side down
and putting it up
should be the task
of college graduates.
But college graduates
would rather
play somebody else's game

in a position
than to create order
out of chaos.

An Unhappy Lot

But the job providers
are not on the job
and college graduates
are disappointed.
They have degrees,
but their degrees
do not give them jobs.
They have been told
that the road to success
is a college education.
They have a college education
and they do not know
what to do
with themselves.
The overproduction
of college graduates
is a fertile ground
for social demagogues.
The unemployed college graduates
are getting sore
at their parents
for sending them into colleges
which have not prepared them
for a changing world.
And they ask themselves
if their educators
know what it is
to be educated.

Houses of Hospitality

In the New Masses
a Communist cartoonist represents
a line of college graduates
receiving their degrees
from the Alma Mater

and joining a soup line
on the other side of the square.
Social reconstruction
will be the result
of social indoctrination.
But unemployed college graduates
cannot be indoctrinated
without first being fed,
as well as clothed,
as well as sheltered.
Houses of Hospitality
for unemployed college graduates
are a pressing need.

Appendix 2

Selections from AJA Gratry, ***La Morale et la loi de l'histoire***, Volume 2, second edition (Paris: Adolph Laine [1871]), Translated by Mary L O'Hara, CSJ

'The purpose of this work is to change the world.' (1)

'What matters to me . . . I want no one to die of hunger.' (23)

'What makes me indignant is that people placed in this second earthly paradise persist, even today . . . in continuing in murder and brigandage on a grand scale, to destroy all the goods for a very great portion of people in every nation. This is the obstacle to freedom.' (23–24)

'To be rich for oneself is to be rich for enjoyment. To be rich for God is to be rich for the good of people, for justice and liberty.' (35)

'We have conquered nature, we must use that power . . . to conquer the social world for justice and liberty.' 'Work enriches and riches corrupt.' 'Humanity, for the first time in its existence has become, for the past 50 years, opulent.' (46)

'It is work that saves and on which a human being will be judged. It is the act of charity which alone suffices for everything and . . . contains all the virtue of the sacraments.' (73)

Appendix 3

Introduction and Part Two of *The Well-Springs* by Alphonse Gratry

Translated from the French with Introduction and Notes
by Stephen J Brown, SJ

(New York: Benziger Brothers, 1931)

Foreword

It is close on thirty years since I first read *Les Sources.* The book made upon my mind at the time such an impression that I resolved to render it available to a wider circle of readers by translating it into English. This translation was, in fact, made a few years later. But, owing to various circumstances, it was not published at the time, and so it has lain for a quarter of a century half-forgotten in some drawer or trunk till the paper has grown frayed and the writing faded.

A few years ago a new German translation came into my hands and stirred up once more the old hope of making Père Gratry's work more widely known. A fresh effort to bring it out has proved successful, thanks largely to the enterprise of its present publishers.

The translation has been revised and in part rewritten. A translation of Part II, not made in the first instance, has been added. Also an introduction and notes. I wish to acknowledge here once for all my indebtedness to the notes of Dr Emil Scheller's excellent German version. My indebtedness to other sources has been acknowledged in the course of the work.

I hope that this little book may be the prelude to the translation, by other hands than mine, of other works by this great writer. If that be so, such labour as this translation has involved will be richly rewarded. It has in any case been a labour of love.

Stephen J Brown, SJ

Rathfarnham, Co Dublin

Introduction

I. The Author

Writing in the eighties of the last century, Dr Pfahl of Eichstadt, who translated into German some of the works of Père Gratry, said, 'We assert with the deepest conviction that in the works of Père Gratry there is from every point of view a rich treasure of which no language and ho country ought to be deprived, and which in the near future will be considered as the common property of the whole world and above all of the Catholic world'. Of all but a small proportion of this treasure the English-speaking world, that part of it at least which does not read French, has hitherto been deprived. For it would seem that only two out of all Père Gratry's voluminous writings have as yet appeared in English. One of these is his little work, the *Month of Mary Conceived without Sin,* published, with an Introduction by Father Frederick William Faber, by Richardson about 1870. It is not, I think, now obtainable. The other is his *Connaissance de Dieu,* published in Boston in 1892, under the title *Guide to the Knowledge of God; A Study of the Chief Theodicies,* translated by AL Alger.[1]

Yet during his life and since his death in 1872, Père Gratry's writings have been most highly esteemed, and their value very widely acknowledged. Though dealing with the loftiest subjects, and that always on a very high level of thought and expression, his works have passed through many editions. Thus the work now introduced to readers of English, *Les Sources,* had reached a twentieth edition in 1923, and there have been further editions since then. It has been translated into German and other languages.

Gratry's eminence as a writer and a thinker has long been recognized in France. Already in 1872 Augustin Cochin spoke of him as

1. His principal works have long since been translated into German.

a great writer. '*Prêtre, philosophe, polémiste, apologiste, apôtre, écrivain, le P Gratry a été tout cela*,' wrote the distinguished critic Camille Bellaigue in the *Revue des Deux Mondes* in September, 1900. 'C'est lui,' wrote Olle Laprune, himself an eminent thinker and writer, 'c'est lui qui, en France, est sans contredit le grand philosophe catholique du XIXe. siècle'. A professor in the Catholic Institute of Toulouse, M l'Abbé Léonce Couture, described him as the most eminent of French philosophical writers since Joseph de Maistre. And it would be easy to quote many other testimonies to the same effect from writers of various types and tendencies such as Père Ramière, S, Père Longhaye, SJ, Mgr Baunard, the Abbé Bertrin, Père At, and Cardinal Parocchi.[2]

Testimonies to the deep and wide influence that he exercised and continues to exercise are even more emphatic. Mgr Baudrillart, at present Rector of the Catholic Institute of Paris, wrote some twenty years ago: 'What Christian is there in our generation who does not owe something to *Père* Gratry?' '*Qui*,' he goes on, '*dans la jeunesse pensante, n'a-t-il pas aidé à traverser les crises du coeur et de l'esprit*?' Even if Gratry had written no book that would survive him, he would have had the great merit of having cast abroad into the world an abundance of ideas that have taken root and sprung up in many a head and heart, and of having been '*un éveilleur et un excitateur d'âmes*'.[3]

For Gratry's wonderful influence was due as much to his personality as to his writings. We have ample testimony from intimate friends and personal disciples such as Henri Perreyye, Cardinal Perraud, and Léon Ollé Laprune. But I prefer to quote more detached witnesses. Père Ramière, SJ, spoke of him in the Jesuit periodical, *Etudes*, as '*Esprit pénétrant, âme ardente, coeur débordant d'affection, nature sympathique, caractère désintéressé et généreux, toutes les qualités qui peuvent rendre un homme capable de gagner et de fasciner en quelque sorte ses semblables étaient réunies à un degré éminent chez le Père Gratry*.' Père Longhaye says in his history of nineteenth century literature, '*L'âme est ardente, aimante, généreuse, compatissante, et communicative à miracle . . . En somme voilà de quoi faire un génie, un apôtre, un saint*.' Finally, the great Pope Leo XIII summed up his worth in a single phrase: 'He was a great mind and a noble heart.'

2. See *Une Ame de Lumière, Le Père Gratry*, by the Abbe Jean Vaudon (Paris: 1914), Introduction *passim*. Also *Essai sur la Philosophie de Gratry*, by B Pointud-Guillemot (Paris: Beauchesne, 1917).
3. L'enseignement *Catholique dans la France contemporaine* (Paris: 1910), 137, 142, 143.

So little is Gratry known in English-speaking countries that a brief sketch of his life seems necessary as an introduction to this first translation of his best-known work.

The standard biography of him is that written by his disciple and close friend, Cardinal Perraud,[4] who deserves to be well known in Ireland as the author of that valuable work, *L'Irlande Contemporaine.*[5] Besides this there are several other Lives—the critical and richly documented biography of Père Chauvin of the Oratory,[6] that by the Abbé Vaudon already mentioned, and a still more recent work, *Le Père Gratry, Essai de biographie psychologique,* by Albert Autin.[7] Besides which we have his posthumous autobiography, *Souvenirs de ma Jeunesse.*

Alphonse Gratry was born at Lille in 1805. In the autobiography just referred to he has related the first thirty years of his life. He was well and piously brought up, but at the age of sixteen he lost the Faith for a time owing to the influence of an unbelieving master in the college of Tours. To another master, this time at the Collège Henri IV, he attributes under God his return. This return meant for young Gratry the immediate consecration of his life to the pursuit of the highest ideals, a pursuit which he never relinquished until his death some fifty years later.

He began with a resolution to devote himself to the study of science with the sole idea of using the knowledge thus acquired in the defence of religion and the apostolate of truth. He entered the Ecole Polytechnique, an institute which stood and still stands very high among the scientific institutes of Europe. He read a brilliant course and passed his examinations with distinction. It was at this period that he passed through a singular spiritual experience, which he has fully described both in his autobiography and in the second part of the present work. The result was a decision to give up the career just opening before him and to enter the priesthood.

Then began for him a period of what we might call successive essays in life, filling the ensuing twenty-five years. He first joined a group of earnest young students who had gathered round the Abbé Bautain at Strasburg. There followed a period of studious and happy

4. First published in 1895 by Téqui of Paris, now in its seventh edition.
5. Translated into English under the title *Ireland in 1862* and published by James Duffy (Dublin: 1863), 620.
6. (Paris: Bloud, 1901). New edition, 1911.
7. (Paris: Librairie des Saints Pères, 1912).

retirement. Then the little group was broken up, and Gratry, acting on a suggestion made to him by one whom he trusted and venerated, entered as a postulant a little community of Redemptorists at Bischenberg in Alsace. Life there was poor and full of hardships, yet he tells us that those three years were the happiest of his career. But it was not to last. In the Revolution of 1830, the little community was dispersed and Gratry returned to Strasburg to teach in the Petit Séminaire.

From this work he was called to Paris to fill the important position of President of the Collège Stanislas. There he remained for the next seven years, 1840–1846. The effects of his rule were seen in a great revival of studies and a notable change for the better in the spirit of the college. There is abundant testimony to the great moral and religious influence which he exercised over the boys. From the outset he let it be clearly understood that his idea of education was the moulding of men, the equipping of them with deep and lasting convictions, the lifting up of their ideals and aspirations to higher levels.

In 1847 the chaplaincy of the Ecole Normale fell vacant. The Archbishop of Paris chose to confide to the Abbé Gratry the spiritual care of this great training college of higher education in France. Here for five years he pursued a line of work similar to that which he had so effectively done at Stanislas. Men who first came under his influence in those days looked to him for the rest of their lives not only as a guide and a friend but as a father. His personality was itself an inspiration.

It was while at the Ecole Normale, when he had reached the mature age of forty-three, that he published his first book. But, during the thirty years of life that still remained to him before he laid down his pen for ever, he poured forth out of his abundance a series of volumes numbering nearly thirty—philosophy, controversy, theology, ethics, sociology, a commentary on Scripture, a book of meditations, a biography. We cannot pause here to discuss the character and value of this output. Let us conclude this brief sketch of the outward happenings of his life.

The final phase of Gratry's life began in 1851 with the revival in France of that glorious institute, the Oratory of S. Philip Neri, the spiritual home of Malebranche and Massillon and de Bérulle, of Newman and Faber. In this revival he himself played a principal part, and though painful differences—not at all unknown among great and holy men—were to separate him from some of his early colleagues, the Oratory was his abiding place almost to the end. Why this word 'almost' must unhappily be used we shall presently see.

The revival of the Oratory in France was due, under God, to four men of very different temperament and antecedents—Mgr Dupanloup, Père de Ravignan, SJ,[8] the Abbé Gratry and M. Pététot, Curé of Saint Roch. The last-named became the first Superior, and around him and Gratry gathered a brilliant group of young men full of ardour and enthusiasm—the two Perrauds, Henri Perreyve, Lescoeur, Cambier, de la Bastie, and many others. The first years of the young institute were almost idyllic. Perfect union and friendship reigned in the little community along with a wonderful spirit of zeal and fervour. Père Gratry's lectures drew the *élite* of Paris first to the little chapel of the Oratory, afterwards to Saint Etienne du Mont. Men like Guizot and Montalembert, Berryer and the Duc de Broglie came to hear him. And the effect upon his hearers was extraordinary.

But these happy beginnings were too good to last. It soon became plain that the outlook and ideals of the first two founders were all but radically different. Père Pététot had been a zealous and saintly parish priest. His idea of the purpose of the Oratory was the uplifting and reinvigorating of the priestly state in France. Gratry's, on the other hand, was to create a sort of workshop or studio of sacred sciences, the purpose of which would be to study and demonstrate to the world the harmonies between religion and science, thus destroying for ever the old bad tradition of the eighteenth century and reconciling the nineteenth to Christ and his Church. This from his early years had been the dream of his life. Thus these two men, equally disinterested and zealous, differed in their conception of the role which the Oratory was to play in the life of the Church. In temperament, also, and consequently in their practical views about the conduct of the religious life, they were in marked contrast.

In his *Life of Gratry*, Père Chauvin has set forth with admirable frankness and impartiality these differences and the results that came of them. We need not detail them here. It will be enough to say that in spite of them Gratry accomplished during those twenty years his great life-work and apostolate of the pen. His dream was never realized to the full, yet, besides his own great contributions to religious

8. *'C'est à cet homme de Dieu que l'Oratoire doit de s'être relevé en ce siècle.'* Chauvin: *Le Pére Gratry,* 150.

literature, he was the inspirer of many others. But for him the works of Henri Perreyve, of Perraud, and of Ollé Laprune might not have been written. It is of peculiar interest to recall that his life-long championship of Ireland and Poland led to the writing of two books that exercised considerable influence in their day. It was on his advice and almost by his orders that Père (afterwards Cardinal) Perraud visited Ireland in 1860, and afterwards wrote his *L'Irlande Contemporaine* (1862). Under the same auspices Père Lescoeur wrote his *L'Eglise catholique en Pologne sous le gouvernement russe*. Portions of his own work, *La Paix*, are devoted to an indictment of the England and the Russia of those days.

His declining years were honoured by his election to the Academy in 1867, and were filled with fruitful work, which included his courses as Professor of Ethics at the Sorbonne. His life promised to close in that peaceful but laborious retirement which he had always loved. Again it was not to be. Two years before his death there occurred that painful episode which has left something of a shadow on his memory. During the Vatican Council in 1870, controversy about the proposed definition of papal infallibility raged in book and pamphlet and in the press. Against the advice and wishes of his other friends, Gratry threw himself into the struggle on the side of his life-long patron and friend, Mgr Dupanloup, in the firm belief that he was thereby upholding the cause of truth. Some time after the definition came. In spite of the veritable agony of soul through which he passed Gratry wrote to the Archbishop of Paris a letter of simple and complete submission: 'I wish to-day, Monseigneur, to tell you simply what, it seems to me, scarcely needs to be said, viz. that I accept, like all my confreres in the priesthood, the decrees of the Council of the Vatican. All that I wrote before the decision contrary to those decrees I now efface.'

The Swiss friend in whose house at Montreux Père Gratry passed away, has left a touching account of his last days.[9] They were days of great sufferings of mind and body. Death brought them peacefully to an end on the 7th of February, 1872.

. . . . . . For a careful and detailed study of Gratry as a thinker I would refer the reader to *Essai sur la Philosophie de Gratry* by B. Pointud-Guillemot.[10] This work contains a useful bibliography of Gratry's

9. *Les derniers jours du Pére Gratry*, by E Mohler (Paris: de Gigord, 1912).
10. (Paris: Beauchesne, 1917), 428 pages.

writings and of books about him. A dispassionate and critical study of Gratry's philosophy will be found in the biography by his fellow Oratorian, Père A Chauvin.

As a thinker Gratry was an inspirer rather than a sure guide. Writing to a friend to whom he had sent a copy of *Les Sources*, Foisset, a writer now scarcely remembered, said very well: 'It was not just by chance that I sent you *Les Sources*. My idea was to give you an angel guardian, an angel of good counsels and of fertile inspirations . . . You need not worry about Père Gratry's metaphysics. That's not the point. The point is *élan.*[11] *Sursum corda. Sursum mentes.*[12] The point is having the sacred fire . . . You must take from a man what good there is in him. Now the good that is in Père Gratry is that he has wings. Don't insist too particularly on this or on that. Have wings. Père Gratry dwells in a loftier region. I don't recommend him to you as a well-balanced mind; but Plato was not by any means a well-balanced mind and yet people talk of the divine Plato. Père Gratry is of the family of Plato. He is a dreamer; but his dreams are of the kind that carry you off into a higher world, of the kind that give me a fever of enthusiasm.'

The real value of Gratry could hardly be better expressed. His role in life was not that of the organiser of action, the leader, the wielder of men. It was analogous to that of the poet. His appeal is rather to the imagination and the emotions than to the abstract reasoning powers, though he never for a moment sought to dethrone the intellect. He speaks to the deepest instincts, the latent enthusiasms of the soul. He ever holds up the highest ideals, so high that one is often conscious of breathing a somewhat rarefied atmosphere. For he has a fine scorn of the practical details, the cautious reservations, the prudent reticences of the matter-of-fact writer. He soars above the earth.

Many a disciple of Père Gratry has felt in various degrees what Père Lescoeur expressed in his diary under date 7 February 1879. 'Dear Father . . . no human being has carried me towards God as you have done. None has inspired me as you have done with the taste for heavenly things, the desire for righteousness, the love of sacrifice, the horror of what is common, low and mean.'

May this book of his in its English garb do some such work for those who shall read it.

---

11. I know no adequate English equivalent for this common French word. It means an impetus or impulse which carries you along or carries you away.
12. Lift up your hearts . . . your minds.

II. The Book

It has been said of *Les Sources* that the book is but a transposition of those *Souvenirs de ma jeunesse* in which Gratry has told the story of his mind and heart. In other words, the great interest of the little book lies mainly in this that it was first *lived* before it was written. Were that not so certain of his 'counsels' would lose their force and be held for the mere theorisings of an unpractical dreamer. As it is we must not take it that these counsels are meant for all and sundry. The author, in his opening chapter, has expressly warned us against such a misapprehension. They could be acted upon in anything approaching their literal purport only by an *élite*. Yet if only an *élite* may derive from them positive guidance in the conduct of life, there is none of us but may gain from them inspiration and an uplifting of the heart.

To the influence which the little book has in fact exercised we have many testimonies, not from immediate disciples only, nor even from Frenchmen, but from men of other nations also. Thus the Italian convert and writer, the most beautiful of whose books[13] was published after he had fallen in the Great War, Giosue Borsi, writes in one of his 'Letters from the Front': 'No gift could have been more pleasing to me nor have done me more good than this admirable volume of Gratry. It was surely Providence which inspired you to send it to me. *Les Sources* has become my book. I have read and re-read it with avidity twenty times over. It has transformed me, has opened my eyes, has made me see depths of knowledge and truth of which I did not even suspect the existence.'

Les Sources was the principal inspiration of that earnest and enthusiastic, though not always prudent and moderate social movement, *Le Sillon*. No doubt it still exercises an influence upon the men who continue in a no less zealous but more orthodox form the movement begun by the *Sillon*.

The immediate disciples of Gratry—Charles and Adolphe Perraud, Henri Perreyve, Alfred Tonnellé, Louis Lescoeur—all testify to the influence upon their lives of the ideas set forth in this book. Their works, too, bear unmistakeable traces of this influence.

But perhaps the most remarkable testimony is that of Léon Ollé Laprune. In his diary under date 27 June 1862, he has recorded a resolution, made after much thought and anxious hesitation, to take up

13. *A Soldier's Confidences with God* (New York: Kenedy, 1918).

wholeheartedly the plan of studies and of life outlined by Père Gratry in *Les Sources*. That resolution he carried out, and it is no doubt to his fidelity to it that we owe that admirable series of works, *Le Prix de la Vie, La Vitalité chrétienne, La Philosophie du Temps présent, Les Sources de la Paix intellectuelle*, and the rest.

I have hinted that Père Gratry as a thinker is not always a sure guide. Even in *Les Sources* ideas are expressed which are, at the least, open to criticism. He was liable to be carried away by the warmth of his enthusiasm and the exuberance of his imagination into Utopias whither we need not follow him. A poetic metaphor, a happy piece of symbolism captivated his fancy and he seems at times to be taking figure and symbol for literal fact. Again, he does not always make due allowance for the existence of original sin. With him, too, the wish is often father to the thought. Intellectual difficulties fade away before the ardour of his desire: stubborn facts take their allotted places a little too meekly in his sweeping syntheses. But I do not think that these defects detract seriously from the value of his work as a whole, at all events of *Les Sources*.

Canon Jean Vaudon, in his book on Gratry, *Une Ame de Lumière*, speaks of *Les Sources* as a book worth more than its weight in gold.[14]

[The remainder of the introduction by S. Brown is omitted in this appendix. His translation of Part Two of Gratry's *Les Sources* follows.]

Part II: Counsels for the Conduct of Life

Book the First

Preparation

Chapter the First

On a former occasion[15] I set before you a plan of studies, I wish today to set before you a plan of life.

This plan of life may be summed up in a single word, which in God's name I venture to address to you, 'My son, be good.'

The plan is a simple one; but you will see that it is as rich as it is simple.

14. 239.

15. *Les Sources*, Part I, published the previous year.

Doubtless only great hearts understand what glory there is in being good. But why should not you, whoever you be, possess already, or dare to ask of God, your Father Almighty, a great heart and great thoughts?

Let us try. We shall see whether you will succeed in grasping the full grandeur and glory of goodness. Let us see whether you really *will* that glory.

Therefore I ask of you, do you will to be good? Do you mean to be that man of good will for whom God longs?

Are you willing to devote your life to justice and truth? Are you willing to accomplish man's true mission on earth?

Will you be generous, brave, disinterested? Would you be proud to become a servant of men, a worker for God? Would you be ready to follow out with unperturbable clearness of vision, with indomitable resoluteness, man's end, God's work?

Whatever be your state of life or your age, your wealth or your poverty, your ignorance or your knowledge, you are capable, if you have a living heart, of conceiving the royal, the divine ambition of throwing into the scales of the world's destiny your full weight of righteousness and of goodness.

Let me tell you a thing that has been for me all my life long a matter of unceasing astonishment.

It is wholly impossible for me to conceive how it is that out of all the multitudes of men who cover the face of the world there are none who have the notion of taking as the real and the sole object of life—righteousness.[16] There are no objects of life, however strange, mean, difficult, or dangerous, but are pursued with ardour, courage, cunning, perseverance by thousands of men. Many men make a gamble of life; some even throw it away; and nobody has the idea of laying it down as an offering and as a force given over to righteousness.

I see human beings whose lives seem to lie within the bounds of order, morality, and religion. They certainly do not wish to lead evil lives. But with them the purpose of life is not righteousness. They have some other purpose which absorbs their thoughts and their powers. They never love above all things God, the right, and the truth.

16. Père Gratry uses the word 'la justice' sometimes in the narrower sense of justice in English, sometimes in the sense of justness or righteousness as it is used in the New Testament.—Translator.

And I am not speaking for the moment of the man who is bound to earth because he must draw from it by his toil his daily bread. I am speaking of the man who is free, master of his time and of his life. I am speaking of the young man of twenty, born well-to-do, educated, with a knowledge of history, aware of the state of the world, and with a heart not yet stifled. He enters life. What is he going to do? I do not know. But one thing is certain—what he will *not* do is this. He will not have the astounding audacity to stand humbly and resolutely before God and his conscience and to say, 'I neither wish nor fear anything; and, because I have neither desire nor fear, I give my life to righteousness and to truth.'

That, I say, is what astonishes me. To say that nobody so much as understands what these words mean—to give one's life to righteousness and to truth! To say that your mind simply does not take in the realness and the fulness of that sublime career! And your heart does not conceive that boundless yet simple ambition!

Well, I am addressing this book to you to help you to conceive that ambition. I will help you and perhaps arouse you by telling you how God gave me the idea of this self-devotion. Do you on your side aid me, rouse me up; demand of me how it is that, having in my soul the germs of these ideas, I have buried them almost all, and they have failed to bear their fruits in me.

II

But how hard it will be, perhaps, to make myself understood. Today in Europe we are cruelly divided; divided by incurable ignorances and inextricable misunderstandings.

Everything is denied, everything asserted, absolutely denied, or absolutely asserted. Voices directly conflict with one another and, as it were, mutually quench each other. And already anger enters into the struggle and the thunderstorm is gathering; the sombre clouds of storm and wrath wrap us round and the light of reason and the serenity of righteousness are extinguished.

But could we not agree on one point? Could we not all of us base ourselves on the evident principle of eternal morality, of infallible and universal religion? To be kind to one another, to be just to one another? To have pity on the vast multitude that suffers and to be willing to wipe away so many tears? Does not the indisputable point lie there? Is not that morally evident and necessarily true? Would not that constitute an unshakable basis, a starting point that is simple, solid, and universally accepted?

I hope so. It is from that will begin the return to peace, to union, to the strength that union gives, and to the miracles that are accomplished by the strength of men who are united.

Yes, we shall unite in an immense pity for the sufferings of the world and in the hope and the will to heal them.

Yes, truth will prove itself anew, leading on once more to epochs of greatness. It will prove itself not by speeches but by miracles. Speeches are played out. Christ proved his teaching by healing men and multiplying the loaves. Genuine, incarnate truth is ready even today to prove itself by healing the nations and by multiplying life throughout mankind. Therein lies a fresh principle of heroism and enthusiasm with which God wills to inspire our times. Let us open wide our hearts and minds to this inspiration and to the power that comes with it.

Is it not time to begin the great changes, the real revolutions, and to impose the law of God on the nations themselves? Thou shalt not kill! Thou shalt not steal! Why should these laws, obviously divine and necessary as they are, be only for man in isolation and not for men collectively? Why are the nations in league against the laws of God? How is it that a people whose laws condemn the wretch who steals a little money continues to organize itself for the plunder of the globe?

It is in presence of such questions that I say to you who want to be clear-sighted and courageous, these words of holy Scripture, 'Take heart, and be a man.'

Chapter the Second

I

But in order to understand this plan of life and above all in order to have the courage to undertake it a fundamental condition must first be fulfilled.

There is an obstacle to be overcome. There is, as it were, a chain that must be broken.

This chain is a universal illusion that binds us to the ancient surface of this world as it actually is.

This chain is the love of money.

But, as it is all but impossible to get any man to understand this, I must explain to you in detail in what way and by what good fortune it has been granted me from my earliest youth to attain to an understanding of this point.

Listen, I beg of you, to the story of the best moment of my life.

I was at the time a school-boy of seventeen. I had just won many honours in my college and was overjoyed at my success. Full of hope that I was, free from suffering and trouble of any kind and moreover very fond of work, it was a joy to be alive. And so it came about that one evening, instead of going to sleep—I remember vividly that dormitory alcove—I began to ponder over my happiness.

Now this reverie was, in a very simple, almost commonplace way, the greatest event in my life. I was little more than a child. An hour afterwards I was a man.

I went over in my mind my recent successes and planned even greater successes for the year on which I was entering and for the year after. I thought I saw these last years of school life closing in vigorous and fruitful work. I saw the powers of my mind growing little by little, I was conscious of budding talents. I left college and began (according to my dreams) other studies which were to be a preparation for my supposed career. In these studies and then in that career I hoped to win the most brilliant successes.

Still, with my youthful pride there mingled also an element of prudence and reasonableness. I saw the huge multitude of competitors which experience of the keen competition of the examinations had taught me not to despise. But having already caught a glimpse of the fact that the little nucleus of hard workers grows rapidly less as life goes on, I put my trust in ever harder and harder work, and thus I reached the topmost places. Then, far from shutting myself up within the narrow bounds of a career, I laid claim to all the honours that literature can confer. Here came in more studies, writings, successes. I foresaw them all in minutest detail and foretasted all their joys.

Fortune came to crown all, solid, superabundant, altogether honourable, being the fruit of hard work and of glory won. Then there opened out before me a vista of wonderful beauty. I saw a splendid dwelling-house set amid splendid natural surroundings; my beloved father and mother lived in it with me. Then the high light of the picture, the very soul of all glory, of nature, of fortune, the ideal being dreamed of from the first hour of adolescence, appeared in the splendour of her beauty, in the supernatural power of the purest love, the strongest, the most religious that ever was.

All these pictures took life before my eyes. God Himself, I think, gave to my mind at this moment a certain creative power. I felt, nay actually fingered, life. I summed up in a moment whole days and years. I held the substance of them, I felt their joys with a power, an intoxication, an intensity such as reality itself does not give. Thus I saw my life unfold itself day by day and year by year, very beautiful as a whole and rich in its details. It was a life full of all the good things that man can enjoy upon the earth. And life went on, ever fuller and more beautiful, as the years rolled by. I counted the number of my years. I went from youth to manhood and then to middle age and then these years of my maturity grew many.

On a sudden I perceived with keen grief that, at the age which I saw myself to have reached, my father's was far beyond the ordinary limits of a man's life. So I saw my father dying and I was at his death-bed. My mother, my all but adored mother, survived to the most advanced age. But at last she too died. Overwhelmed with grief I closed her eyes.

My sister and my friends followed one by one the common path and left me.

And then came the turn of the fair and noble companion of my youth, the soul of my life. On her too winter fell. She prepared for departure. Should I survive her also? Yes, she died. There she lay cold and dead before my eyes.

Broken down with grief I clasped my sons in my arms. They had long been grown men. I was myself of an advanced old age. Should I survive them too? Alas my life is inexhaustible! I harden and wither but I do not die. Like the hollow trunk of an ancient tree I hold together merely by my bark. And so I see my children die.

I find myself alone without branches or offshoots, but I vegetate yet a little while. At last my hour comes and I am on my death-bed. Yes, the moment will come when I shall lie stretched upon my bed of death, I shall struggle in the grip of death, and I shall die.

At this point of my waking dream God, who willed to make me pass through all life and death within the compass of an hour, gave to my thought a more and more creative power. What I thought seemed to be enacted before me.

I saw intuitively all these things. I experienced them all. And everything was more vivid than reality. It is impossible for me to describe with what realism I saw death. Death was shown to me unveiled, it was laid bare before me. I do not think that in my last moments I am to see and feel it as I tasted it at that hour. So all is over, I cried. All is come to naught. Father, mother sister, friends annihilated! Beloved of my soul, companion and partner of my happy life, you too annihilated! Cherished beings, my offspring and hers, annihilated! I myself was vanishing.

No more the sun! The world no more, nor men. Nothing any more.

For a moment I have passed back again into life. From my bed of death I reach out and touch my cradle. Assuredly it is not far from birth to death however long deferred. It is but a day, or rather it is a dream. Those old and trite sayings of the moralists are after all the barest truth.

There is Life for you. Thus are all men born and thus they die, from the beginning of the world, even to its end. Generations succeed one another, pass swiftly, and are gone.

And I saw in a light and under forms that nothing shall ever efface from my memory countless multitudes from the beginning of the ages even to the end passing, passing like herds that go to the shambles all unawares. And then I saw them flow like the waters of a river nearing a great cataract and an abyss. All the waters reach it in their turn, they fall, only to hide beneath the earth and see the sun no more.

In this river I saw tiny wavelets that rose for a moment and for the duration of a flash caught a sunbeam, then faded out and sank. That wavelet was myself. Those that for a moment gleamed beside me were the beings whom I had loved. But all are long ago beneath the earth and within the great shadow.

At this sight I was motionless, transfixed with astonishment and terror. But what does all that mean, I cried? Why do not men league together to seek out above all an explanation of this frightful enigma and transform it all? Nobody troubles about it. Everybody passes on without taking the trouble to find things out for himself. People live like the gnats that hum and dance in the sunbeams. What is the purpose of these momentary apparitions in the midst of this on-flowing river? Why do men pass on? Why did they come at all? What is the use of anything that exists?

I was in despair for myself, in despair for all mankind. I kept gazing in terror at the abominable and insoluble enigma.

Then an immense despair forced me to collect my ideas and all my powers so as to break a way out, by a sort of violence if need be, and find somewhere an explanation of it all. Can it be that that is all? Can it be that all is absurd, useless, and void of sense? Have things any *raison d'être*, and if so what is it? If what I see be not all, then where is the rest? And what is the use of what I see? Is it not possible to shatter this dream?

But I heard no answer to these questions.

At that time I had no religion. I believed in nothing, unless, perhaps, in God. I felt towards Catholicism all the horror and all the disgust that any of its blindest enemies have ever felt. Nevertheless I began to think of God. O my God, I cried, do you hear me? No answer. Heaven is deaf and empty. And in deeper and deeper despair I tried a fresh effort.

Soon under the stress of this tremendous effort my whole being felt as it were a powerful drawing together, a flowing back of life to its centre. It seemed to me that I entered into my soul and that I penetrated into myself to fathomless depths which I glimpsed for the first time. Even to this day I still seem to see those strange depths. What I have been saying is not expressed in studied phrases. You must have felt that all along. I have simply described facts which are still, and will ever remain, ineffaceably before my eyes.

Suddenly out of the mysterious and fathomless abyss there came forth a cry piercing, heartrending, repeated, capable, it seemed to me, of reaching the uttermost bounds of the universe and of shaking everything that is. It seemed to me that at the bottom of my soul a most powerful being other than myself gave irresistible energy to this great cry of my whole nature stirred to its depths. 'O God! O God!' I cried, 'explain to me the enigma. My God, I promise, I swear it, only make known the truth to me and I will devote my whole life to it.'

Straightway I understood that this tremendous effort and this great cry of the whole man had not been in vain. I felt that an answer would come to me; but from what quarter I knew not. Still that of itself brought calm to me. Truth must exist. Truth does exist. It is beautiful, it answers everything. Yes, I will seek it, I will come to know it, and I will devote my life to it.

Then I perceived that I was still at college in my cubicle. But I was no longer a child.

Such is the first part of the story.

Here is the second.

II

After the great inward experience which in an hour made me pass from childhood to manhood, I remained for more than a year without drawing any explicit conclusion from what I had felt and seen. But the moral direction of my course of life was altered. I had no longer any illusion, nor any hope in the ordinary sense of the word. All that had attracted me but yesterday had come to nothing. All the palaces, all the treasures, all the honours of the world, all the power and all the grandeur of kings, all the glory of heroes, all the fame of letters, the whole thing seemed to me merely childish. Had an empire been proffered to me at that moment I should have spurned it. The whole of life seemed to me so barren and empty that at times I thought of quitting it. I had become very serious, very critical, and very proud. All men appeared to me so many unintelligent nonentities. In my eyes reason was in them only in germ not in actual use. In their entire lives, their habits, their moral and intellectual doings, I saw them but little different from the brute beasts.

To-day all that, doubtless, seems to me true in part; but I feel it in a wholly different way, and besides I now know better.

It would be too long to tell you how I was brought back from critical despondency and from pride to the esteem and pursuit of that state of love and kindness which is the state into which the Father draws the souls of those who are willing to become His children. I will not tell you now how I was led to what I know to be the light. I confine myself to the story of this thrice blessed beginning of my education by God.

When I had grasped the truth that the world and mankind are perfectible; that the beast-like condition of the human race may be and ought to be transformed; that reason should cease to be merely in germ and that it ought to come to reign over the world. When I understood that there is a reign of truth and justice that is drawing near and whose coming depends upon our efforts; that holy compassion for so many tears and sufferings will not always be barren:

that finally the Gospel of Christ is the announcement of that future, the instrument of those transformations, the new law of that better world. When I could contemplate that law of God in itself and when I saw with a certainty that seemed necessarily and absolutely unerring, that that law is light itself, that very light for which I had begged—then with intense and unspeakable joy, seizing upon my good fortune with all the powers of my soul, I consecrated my life, as I had sworn, to make this truth known, this truth that is the hope of all the nations, the great mainstay of all men in life and in death.

But, I ask you, resolved as I was to devote my life to truth alone—a consecration that was my happiness and sufficed for me—what time could I spare for anything else? It is clear that I had no attachment to this world as it is, still less to its god which is money. I had no time to spare for the amassing of wealth.

And then, in view of the fact that the immense majority of men must earn their living day by day by dint of hard work, and possess nothing whereon to live a single day without working, I refused to be an exception and a privileged person and chose to be poor as nearly all men are.

Christ was born poor and chose to live and die poor. He toiled with His hands for thirty years to earn His daily bread. When He left off His work in order to begin His preaching He had nothing: He received His humble fare from His friends or else from the crowd that surrounded Him or from the women who followed Him ministering to Him. He passed by, blessing and teaching, but had neither land nor house in which to dwell. 'The foxes have their holes,' He said, 'and the birds of the air their nests, but the Son of Man hath not where to lay His head.'

That saying pierced my heart through and through and filled it with enthusiasm. Like Him, I too could pass through this world in the footsteps of the Master doing some little good, without ever possessing where to lay my head. And that seemed to me good and beautiful. It seemed to me that by giving up everything—that everything which I knew to be nothing—I gained God, goodness, light, liberty, and that I received power to propagate the truth.

One day, therefore, after carefully weighing the hardest consequences of evangelic poverty, I freely accepted them. Then, to give more solemnity to the act that was about to determine my life, I entered a church, and there, as I was alone, stretching out my arms towards the altar, I made a vow never to become rich, to have but one purpose in life and possess no other property than truth and, if it might be, righteousness.

You understand why it is that I tell you this story. It is to show you, if I can, how at the outset of life one must be able to free oneself from the barren routine of this old world and keep all one's strength for the purpose of seeking the one thing necessary, the only lasting and fruitful life.

Moreover, I know that there exist in several quarters a certain number of men of heart, in whom reason is highly developed, and who really do love righteousness and are willing to devote themselves to its triumph. I wanted to make myself known to these, not in my inconsistencies and shortcomings, for which I ask pardon of God, but in the right and good intention which from my youth has guided my life, so that none of them could have any doubts as to my starting point or as to my purpose.

Let them understand that in all these political, social, philosophical, and religious questions I am as free from prejudices and from narrow and evil passions as a dead man could be. Indeed to all intents and purposes I have actually passed through death.

Let them understand also that this story which is mine, literally true every word of it, is, with but little difference, that of thousands of priests in France and the world over. Only, these generous and venerated brethren have almost all known better than I have how to use the gift of God.

Chapter the Third

I

And now I repeat my question: Do you wish to be *good*? Do you want to follow out God's plan? Do you want to devote your life to justice and truth?

If so the first step to take is to overcome the obstacle. It is to break asunder the chain that holds men and nations in bondage. It is to be free from this world as it is.

Take this well in: men bound by the tradition of this old world and carried away by greedy selfishness are deceived almost all of them and almost always, just as if they had not the use of reason. They still live, for the most part, eaten up by appetites that are almost bestial. That constitutes their chains, that is, paganism, and slavery still flourishing.

There are for the individual as for society two ways, two objects, two sorts of worship. There is God and there is the idol. And what, according to the Gospel, is the idol? The Gospel says that there are two masters which cannot be served at one and the same time and these two masters are God and money. You cannot serve at once God and money.[17]

So it is money that is the idol.

But it is just here that the world laughs at the Gospel. And it is here that we ourselves have need of courage to preach the Gospel and keep repeating the great law: 'You cannot at the same time serve God and money.' But the Gospel explains the law and in a single word, lays down the principle—riches of *iniquity*, it says, *mammona iniquitatis.*

Therefore what is condemned is not the toil which accumulates the forces or powers represented by riches, but the iniquity which destroys them. Mammon, that idol which must not be served if we are to serve God, is the worship of unjust riches, the worship of riches used for mere enjoyment, a, worship which shatters the powers of labour and ruins the nations.

In this sense, therefore, money is truly the great and universal sacrament of all false worship and of all idolatries. More than Fate, more than Jupiter, it is ruler of gods and men. It is evidently ruler of Jupiter, god of power; of Mars, god of war; of Venus;[18] of Mercury, god of thieves, gamblers, swindlers, and also god of eloquence, that is of the throng of writers and talkers. Money is thus the great idol and the sacrament of all evil and the arch-enemy of God.

Now so long as individual men and peoples will not come back with faith to the worship of the true God and will not shatter the idol, all progress whether of individual men or of the world is absolutely impossible. The triumph of the Kingdom of God is not even conceivable. Justice and truth can take no forward step.

17. *Non potestis servire Deo et mammonae* (Lk 16:13).

18. On this subject I dare not quote the saying of Bourdaloue in his Sermon on Riches.

Therefore to trample the idol under foot is the beginning of the moral life, it is the indispensable prerequisite of all progress of man and society.

It is not without wonder that on opening the Gospel I find that the first sentence of the first discourse of our Saviour is, 'Blessed are the poor, for theirs is the Kingdom of Heaven.' Elsewhere I read this astonishing condemnation, 'It is impossible for a rich man to enter into the Kingdom of Heaven.' That is to say it is impossible that the worshipper of money, the man who has not vanquished that idol, should enter into the Kingdom of Heaven in justice and truth and should ever reach the light and the bliss of eternal righteousness and eternal truth.

Indeed, do you not see that in every soul there are two things, reason and passion? I call passion that inveterate proneness to seek pleasure and excess in pleasure; to shun work for the sake of pleasure; to abase oneself, degrade oneself, to crawl, to lie, to deceive, to rob, and to slay for the sake of pleasure and self-indulgence, and in order to grasp the great universal sacrament of all pleasures, money. Such is the worship of the idol. But, I ask you, what do these pagans gain by their abominable worship? Obviously every possible evil, physical and moral.

Science and experience tell us that in the human heart and blood there is a fierce and hungry instinct, a hunger and thirst for joy which is ever tending to sweep us away. Science adds that the man who gives himself up to this tendency murders his body. He hastens towards every sort of disease, premature old age, and an early death. Nearly all men thus hasten prematurely towards death. And that is why science adds: Man does not die, he kills himself.

But, if he resolutely slays his body, does he not slay his soul more swiftly still? A slain soul—what else is the soul devoid of self-respect and truth, without strength against passion, a soul in which there reigns a hopeless baseness, a ceaseless thirst for pleasure, fierce egoism and contempt for the rights of others and for their very lives, when there is question of money for self, pleasure for self. Clearly, all men are born in this state of 'passion,' in this leaning towards self against everybody else, in the longing for this evil fire of pleasures that burn up life, devour body and soul, and bear us on towards hopeless decadence, towards suffering of every kind both for self and others.

But, thanks be to God, there is in our hearts and in our souls another force. It is what for the moment I have called reason. I am speaking of true reason, of the eternal reason! Reason, I say, speaking in conscience, is the power that struggles against decadence, which breasts the current of evil, and if need be breaks through all obstacles. Labour, courage, hope, virtue, justice towards others, victory over cowardly and cruel selfishness, temperance, self-respect, the growth of the mind in wisdom and enlightenment, and that of the heart in goodness and righteousness—that is what I mean by the effort in the conscience of "reason" blessed by God.

Is it not evident that the obstacle to all good and to all progress is the hungry craving for enjoyment and possession? The obstacle is that avidity of mind and heart which one might call in one word the spirit of lucre or the love of riches. And on the other hand the regenerating force, the mainspring of progress, moral good, is obviously that spirit of self-restraint, of disinterestedness, of self-respect, of vigorous resistance to selfishness, which one may call in one word: the spirit of poverty.

Hence, as the Gospel says, it is impossible that a rich man should enter into the Kingdom of Heaven, and on the other hand it is evident that 'Blessed are the poor, for theirs is the Kingdom of Heaven.'

The spirit of poverty is the salt of the earth. It is the only path towards that regeneration of society which is the will of God to-day. It is the only force that can accomplish man's mission on earth, to wit, the restoration of the divine order in the world.

II

But let us come to an understanding as to what precisely is this 'spirit of poverty.' That is the first thing to know and to practise at all times but especially in these our days. It is, as I have already pointed out to you, the first saying of the first discourse of Christ our Lord.

It is often said to me, There is something that rings false and which cannot be generally accepted in that axiom which is the Christian axiom, to wit: 'Be miserable in this life in order to be happy in the next.' I answer, What you choose to call the Christian axiom is not Christian at all: it is nonsense. Now the Gospel is, everywhere and always, reasonableness itself, and the Gospel says, 'He that leaves all things finds all things a hundredfold even in this present life.'[19] It says again, 'The meek shall possess the earth.' And St. Paul, 'Our law is useful for all things, for the present life and for the life to come.'[20]

But what is this evangelical spirit of abnegation, detachment, poverty? It is this—one cannot serve God and mammon. It is God that must be served, not mammon. Justice, truth, honour, virtue, morality, self-respect, liberty—all these things must come before money. Can there be a doubt of it? Before it, too, must come science, art, wisdom, work, and when it comes to a choice a man must resolutely trample money under foot and choose righteousness. Once more, can there be a doubt of it?

Do you think, my son, that the Christian, when he is choosing his future path conscientiously and freely, ever says to himself, 'I shall be miserable in this life so as to be happy in the next.' On the contrary he ought to dare to say to himself, 'I want to possess the sovereign good even in this life.' To that end let us cast aside what is neither good nor happiness, and let us take hold of the truth which is the source of true happiness.

But according to the ordinary ways of men in this world, is it really happiness that men seek and that they find? Is it not obvious, on the contrary, that nearly all of them go wrong, led astray by gross blindness and almost animal cravings? Like animals men fling themselves upon material things and fight for the biggest shares. Life such as we have made it is like a feast of savages in which the coarse guests snatch the food from each other instead of helping one another. Ought we not to change this manner of seeking the good? Might not life become some day an *agapé* or early Christian love-feast, in which each would offer instead of taking; in which the man who grabbed things for himself would make himself a laughing-stock; in which good men would think it the right thing to accept but a modest share; in which while the poor folk, if there be any left, would attend to the repast, the people of light and leading would enliven the feast by their charm and their wit? I do not see why the whole of life should not take on this form, this beauty and this dignity. When it comes to be understood that money and bread, very necessary things assuredly, are neverthe-

19. Mk 10:29, 30. *Nemo est qui reliquerit . . . Qui non accipiet centies tantum, nunc in tempore hoc.*

20. Godliness is profitable to all things, having promise of the life that now is and of that which is to come (1 Tim 4:8).

less the least of good things, and that mind, wisdom, science, and above all goodness, courage, liberty, love are far and away the most powerful forces making for present and daily happiness, there will be then, I hope, a more ardent pursuit of the greatest goods, a less ardent of the lesser, and then bread and money will be less greedily sought for and less shamefully divided up.

III

So you see that the only way to give the world a forward impulse is to shatter the idol in your heart, the idol of all times and of all places, and to understand the first sentence of the first discourse of Christ, 'Blessed are the poor in spirit.'

But now, to speak more accurately, what is poverty? Poverty is not abject misery, it is not absolute want, it is one's living earned by work. Thus defined poverty is manifestly a holy and a sacred thing which all of us ought to respect, esteem, and seek.

Think what would have happened if God our beloved Father who rules us by His Providence had chosen to send us, being what we are, into a rich world (our actual world is poor, and God-made-man willed to be poor also); had He placed us in a world of opulence obviously we were all lost. What sort of a world would that have been which would have spontaneously offered to our needs and to our desires all that they craved? It would have been a world without efforts, without work, without courage, heroism, or genius, deprived in fact of everything that goes to make the Man.

Accordingly our Father placed us in a vigorous world, in a hard school, in a world of poverty wherein His well-beloved children may develop the soul and the heart, their genius and their heroism. A world devoid of struggle, of obstacles, of danger, and of death could have made of us but a contemptible set of human beings. But the world in which we find ourselves makes for strong souls, men who have steadfastness, effort, energy, courage, and devotedness, everything that is beautiful, worthy, and glorious. That is poverty for you. She is the mistress of work and of effort, the mother of every virtue. She is the teacher of the human race.

Now there are men, those whom the Gospel describes as the rich and of whom it says, 'Woe to you rich.' There are men who despise these great benefits, men whose life-long concern it is to shun poverty, that is to say work, that is to say the effort that brings out what a man has in him, the courage to strive, to brave danger and to overcome obstacles.

Man has been placed on this earth to keep it, defend it, and cultivate it.[21] So much is evident. Now there are men who shirk that labour and that strife. You who read these lines, those of you who are rich and who have hitherto lived merely for pleasure, who are throwing away your life in immorality, in futility, is that, I ask you, the role which you accept definitely and after taking thought? Do you mean to hide for greater safety behind the mass of men who are fighting and dying? May I venture to ask you whether, when a visible war is being waged, you lose courage and run away? Surely when fire and sword have to be faced you put yourself at the head of your soldiers without being compelled by any law of conscription. You are the foremost at the posts of danger and you would think it strange were a soldier to offer to shield you with his body. You are brave and generous and noble then.

But then why bury yourself in shame and desertion and treachery when there is question of that universal and inevitable warfare—Life? Do you know what you are doing, you who have within your grasp money, that is to say a weapon or a tool, you who by that very fact grasp the power of a hundred or of a thousand men, you who by yourselves alone are a veritable legion in virtue of the money with which you are armed? This is what you are doing—you are deserting in the very middle of the fight and then your brethren are beaten. The leaders desert, those who are well-armed make off: then poverty which had been a source of energy and strength changes to misery, weakness, destitution, slavery: the vanquished perish of starvation.

O rich men, do you now understand what poverty means? Do you at length understand that it is a universal duty, since it means daily work, struggle, and effort? In this sense all men ought to wish to be poor and even to become poor, for it is in this sense that it is said, 'Woe to you rich.' Do you understand likewise what riches are in themselves and what property means? Do you understand that property, capital, is the wages of a hundred or perhaps a thousand working men given in advance to a captain of industry? And this captain of

21. 'And the Lord took man and put him into the paradise of pleasure to dress it and to keep it' (Gen 2:15).

industry must render an account to God for the use to which these wages are put, just as, like everybody else, he must render an account of the use made of life.

And from this point of view, when one is preaching the contempt of riches, might one not also, with a view to reaching the same end, preach the esteem and the respect of money? What *is* money and whence does it come? Money is accumulated labour, it is so much time, it is so much human life, it is so much blood, sweat, and tears. That is what you hold in your hands. What will you do with it?

Do you not see in this one point the whole Gospel, the judgement of God? The Gospel calls rich, rich and accursed, the man who, holding in his hand this blood, these tears which are commonly not his own, prostitutes them, pours them out for his own pleasures. The Gospel calls poor, poor in spirit, the man who knowing what he holds in hand, respects these sacred things and gives them only for the salvation of men and the progress of the world. And thus one begins to understand why morality like the Gospel may be summed up in a single question, 'What will you do with the blood of men and with their tears? Shall it be consecration—or desecration?'

Chapter the Fourth

I

Yes, men of noble heart, you understand these things and, I hope, appreciate them to the full. You are on the side of righteousness and you feel that you will be able to love your duty in that heroic struggle, the onward march of mankind towards its true goal. You understand what honour and real glory there is in marching in the vanguard and in leading others bravely towards that land of the future, a better and happier age. Perhaps, even, you have in your heart courage of that impetuous kind that is capable of daring everything and making every sacrifice in order to overturn all obstacles and reach the goal.

If that be so, there is another virtue that must be combined with your zeal for the right—wisdom. If you want to become a soldier of progress, a worker for the right, then to disinterestedness and courage, which is the first condition necessary, you must unite that tranquil and luminous wisdom which clearly sees the work to be done and the goal to be reached, throws itself only into genuine efforts, does not lash itself into useless violence, and does not root up the wheat along with the tares.

Let me speak more clearly still. If to-day you wish to labour for the good of men you must first forswear that worst mental aberration of our days, the fierce and blind mania for smashing and overturning. To smash up everything in order to build all over again on some new plan, that has been among us the absurd, cruel, and criminal notion of the fierce and ignorant zeal of the great mass of misguided reformers. If you are unable to cut loose absolutely from this stupid madness, you can do an immense deal of harm but you are powerless for good. You will not wipe away a single tear, you will set many flowing.

II

Friend, when I was young and ignorant, but already resolved to work for the right, I had at first this bitter, sombre, and barren zeal which wants to tear up everything and curses the good at present existing for want of understanding its greatness. Listen. Here is a mystery of which I was long unaware, blinded as I was by the madness of the times. Indeed it is, I must admit, only within the last few days that I have come to understand to the full its splendid clearness. It is this, that in all things God has done much more for us than we know. We are closer to all good things than we can possibly suspect! We are held apart from heaven and from the promised land only by a moral obstacle which we are free to break down. Everything is given but man does not yet know how to take it. Our blind ignorance, our ungrateful despondency are unable to see that in every order of things, even in the social order, God gives us everything. 'If thou didst know the gift of God!'[22] says the Gospel, a universal saying, true everywhere and always. 'This place is holy', cried the patriarch in his vision, 'and I knew it not'.[23] Yes, we almost all of us know not how much holiness and sacredness there is in our present world as it actually is.

Men's life on earth is no more given over to mere chance than is that of nature, or than is the life of the heavenly bodies. God's goodness gives the germs of all things, and the holy laws of His Providence are ever at work, developing them. What then is wanting? What is

22. *Si scires donum* Dei (Jn 4:10).

23. *Locus iste sanctus est et ego nesciebam* (Gen 28: 6).

amiss? Where is the obstacle? It is this—our blindness and unrighteousness! blind unrighteousness! This is the only obstacle there is, the sole enemy that has to be fought in order that what is good many develop. The whole of human endeavour is summed up in this divine and marvellous saying: Seek first the kingdom of God and all things will be added to you.[24] Yes, all the rest will be given, or rather is it not already given?

III

Ah, if you but knew the gift of God! God's grace is given to all from the outset. God outpours His sunlight and his dews, says the Gospel, on the wicked as on the good.[25] Take away the obstacle of unrighteousness and the spirit of God fills the soul.

What dogma teaches about grace and the spirit of God is true of all the sources of life. Bread, the nourishment of the body, is given to us. Warmth is given to our limbs, light to our eyes. The germs of things are sown lavishly in the immense bosom of the nurse of mankind. Water, electricity, light, heat are poured out on her in floods. The mother's milk is given to the lips of the child as soon as he can draw it to him and take it. And when he was unable to take anything the blood itself was given, the maternal (and providential) blood flowed in him without any doing of his own. And as for the light of reason, it enlightens every man that comes into the world. Truth also is given to us; we are inoculated with certitude. But the restlessness of our feckless minds breaks away from it and eludes it. And our clumsy and distrustful thought, by some blind effort or another, reaches doubt and error.[26] Why should not God have done for the mind and heart of man what He obviously has done for his body? True wisdom is given in its necessary bases, and the sophists who try forsooth to create the beginning of wisdom, are destitute of gratitude and of understanding.

24. Words of the Master, Matt 6:33, Lk 12:31.
25. Matt 5:45.
26. The angels of the little ones, says the Gospel (Matt. 18:10), see without ceasing the face of the Father in Heaven. Is that not as much as to say that a bond of light binds all innocent souls to God? And when Christ speaks of those little ones who believe in Him, does He not seem to teach us that as the innocent souls of children possess implicit reason, so they have also implicit faith and the germ of everlasting light?

True religion is given, and, if man liveth not by bread alone but by every word that cometh forth from the mouth of God, I infer that the word of God is in our midst just as much as is bread. I hold that it broods over the world and that it reaches all men, be it explicitly or implicitly. Religion is true. There is only one religion. It is the religion that is a rounded whole, universal, of all times and places. Yes, true religion is in our midst lavishly outpoured like the benefits of nature. Nay, God Himself is given. The heavenly ideal, the supreme good which every heart yearns for and every mind dreams of, that is to say God, God offers Himself to us, takes flesh, unites Himself to the soul and the mind, to the whole man, gives Himself to us to breathe like the air,[27] distributes Himself like food and drink: immortal blood of the life to come which during this earthly life penetrates into us without any doing of our own,—just as in the life preceding our birth the maternal and providential blood flowed in our physical frame without our doing.

And, in our days above all, benefits are given us even to the extent of luxury. To say nothing of the marvels and beauties of art, true science is ours to-day. Immense regions of wonderful and pregnant truths are accessible to everybody. The vast domain of the mathematical sciences offers to the human mind an almost boundless world of affirmations which are capable of application to the conquest of nature. The form of the visible sky is known in the detail of its movements and the principle of its laws. We calculate the distances of the stars: we know their weights. Then come the contemporary wonders of scientific applications and above all man's conquest of space and the human race brought to have henceforth but a single dwelling-place where soon all men will be able to hear one another as in an assembly.[28]

IV

And, after all that, the friends of humanity, the hearts athirst for righteousness, those that observe what men's charity is and who, like Christ Himself, weep at the sight of their sufferings, those generous souls

27. *Spiritus oris nostri Christus.*

28. [How wonderfully this is being fulfilled by the discovery of wireless transmission.–Translator].

enlightened above the common, are they to be supposed not to suspect that, even in the social order, numberless benefits are bestowed, and that powerful and holy laws exist and are at work for the development of those benefits? Have they no suspicion that the evil, that the obstacle that bars the way is our blind ingratitude which does not see the benefits, does not understand the germs of good, and tramples the laws under foot! Have they not the happiness of discovering that our task is simple—to sweep away the obstacle of unrighteousness, that is to practise simply, as between man and man, between people and people, between rulers and ruled, those great moral laws that are essential, known eternally, perceptible to every conscience, visible to all men's reason? Do they not understand, in a word, that if a man seeks righteousness alone, all is given or will be given him?

Friend, understand therefore with the holy and ample logic of the heart, with the sane reason of an unmutilated nature, that, since you found in this world on coming into it that marvellous creation of God, the family, and, as an outcome of a fatherly love and a motherly Providence, life given to what was not, nurtured and fostered in what had no power of its own, that alone might well convince us that there exists an eternal and all-powerful fatherhood for all men taken together, no less than for man in isolation.

There is a fatherhood, an invisible family, as it were, watching over us, over us, i.e. over all mankind. And this 'family' at the outset gives us everything without any doing of our own and subsequently develops everything along with and by means of us, provided we put no obstacle in its way and are willing to work.

V

Let us hope that the serenity which is born of the contemplation of such truths as these will unite with your zeal and your courage. Man and the world, as they gradually rise, progress from terror to confidence at the same time as from blindness to light. Light shows forth the beauty of things which had been hidden in darkness. One of those vices of human nature that have not been sufficiently noticed is the abusive, scoffing spirit[29] which sees everything black and makes out

29. The word used by Père Gratry is '*le blasphème*,' which in French is occasionally used without the full meaning that it bears in English.

that everything is black. As St Paul wrote to the early Christians, 'Let all bitterness and wrath and anger and clamour and abusive language[30] be removed from you and all malice' (Eph 4:31). Yes, according as man is renewed in God, such an attitude ceases and gratitude comes with the light. Man ceases to see nothing but the dark side of this garden of the earth and to speak ill of life and of its Author. Little by little he discovers the immeasurable beauty of things and sees in present benefits an earnest of magnificent promises for the future. Let us beware of impatient ideals of absolute perfection and of the contempt of present benefits however merely relative. How many men ruin themselves physically by impatient striving after perfect health, by the contempt of the sufficient powers that they possess but will not use. And in the soul-life how many souls are there not who, at the very moment when God is inspiring them, draw away from Him with a certain churlish coldness, under pretext of unworthiness, while awaiting better times! And when one has lost one's powers of soul or body in this barren inertia, one begins to feel that before that loss one possessed life in sufficient abundance to be capable of winning more ample life. As for me I know too well by long experience that one of the greatest obstacles in my life all along has been ignorance and disdain of present goods. We are always waiting for a better present in the hope of making the most of it when it comes, and this better present can only come from a real and actual present which you are neglecting and destroying. Both the wicked by their dark and sinister spirit and the good by their excitable impatience or their barren restlessness conspire together in this disdain.

True wisdom in its serenity sees things otherwise. It sees in man and in the world three things—magnificent germs or seeds of good, laws which evolve these seeds, and the moral obstacle which arrests development. It sees that in everything the state of the world of peoples and of every man is just what the moral life which that people leads admits of. You speak of slavery! Are you fit for freedom? Be fit for freedom and say, Let freedom be. Freedom *will* be and all the rest as well.

Consequently there is no place for that sombre violence that must needs smash and slay in order to succeed in giving life. There can be no question of destroying contemporary society so as to rebuild it on

30. The word used in the Greek text and in the Vulgate Latin is *blasphemia*.

a better plan. Hopelessly astray are those absurd and impotent efforts of mad genius and scared heroism spent with a view to creating the real social organisation. The real social organisation, my brother, long before you were born was from the beginning of things created by God, bestowed by God in its essential bases and in the laws that develop things therefrom, just as the organisation of your body was created by God in the mother's womb long before it was possible for you to know and will it.

Understand once more. What is done in us and in the world, without us or in spite of us, by the goodness of God and His providential laws is always much more than half the work. It is for us to grasp, to understand, to follow, to obey, and to continue. But above all—and therein lies our greatness and our royalty—it is for us, by reason and liberty and heroic enterprises, to know and overcome the obstacle, that moral obstacle which comes between man and the gifts of God.

Therefore morality, absolute, necessary, evident morality, in a word, all-round righteousness, that, in every order of things, is the holy and simple condition of all progress and of all good.

Book the Second and Last

The Aphorisms of the Science of Duty

Chapter the First

The Science of Duty

Courage! the human mind is really marching forward and that in this present age; it is working out a science which will have more influence on the world than the science of the forces of nature has exercised during the past two centuries. This science is the science of Duty.

What I mean is this[:] that in this present age History, Politics, Economics, Law, Sociology, and all the sciences that are bound up with eternal righteousness are tending to combine into a single higher science which will be the science of Duty. And this great science, the most fruitful of them all, will bring into full relief, and by descending to details and applications will develop, the rich beauty of the primitive inspirations of men's consciences and the divine fruitfulness of the precepts and counsels of Christ our Lord and of the Church.

Conscience is bestowed on everybody, at all times and in all places, and it suffices. Each man will be judged according to what shall have been bestowed on him. But the just man must endeavour to enlighten his conscience daily by knowledge, and knowledge ought to develop from age to age by the efforts of reason and liberty.

The principle of this science is simple, as, in astronomy, is the principle of attraction and its law. But the applications of the principle constitute one of the most extensive and varied of sciences. This principle which is in the science of Duty what attraction is in astronomy may be thus formulated: *Assistance due by every being to every being.*

Assistance due by every being to every being! It is only another way of saying with S Paul, 'For all the law is fulfilled in one word: Thou shalt love thy neighbour as thyself' (Gal. 4:14). It is another way of saying, 'Do unto others as you would that they should do to you' (Matt 7:12). That is the principle of Duty. And it is on purpose that I leave in the formula the word *being* instead of the word *man* which is less general. That boundless scope of the object of duty recalls to my mind the saying of our Lord, 'Go into the whole world and preach the Gospel to every creature' (Mk 16:15). The reason is that duty is not only between man and man but between man and the whole creation, every being without exception.

Duty means going towards the goal and leading all creation thither. And we ought to go towards the goal which is the union of beings among themselves and with God 'with our whole soul and with our whole heart, with all our mind and with all our strength' (Matt 22:37; Mk 12:30). And I dwell with pleasure on the unrestricted universality of the formula, 'by every being to every being.' I bear in mind the insistency with which S Paul calls on Christians to succour and to be mindful of and to pray for 'ALL MEN; for God will have all men to be saved . . . for Christ gave himself a redemption for all' (I Tim 2). And this principle of the universality of duty and of the object of it comes also into this sublime saying, 'Christians, you will render an account not of yourselves alone but of the whole world.'[31]

The absolute universality of man's duty towards the whole human race is a thing which, now that mankind has been brought back to unity, must be inculcated by education on every man coming into this world. Why? Because this sublime way of looking at things might well conduce to increase tenfold in men's hearts enthusiasm and

31. *Non de vestra tantum salute sed de universo orbe vobis ratio reddenda est* (S John Chrysostom).

effort. Why again? Because it is easier to reduce the whole world to order than a single state or a single town. Nations will not be saved in isolation any more than will individuals. In this age of ours what God demands of the human race is a movement all together. And I repeat with a feeling of deep joy that God wishes to give to Europe to-day in detail and in its applications this science of Duty which is necessary to that great movement. This science but yesterday only a sapling, to-day puts forth branches and fruits. The Master said, 'If you keep my word you will know the truth.' Yes, the word of the Gospel (implicitly the whole truth) which has been kept in the Christian world has borne fruit and to-day we are coming to the visible light, to a scientific knowledge of at least a part of that truth.

In this chapter which I have entitled Aphorisms of the Science of Duty I shall endeavour to set forth in a series of résumés, succinct but not dry, the principal scientific conclusions of a moral nature which the public opinion of the European peoples has reached or will reach I hope within the next hundred years.

I

This then is the simple first principle of the science of Duty, *Assistance due from every being to every other being.*

II

The fulfilment of Duty in the full sense of the word is the effort of the whole man to lead all creation towards its goal.

III

The effort of the whole man, the act of the soul in its entirety is called in the language of the Gospel which is the language of God, love. That is why it is written, 'Thou shalt love the Lord thy God (the goal and the end of all beings) with thy whole heart and with thy whole soul and with all thy mind and with all thy strength.' The act of love, the effort to help is the general action of the soul in light and freedom. Love is not passion but an act of the soul.

IV

Love, as the divine formula lays it down, ought to be the love of the neighbour, that is to say the effort to be a help to every being ought to conform itself to the hierarchy of duties. Consequently the rule is to go to what is nearest, to love according to proximity, as attraction is exerted in proportion to distance. But this must be rightly understood.

V

Man owes himself in the first place to the neighbour. But who is my neighbour? Christ was asked. And Christ answered that one's neighbour is the man whom you find lying wounded by the roadside.

VI

But the law of the love of our neighbour is stated in most absolute terms. The endeavour to help or to love is really regulated by the law of nearness, not physical, but moral and metaphysical, nearness. According to this law well-regulated love begins with God who is more intimate with me than I am myself: then it descends to myself, for I am primarily responsible for myself; and next it extends to the neighbour who comes in contact with me, then to country, then to the human race.

VII

Yes, assuredly the first of all our duties is to love God above all things. Yes, *to serve God*: the expression is a good one. I will even say *to help God*: for the Incarnate Word says to us: 'It is me myself that you are helping.' *Et mihi fecistis*. To help God! That is St Paul's own expression. We do aid God. *Dei adjutores sumus*. Yes, to aid God, that is to say to open souls to Him, my own first of all and then those of others, to make an entrance for Him into all beings that are shut against Him by perversity, to aid and assist Him to attain His object and bring all creation to its goal, so that He who is the supreme goodness, the absolute truth, beauty, bliss, love, may be all in all.

VIII

Yes, I aid Him thus and serve Him who is the source of all good by ever endeavouring to know and love Him and to be His and to abide with Him with my whole heart and with my whole soul, with all my mind and with all my strength.

IX

And that of itself, if I succeed in carrying it out, is a doing of my whole Duty towards myself and gives all the aid that I owe to my entire being. For, ceasing not to draw upon God by love and effort, as the new-born babe clinging to its mother's breast, I drink in life from an infinite well-spring and I draw it down into all my energies and faculties. I draw it down into my soul, then into my mind, and finally into my body.

X

And it is not in vain that the Gospel tells us that the two great precepts of loving God and loving our neighbour are like and indeed are but one. For in reality the love of God gives love of the neighbour and the service of God serves the neighbour. For what do we draw from God by the act of the soul if it be not faith and light, liberty and love? Now these are the forces that call blessings down upon the world, which make us rich for the succouring of the human race, make us clear-sighted and resolute to urge the world towards its goal.

XI

He therefore who fulfils the first duty, who draws from God faith, certainty, light, and liberty, wills and even performs his whole duty, for he wills and performs with his whole being the helping of all beings.

XII

Thus my first duty, my duty to God, if it be fulfilled, implies the fulfilment of my duty to myself and others. For if I am a co-operator with God in His undoubted will to lead me to the goal, it is myself that I am helping on. And if God's life abides in me, that is to say if I have succeeded in attaining to righteousness, it is once more obvious that I have worked for others.

Thus the three duties are identical. Nevertheless let us take them separately so as to come down to details.

Chapter the Second

Duty to God

I

I say to you solemnly, Here is the basis of things, the whole perfection of life. Thus speaks the Gospel: 'I am not alone; my Father is in me . . . My Father worketh even until now and I work. And what I see in my Father, that I do.'[32] Thus speaks He who is the God-Man.

II

I, too, the last and least of men, bear within me my Father, my Creator, the eternal well-spring of my life. My Father ceases not to work in me and to urge me towards the goal by constant inspirations and impulses. The irresistible longing for happiness and the perpetual restlessness of every soul are the effects of this incessant working. It is for me to feel and to understand what the Father wishes to work in me and to act accordingly with my reason and liberty.

III

God who bears us up, who is in us, who is our principle and source, prepares and even sets going our thoughts and our actions. He has lived beforehand eternally within His own Being what He wills us to live in time. The idea which He has of us, His eternal will in our regard constitute the ideal history of each one of us, the great possible poem of our life. This fair poem our Father, in His love for us, never ceases inspiring us with deep down in the hidden aspirations of the soul, in conscience, in the light of reason which enlightens every man in this world. In that motionless, simple, infinite activity of God's Providence, is contained from all eternity all possible details of our acts and of our movements. Our life as it works out in time and space must be an image of that idea of God.

32. *Pater meus usque modo operatur et ego operor* (Jn 5:17).

IV

I pray God to open the eyes of all thinking men so that they may league together in order to understand and get others to understand this truth: THE FATHER IS WITH US; OUR GOD IS WITHIN US. He lives in us and He wills to guide us, and we His children, free that we are, follow or resist. Will not the deep attractiveness of Pantheism combined with its manifest absurdity succeed in opening our eyes? Do you not understand that most certainly every being is not God but that God is in every being, above all in the intelligent and free soul wherein He works, enlightens, inspires? That is the common basis of metaphysics, logic, morality, and of the entire science of duty.

V

Yes, my Father is in me, in the midst of my soul and at the very source of my being. And there He enlightens and works and inspires and fills my youth with holy joy.[33] And this youth of mine is not only the beginning of my years, it is also that deep seated youth which, be our age what it may, is ever in the centre of our being, at the beginnings of our impulses and inspirations. Happy they who, by grateful tenderness, by humble recollection, cease not to refresh their being in that well-spring! Thus it is that my Father unceasingly renews my youth. He that can no longer renew his youth is drawing near to death.

VI

By loving God, that is to say by eliciting unceasingly the act of my soul which serves God and aids Him, it is myself that I am aiding, it is to myself that I am giving life. I draw from God in the first place the root force of life, that is the ever growing energy of light and happiness, righteousness and truth. I draw from Him that fundamental gift, certitude, faith. I draw hope and the joy of effort. Thence there flows into my intellect increasing light and into my will ever growing freedom. The fountain of living water, that living water about which Christ spoke to the Samaritan woman, has begun to well up in me.

33. *Ad Deum qui laetificat juventutem meam.*

VII

The moral effort that one must make in order to draw upon this source is prayer, a sacred name, the one best adapted to express the fundamental act of free and rational life. Continuous prayer is therefore the essential, universal, and principal duty of all men, just as the duty of the green leaf is to draw up the sap and breathe the air, without which it will wither and die.

VIII

We must here recall that other pronouncement of the Gospel: 'And all things whatsoever you shall ask in prayer, believing, you shall receive' (Matt 21:22). And again, 'Whosoever shall say to this mountain, Be thou removed and be cast into the sea, and shall not stagger in his heart, but believe that whatsoever he saith shall be done, it shall be done unto him' (Mk 11:23). Such is the complete idea of prayer. The Gospel teaches us that prayer, that is to say the Soul's fundamental act, is on the one hand something asked of God and on the other a command to things. The soul begs of God to send life and it commands the world to receive life and obstacles to disappear, thus by faith moving aside the mountains that hinder the onward march of the world.

IX

Whosoever, therefore, fulfils the great duty of prayer to the full extent of the Gospel meaning, fulfils all duty. He who prays helps all the souls of men, he helps his brethren by the saving and powerful magnetism of a soul that believes, knows, and wills. He performs, what S Paul calls upon us to do above all things, prayers, supplications, and acts of thanksgiving on behalf of all men.

What is the scientific meaning of this? It is that in a very real manner, as Fénelon has said, men touch one another from one end of the world to the other. They are in contact with us. That, then, is the neighbour whom, we must help. Now in this real communion between souls are the impulses of my heart, my certainties, my resolutions, my lights in no wise communicable? Surely if bodies are in contact and communication with one another from end to end of the world in electricity, must I be expected to believe that souls have no intercommunication. Indeed the contact between souls is to-day ascertainable by experience, if it was not certain beforehand by reason and faith. Here again I who write these lines *know*, I have *seen*. Well, if you have within you the fountain of living water, the fountain of rays of light, of impulses, convictions, hopes, how could these living waters not flow out from your soul upon all souls? There, indeed, is the real succour and assistance! That is why Isaias said: 'When you shall have poured out your soul into another soul that was about to perish, that will be righteousness and the fulness of Duty.'[34]

X

And S Paul requires of us unceasing watchfulness in the essential and indispensable fulfilment of this duty—the assistance given by each soul to every soul. Hear him, 'Cease not to pray and to make supplication at all times in the Holy Ghost' (I Tim 2:1). And again, 'By all prayer and supplication praying at all times in the spirit; and in the same watching with all instance and supplication for the faithful' (Eph 6:18). And does it not seem that if you cease to watch, to insist, to make efforts, to hold fast, everything will relax, the world will relapse, your brethren will feel in themselves less strength and support? Yes surely it is so: Each one of us in a measure bears up the world and those who cease to work and to watch overburden the rest.

Therefore once more duty to God implies everything. Every duty involves every other. But there are further distinctions to be made.

Chapter the Third

Duties of Man Towards Himself

I

Our duty towards ourselves is to educate ourselves, to bring ourselves up, so to speak. There is a sort of primitive, *impersonal* education which comes from God, from nature, and from society. But if God begins our education Himself or through His creation, He expects us to complete it by thought and liberty. And that is *personal* education.

34. Isa 48 [*sic*] [more likely 58—Editor].

II

Herein lies the first part of Duty, viz. profound respect for what is begun in us, without any doing of our own, by God, by the family, by society, by the Church. It is the laborious assimilation, the taking up by free choice, of what was in the first instance imposed on us or instilled into us. Here begins the crisis of personal education.

III

That crisis, above all in our days, is not rightly weathered by the most of men. They are wanting in respect, they do not accept, and they make no effort to go deep into things. They despise and trample under foot the benefits generously bestowed by Providence. Instead of imitating the Apostles by hauling in the full nets; instead of taking nearly the whole catch, merely throwing aside a few worthless fish, they cast back into the sea the whole of that abundance that had come to them by God's favour. After which the most of men live their days poor in moral life, poor in faith, and only the weariness and sadness of the evening of life bring them back to seek and find some scraps of those riches which in the morning they had caught in their miraculous net.

IV

Many men, it is true, lack the benefit of that primitive education. They come into the world without any moral inheritance and have perhaps received nothing but evil example and evil maxims as an outfit for this hard life. But reason and the Gospel say that there shall be demanded back from a man only what has been given to him. God asks of every soul one thing which is always possible and is always called forth from us by conscience and the actual impulse of the Father, to wit, an effort to turn towards the right and the good, starting from whatever point we may have reached at the moment.

V

At every point at which a soul finds itself two ways lie open before it. This is ever and always true: 'God made man from the beginning and left him in the hand of his own counsel . . . Before man is life and death, good and evil. That which he shall choose shall be given him' (Eccl 15:14). The first act of personal education, an act on which everything depends, is the original, fundamental choice between those two ways: right or wrong, good or evil, life or death. Do you will to be *good*? That is the first question.

VI

Uprightness, the instinctive turning towards the goal, some practice however slight of goodness according to one's lights, some little love of the glimpsed truth, that is what will lead man on and on whither God wills, if only he will persevere, keep up the effort, and march onward.

VII

Let him then march on and make efforts and, starting from the point at which he finds himself, let him undertake the education of his entire being, mind and body.

VIII

People sometimes speak of duties towards our bodies. Why not? Now the primary duty towards the body is the right choice between the two ways—good or evil, life or death. Health, long life, beauty are things that for the most part you give to your body by the choice you make. The great majority of men kill their bodies by vice. Science has laid down an axiom that we must keep on repeating: Man does not die, he kills himself. And as for beauty, it is the soul that transfigures the body and gives it a meaning. The expression of a man's countenance is only the resultant of his habits. Therefore help this poor body of yours, sustain it, transfigure it, if possible, by serenity, purity, peacefulness, by courage, by intellectual effort, and by the nobleness and loftiness of your desires and habits and resolutions.

IX

A further word on our duty towards the body. Remember these three sayings: 1. 'Wisdom will not . . . dwell in a body subject to sins' (Wis 1:4). 2. 'If then thy whole body be lightsome, having no part of darkness, the whole shall be lightsome and as a bright lamp shall enlighten thee' (Lk 11:36).[35] 3. 'As the lamp shining upon the holy candlestick so is the beauty of the face in a ripe age' (Ecclus 26:22). Bear in mind that it is the whole man, soul and body, that acts in everything, even in moral and intellectual matters. Lastly do not forget that Holy Communion is given for the protection and sustenance of both body and soul: *Ad tutamentum mentis et corporis.*

X

But let us come back to the soul. The choice once made, death set aside and life accepted, at least in principle, by the rightness of the intention, then, if this fundamental act of personal education is to bear fruit, you must act and work and bring out the powers that are in you. It is the moment when conscience says to us, Take courage and be a man, *Confortare et esto vir.* This is said to every man at the threshold of life, as it was said to the prophet at the threshold of the Promised Land. What has to be done is to undertake, and that by ourselves, the education of the mind and the education of the will with a view to the conquest of truth and of freedom.

XI

Truth, freedom, how splendid a goal! The Europe of our day has not yet reached that goal. The world has not yet gone far enough with the Gospel to know it for the truth, still less to draw freedom from it. The vast and luminous regions that have already been conquered are scattered about as separate sciences, have not yet been brought together as truth, nor brought back to God and the soul, and to duty, as the source and instrument of liberty. But I never tire of saying that we have reached that crisis and that 'the eagles' are endeavouring to gather together.[36] Sciences are converging and it is in the science of Duty that, it would seem, they tend to unite. Many minds are glimpsing this and longing for it. All credit to the workers of the mind who

35. This is the Douai version. Père Gratry's text reads: *Lorsque votre intention est simple et droite, dit l'Evangile, tout votre corps est éclairè, et il devient pour vous comme un réflecteur de lumière.*
36. *Cf* Matt 24:28; Lk17:37.

will discover in advance of their age the great passage to the Promised Land, the passage by truth to justice and liberty. That is the duty of genius.

XII

But what we are concerned with here is ourselves, all of us, the least of us. To seek light and leading, to seek truth, is the duty of all men. What is to be done if genius, if the most advanced peoples are still seeking? Now that which is the supreme duty of genius is also the first and simplest intellectual duty of every man. And for every man duty is possible of fulfilment—in this way, 'Seek first the Kingdom of God and his justice and the rest will be added to you.' There is the whole method, a method of reaching truth which is as simple as it is necessary.

Seek righteousness, truth will be given over and above. Seek the knowledge and practice of duty, for that is the right beginning of the road that leads to all truth: it is a step towards that supreme knowledge of which Christ said, 'If you keep my word, i.e. if you practice righteousness, you will KNOW THE TRUTH.'

XIII

Morality[37] social and individual, national and international, its consequences and its sanction, its consequences not present only but eternal, what science is there that does not come within that science? *Hygiene* comes within it, and how necessary it is to teach hygiene to everybody. Is *political economy* anything else but ethics—the science of labour and wisdom, of equity and liberty, and of the immediate, material, and manifest sanctions[38] of labour, wisdom, equity, and liberty? It is in fact one of the most striking aspects of the science of Duty. *Politics* is identical with ethics; those who do not know that are out-of-date politicians. And is not *history* morality in action? What are we to see in it if not the onward march of the human race hastened or hindered by good or evil? And as for *geography*, inseparable

37. '*La morale*.' The word may be rendered 'ethics' or 'the science of morals' or 'moral science,' as in the phrase Mental and Moral Science.

38. That is, punishments and rewards.

as it is from history, does it not imply the knowledge of all nature, thus bringing to ethics an important contribution? What is to be said of *Logic*? Is it not really inseparable from moral science, as are the intellect and the will, those two faculties of a soul that is one and undivided?

Thus our intellectual duty is to seek above all that science which is a rounded whole and which we call truth. And that summing up turns out to be clearer than the details and that whole richer and less ponderous than its parts.

XIV

But in reality intellectual duty consists less in the acquisition of knowledge than in the education of the faculties. 'The life is more than the food,' says the Gospel, 'and the body more than the raiment' (Lk 12:23), a saying which is capable of general application. Consider your mind as a being to which you owe assistance and understand that it is better to give it strength than clothing, health than riches, virtue than all the rest besides. Make your mind just, active, prudent, upright, sincere, disinterested. Acquire what S. Thomas calls the intellectual virtues and you will have given your mind something more than knowledge. You will have given it light and liberty, and you will have endowed yourself with a steadfast mind, capable of standing upright amid all the storms of opinion and passion.

XV

God in His Providence has willed that this primary intellectual duty, the cultivation of the virtues of the mind, should be much more accessible to every man rich or poor than is the acquisition of knowledge. Read Channing's admirable pages on the personal education of the working man. Knowledge itself, moreover, will be, when people choose, much less inaccessible to the common run of men than one would be disposed to think possible in view of the state of pedantry in which our sciences are at present. The expounding of science and of knowledge generally in language understood by the masses is one of the most urgent intellectual duties of great minds and of friends of humanity.

XVI

And bear this in mind that of all the intellectual virtues[39] the most fruitful and the most necessary is faith, faith in every sense of the word, including its great theological meaning. Faith is the free, habitual assent of the mind and of the will to the truths that God reveals. Whether He reveals them to conscience, to reason, to the human race, or to the Church, by nature or by history, by tradition or by inspiration, naturally or supernaturally, faith is a virtue of the soul which perceives in all things what is of God, which feels it, is drawn to it, and takes God Himself, real and present, as the foundation of its magnificent certainties. Faith, that divine tenacity of the soul, clings to God, to God who is the source of truth and of liberty. Faith is the turning of the whole soul towards truth. It knows beforehand that TRUTH IS, that it is beautiful, that it answers everything. Faith lays hold of truth before having seen it and holds on to the core of it even when it cannot make out the details of the outer surface.[40]

XVII

And it is in this way that the intellectual are bound up with the moral virtues. Faith is the common root of both. Faith is precisely that saying of our Lord, 'If you keep my word you will know the truth and the truth will make you free' (Jn 8:32). It is surely here, if anywhere, that the effort towards personal education is called for. A man's freedom is at issue here and his very dignity as a man. It is in this connection that we must say: 'Help yourself and Heaven will help you: take courage and be a man.' Courage, friend, were you bent all day to the earth in toil, were you buried in the mines, courage, lift up your head and let your heart bound within you. Moral education, far more important still than even intellectual education, is always within your power. You have God, reason, and faith, uprightness, good will, prayer: you may make of your mind an ever growing light and of your whole soul a free soul. You may become a man, a sage, a saint, a benefactor of mankind. Yes, simply by the steadfastness of your soul in God, in righteousness and truth deliberately chosen, in the courage that

39. See in Gratry's *Logic* the section entitled '*vertus intellectuelles inspirées*'.
40. This is perhaps hardly an adequate rendering of Père Gratry's words: '*Y tient par le centre et le fond quand la surface de réflexion n'en analyse encore aucun détail.*'

freedom gives, you bless implicitly and you help the souls of all men. You are among souls like a magnet among filings magnetising and orientating all around you.

And here we come to your duties towards others, though indeed they are almost fulfilled already by the fulfilment of your duties to God and to yourself.

Chapter the Fourth

Duties of Man Towards Others—The Family

We must help and love all—the family, our country, the man whoever he be who falls wounded beside us, the human race, the Church, that is to say the assembly of men united among themselves and with God. What objects to love, to serve, and to aid in our journey towards God!

I

But for the accomplishment of all these things, after your personal education, blessed be God, you are not alone. Were you alone how heavy the task would be! Woe to the moral being who is alone! But man is not a solitary being: he is social, living in groups. The bunch of grapes, the ear of corn are better symbols of us than the pearl or the diamond. Yes, friend, there is the family, the family from which you are sprung and the family which you yourself will found.

II

The family. Let us talk about the one that you will found. Perhaps you will understand things better thus. Yes, to fulfil these duties and to aid you in your efforts you have a helpmate who is almost yourself: '*Adjutorium simile sibi*.' You have a permanent resource, an ever present recompense, a visible object for your love, to whom God Himself has joined you by a contract that is natural, social, legal, and sacred. There lies your strength.

For, says Christ our Lord, when two of you join together in my name upon earth, whatsoever they ask, it shall be given them.[41] Every-

41. Again I say to you that, 'if two of you shall consent upon earth concerning anything whatsoever they shall ask, it shall he done to them by my Father who is in Heaven (Matt 18:20)'.

thing then is possible. Friend, are ten years of work and of assiduous personal education too much to make you worthy that God should give you His daughter as partner of your life? Are you not aware that Christian marriage in its holy condition really implies that—God Himself bestows His son or His daughter and a dowry worth a kingdom?

III

That condition is thus defined by our unknown theology (it is public and written everywhere but unknown): Marriage is a sacrament of the living, that is to say that it is necessary that people should be in a state of grace when getting married as when going to Communion. Who among us dares to communicate unworthily? Nobody. How then do you dare to get married unworthily?

IV

Yes, look at her, this king's daughter, who deserved that you should toil in order to win her, and that to win her heaven-born love you should be pure, courageous, intelligent, free, honoured, a friend of God, capable, so far as character and talent go, of guarding her, helping her, glorifying her and the children that shall be born of her.

V

But these things are so great that love alone, the love of a pure heart, can understand them. Happy the age, not far off let us hope, which will have a practical reverence and an understanding of this sacrament of the living. When that comes about it will be possible to talk about a Return to God, the beginning of the social epoch of Christianity by the transformation of the family, by Christian marriage understood at last.

VI

True marriage, holy matrimony, marriage with the son or daughter of God, what good fortune; what a future it means! But are not the most ordinary of men called to it? Glory to God. All men have a great mission. Social differences disappear before this grand equality of royal marriage with the son or the daughter of God, that is offered to all.

VII

And what if I were to speak here of those who by a yet more marvellous mystery enter deeper still for life and eternity into God's intimate adoption? Such as these may well say: 'I am not alone because the Father is with me.'

VIII

But it is above all when a man becomes a father that he comes to know what benefits God showers upon us in the family. As for me it is only as I advance in years that I come to understand the greatness of these primary benefits. Happy the little children, fresh flowers that have not yet withered. Of them the Gospel says: 'Their angels always see the face of the Father who is in Heaven.' Yes, the pure inspiration of the Father who is in Heaven and in their hearts flows without let or hindrance into their innocent souls. Their angels see God. They themselves know nothing of it all, but they live by it and thrill with happiness in that universal light of the Father in which they grow, full of presentiments, germs of thought, exquisite impulses. Now who is the priest, I almost said the visible God, of this first period of life? It is the Father.

IX

Yes, I have full and happy memories of it, just as if it was yesterday, and many people have told me facts about their childhood in sufficient number and with sufficient accuracy to form a scientific basis for conclusions. Yes, the pure soul of the little child sees in its father a divine being, all-wise and all-powerful, and in its mother all the treasures of goodness and love and beauty. I know nothing more profoundly true than those words of Christian piety repeated to children at school and in church by priests and nuns, 'My dear child, see Jesus Christ in your father, and our Blessed Lady in your mother'. The family is a sort of primitive and private church, it is natural religion, and as such an admirable symbol of, and a powerful preparation for, supernatural and universal religion.

O man, O companion of man, see what these little ones think of you. That is what God makes them think, God who in showing you to them means to give them holy visions and divine ideas, the grandest, truest, most fruitful that they shall ever have. Tell me, is that mission glorious enough for you? Your duty, then, is to represent, to stand for, God. To be for them a visible God, filling them thus with joy and faith and trust and ideal aspirations, and heavenly images, and often, even in earliest childhood, with ineffaceable ideas of justice, heroism, and honour. That is what you owe to them. It constitutes for them the first push, as it were, into life; do you not want to make it, for these poor little ones whom God has confided to you, a powerful, right, and holy impulse? God be praised, there are fathers and mothers who do fulfil this admirable priestly office in spirit and in truth. Do you not want to do so too? You owe them, then, the sight of moral beauty of every kind. Will you give them that if you be not yourself pure, self-respecting, just, temperate, and religious, master of yourself in meekness and kindness? Take care! they perceive the all but imperceptible; they see everything and take everything in.

X

A thousand times happy are they who have received from their parents and hand on to their children these images and memories as a heritage. Blessed power of sacred family traditions, how great you are and how rare! To-day the various generations are greatly broken up and live apart, and families no longer form, in the social warp and woof, those clear-cut, continuous lines which knit the whole solidly together. How comes it that people do not understand what nobility is? And how is it that everybody from the king down to the humblest shepherd does not desire it and labour to found it? Yes, nobility for everybody. It is open to all by way of hard work and virtue. Ancestor worship—a fine word and a noble thing. Has not every man somewhere in him a deep and providential desire to leave a blessed memory behind him? Christ Himself when He was, as it were, passing on His precious Blood to the new generations of mankind said, 'Do this in memory of me'. Ought not every father likewise to be anxious to pass on, along with his blood, a noble, holy, and beneficent memory?

XI

Of late years the art of fixing the image of the human face has become so popular and so easy that painters, with the help of the sun, are going about Europe even to the smallest villages and often leave in the countryside scarcely a human face that they have not caught. Well, there you have ancestral portraits. What a few centuries ago was possible only to kings and lords will soon be realised for everybody; the uses of these collections will be extended: names and dates will be inserted and perhaps a few outstanding facts—offices held, honours, services, deeds of devotedness. Mayors and priests will sign the portraits and witness to the memories which they enshrine. There you have the family deeds, titles of nobility. My brother, whoever you be, become the founder or at all events the regenerator of a noble line. Carry on vigorously to its great goal, viz. the multiplication of the just and of the children of God, that particular human line of which you are a single link. In that, if in nothing else, you will be a benefactor of the human race.

XII

Yes, we shall do these things and many others when the Gospel light and the heavenly sap shall have come back into these dried-up masses of mankind like the sunlight and the showers of Spring to the countryside when Winter is past. Yes, it is my dearest hope that before three centuries have gone by, when the present chaos has been overcome, when the science of Duty shall have made the hoped-for progress, the nations will grow nobler and that nobility will penetrate even to their very marrow.

Conclusion

The will to abolish destitution leads to the Gospel and from that to the Catholic Church.

Earth overpeopled and grown too small tends towards Heaven.

At bottom the great terror and the great sorrow is death.

The great consolation, therefore, will be immortality made manifest.

I ask of the contemporary world one thing only—a determined will to do away with abject poverty. Let it be resolved publicly and solemnly to take as a motto those words of Moses: 'O Israel, there shall be no poor nor beggar among you: that the Lord thy God may bless thee in the land that He will give thee in possession' (Deut. xv, 4).

Let all peoples, sects, and parties agree on this one point and pursue it without ever desisting, and it is enough. I say that by that very fact Christianity and Catholicism (which is integral Christianity) would rule the world.

How can that be?

It is that integral Christianity may—it is impossible to repeat this too often—be reduced to a single point: I was hungry, says Christ, and you gave me to eat—you are saved. I was hungry and you gave me not to eat—you are judged and condemned. That is the point. According to the Gospel everything lies there, not in the sense that this one point excludes the rest, but in the sense that it implies everything. It implies and presupposes all religious practices, every Christian virtue, and the true life of the soul in God.

Therefore, if to feed or not to feed Christ our Lord, that is to say, the least of men who suffer, is the entire basis of the last Judgement, the whole question of eternal salvation, it is quite clear that this one point is and implies the whole of Christianity. Therefore individuals and nations will be putting Christianity, that is to say Catholicism, into practice as soon as they set to work with their whole heart, with all their might, with perseverance to the point of success, to feed with bread the mass of men that are consumed with hunger. Therefore once more it is the essential function of Christianity that human society will be undertaking when it undertakes to banish misery from its midst. Is it not evident?

Suppose you endeavour to multiply the means of subsistence in Europe, in any nation, suppose you try to drive misery out and replace it by decent comfort or at all events by poverty that is bearable—I mean the poverty that does not slay, surely that is not asking too much; suppose I say that you undertake this, then from the very outset you will see with your own eyes that it is absolutely impossible to improve in any way the condition of the suffering masses, unless you moralize them. You will see with your own eyes where lies the obstacle, the great, fundamental obstacle, almost the only one there is—the moral condition of the poorer classes, ignorance, sloth, and vice. You will see with your own eyes the absolute impossibility of modifying in any respect the condition of those who are suffering unless you make them better.

Once you have realised that, then attempt this second task and you will at once get at the core of the difficulty; you will see whether it is possible to make men better without religion, whether you can transform the family, uplift man, woman, or child without God, without law, without faith. Yes, that familiar challenge of the priest to the philosopher, that well-worn axiom—*No morality without religion*, is of the most perfect accuracy. Rightly understood it cannot fail to become in course of time a method of proving the truth of Christianity and Catholicism which will be both experimental and scientific.

A thousand years of effort by means of abstract and purely philosophical morality will not bring people a step further. But twenty-five years of good will in the propagation of the true religion would be able to change the whole condition of a people in a single generation.

But of what religion is there question?

There is only one in the world—Christianity: the others are negligible. Therefore by persevering it may be proved that in order to live by bread people must first live a moral life, and that to live a moral life they must live by God, the God of the Gospel. It will be proved, I say, that God alone multiplies the loaves, and it will be seen by experience that God, God incarnate and really present in the Catholic Church, is the only power that can multiply the loaves, Jesus Christ alone multiplies the loaves.

And such, I hope, is the course that the history of European peoples will really follow, nay is following even to-day.

II

Among us there has been for a long time past general and increasing good will to ameliorate the lot of those who suffer, that is to say of the great mass of human beings that covers the earth. But the men of a hundred years ago, such as Voltaire, who talked most about humanity and the relief of the oppressed, hoped to set the people free and bring them happiness by giving them up to nature and voluptuousness, by granting them boundless licence and breaking the yoke of the moral law.

To-day, thanks be to God, if there be one point more than another that the fieriest popular orators ardently maintain in the light of evidence and with the details furnished by knowledge, it is that morality is the sole source of progress. To-day the time-spirit says, No progress, no happiness without moral law and without the austere cult of righteousness—work, continence, temperance. Justice and the moral law! That is what they all maintain. But there are those who cry, 'But no religion, please'. Now in process of time everybody will come to see that if the life of the body, if daily bread is not to be had without moral life, moral life in its turn is not to be had without religion.

I know a man, a man of some consequence and well known, who told me that he became a Christian by this way of experience. 'I became intimate,' he said to me, 'with certain poor families. For several years I followed their fortunes closely, watching all the details of their daily life and wondering how I should bring well-being to them. I saw clearly that progress in well-being depended on moral progress and moral progress depended on religious progress. To my mind this is a scientific conclusion from experiment as certain as any of the physical laws. I did more. I recommended a similar course of action to some young men who were undecided in their convictions. I told them to undertake without prejudices or partizanship a consecutive and detailed study of some poor families and to seek out the cause and the remedy of their poverty. Their conclusion never varied: no progress in prosperity without moral progress; no moral progress without religious progress.'

A writer who ordinarily raves but has occasional lucid intervals once addressed the following exhortation to the Catholic clergy. After arguing powerfully that the source of abject poverty is simply the lack of balance in the reason and morals of the people, he said: 'There you have, O priests, a truth which it would become you to proclaim in all your churches. That is, in these days of ours, the most eloquent commentary on the Gospel that you could make; those are the truths which, if proclaimed by you and if they became part of the people's faith at the same time that they are scientifically proved, would end the present crisis peacefully and would make you the natural leaders of progress. And at the same time that you would address to the rich the Gospel exhortation, with a commentary based on scientific observation, we leaders of the people would tell them that the cause of their sufferings is the universal immorality and that the first thing to be done in order to do away with pauperism and guarantee employment is to return to good living. We would point out to the people by means of statistics which they would be able to grasp that in the most favourable conditions, supposing all the fortunate influences of climate, soil, order, and freedom acting together, they cannot hope for a sum of material wealth equal to an average of one franc fifty centimes[42] a head per day for a population of thirty-six millions of human beings spread over a territory of 27,000 square leagues. That consequently the greater part of their happiness must be sought for within, in the joys of conscience and of the mind. And having thus disposed them to moderation, we should try to get them to understand that, as no man, no class of society, can be accused of the collective evil that exists, all thought of reprisals should be given up, and that, after having for so long gone aside from justice, our duty is to return to a state of equilibrium by a gradual process which will stir up no anger and will not make either criminals or victims.

'While we are preaching thus to the proletariat will you on your side, O priests, undertake to preach to the rich and powerful? That would be a great day and peace would soon be made.'

Oh, yes, we shall do it. We have done it already for centuries both to the poor and to the rich and powerful. It is we, it seems, who have taught you all that. But it is a good thing that you should understand it at last, while thinking that it is you who have discovered it.

Yes, it is thus and only thus that peace and progress will come, and that an end will be put to the crisis which has lasted for nearly a century, and this will be the greatest, most powerful, and most convincing proof of the Gospel and of the Catholic faith that has ever been set forth.

With a firm determination to come forth at last out of this universal misery which is the real leprosy of the world, the peoples of these modern times will see in clear-cut detail, as you see bodily objects, that the real cause of the evil is universal immorality and that the one resource of the world is to come back to right living. And very soon they will see that the only light that can light up the way towards right living is the light of the Gospel, and that the power that can speed us on the way is the efficacious regenerating power of Catholic virtues and Catholic sacraments.

That day the greatest revolution in the world since the coming of the God-Man will have come to pass: that day will begin in real earnest the effect of the universal Gospel prayer: 'Thy kingdom come; thy will be done on earth as it is in Heaven; give us this day our daily bread; deliver us from evil.'

42. About one and threepence in English money at the time.

III

Then will the whole human race, with ever growing power, light, and liberty, go forth to fill and dominate the globe—'Increase and multiply and fill the earth' (Gen 1:28). And when our earth, at length fully peopled and cultivated, will afford a livelihood to ten milliards of men, the human race will once more begin to perceive that the world is small and no longer suffices. If the world continues to exist, a time will come when men will understand that a stop must be put to the increase, and as happens to every man at the summit of life, growth will cease. Equilibrium will set in and perhaps a certain decrease.

Then it is that people will recognize the duty of transfiguring by chastity the last third of life, no less than that of maintaining the first third in angelic purity. Then it is that the Catholic marriage laws will appear as the truth itself, as the true social law. It will be seen what a holy thing virginity is, what a holy thing marriage is, what a great thing it is to bring a human being into the world, what a divine thing it is to sanctify a human being, and how man is raised to Heaven even in this life by the divine inward development that comes of chastity. 'To raise oneself to Heaven' is a phrase that the human race will come to understand when it sees that the world is not big enough.

Bring before your mind then what state the mind of man will be in and where it will turn when the universal preoccupation of the peoples, of science, and of politics will be. The whole world is occupied, land is beginning to fail us. And the human flood continues to rise. Ever increasing sobriety and continence—therein lies justice, virtue, and necessity.[43]

But what then? Man will want to go on increasing in happiness, and he is right. It is then that it will become plain to the whole world: *that the greater part of man's happiness must be sought in the soul and in the joys of conscience and of the mind.* But men want a concrete happiness, and the joys of conscience and of the mind, if the meaning of these words be not rightly understood, are an abstract sort of resource such as man will refuse to be satisfied with, for his thirst for happiness will grow with increasing enlightenment.

---

43. [Père Gratry could not have foreseen the immoral and socially suicidal solution that certain elements of our contemporary society have found for the situation he foresees. The inevitable reaction may yet take the form that he envisages.—Translator].

But if these joys are recognised to be the love of God and of souls, the love of the living God infinitely rich in the benefits which He lavishes on us, the love of personal beings, immortal in life and beauty. Yes, then mankind will have found a way out. Then the human heart will ask, as I, who in age and in thought have passed through life and the world, am asking myself to-day, if there be not some possible prolongation of this short life, some extension of this petty world. People will begin to scan the heavens—the visible sky and the Heaven that is unseen. They will look for the living links, the possible intercommunications between the earth and what surrounds it. They will seek and find.

Thanks to the wonderful development of the sciences of light we shall perhaps come to know something about the use of the stars, something about the actual life, the common destinies of the entire universe, something about the intimate life of the radiant sun which bestows fruitfulness upon the earth.

And who knows whether the other worlds will not prove a resource for us? Who knows all that can yet be drawn from the sun or what work its rays will one day be made to do? Who knows to what extent Christ may yet multiply the loaves and above all the rays of the Holy Spirit, and whether His was but an empty promise when He said, 'O Father, I say these things to the world that my joy may be in them and their joy may be full' (Jn 15:11).

Again, who knows what all-powerfulness prayer may give to the human race when it will say, Up to the present we have not prayed. Now that this earth of ours has become but a single temple in which we are all in closest contact, now that we are always gathered together, let us pray so that our hearts, too, may be in closest contact, and that the intensity, the divine energy, the ardent, continuous prayer of all men's souls may become a support, a moral and even physical power, almost a food for the poorest and the weakest.

Yes, our divine Lord said, 'Hitherto you have asked nothing in my name, ask and you shall receive that your joy may be full' (Jn 16:24). Let us ask for this full joy. And who knows whether the grand effect of this prayer and of this fulness of joy may not consist in believing and knowing that we are all and for ever one life, one love, as the Father and the Son are one in the unity of eternal love,[44] and that every man

44. Jn 10:80; 17:11 and 21–22.

may and ought to say with Christ, 'O Father, I desire that where I shall be all those whom you have given me should be also' (Jn 17:24).

Who knows, I say, whether this full joy, the supreme joy of the Holy Spirit the Consoler, will not consist even in this life in the clear vision to be given to the human race that this prayer is the truth and that men are living and will live, and they will be together in a place where they will see one another, in that place which Christ our Lord, first-born of eternal life, when He was leaving this life, promised to prepare for us, 'I go to prepare a place for you' (Jn 14:2).

Finally, who knows whether science and faith and revelation and the light of the Holy Ghost will not all point to the existence of the heaven of our immortality, its nature and its relation to the universe, and whether living, real, personal relations with the immortals of the other life will not be the consummation of the great joy!

Then mankind will be able to say with the apostle of the Gentiles, 'All things are yours . . . whether the world or life or death, whether the present or the future, all are yours' . . . (1 Cor 3:23). Yes, we are in life and we shall stay there. At bottom the great terror and the great sorrow is Death. The great consolation will therefore be manifest immortality. Why should not the vision of immortality be given us some day, as every day we have the vision of death?

But after all is not the very foundation of Christianity this vision of eternal life, the vision of the risen Christ? Is it not thus that Christ sets us free? By showing himself alive, said St Paul, He set at liberty those men whom fear of death had held captive all their lives.[45] Yes, this is my hope. If mankind becomes righteous, if in the final stage of its earthly life it is truly reborn of the Spirit as God wills that it should be, then I hope that it will be thus. And mankind upon this earth shall end like a saint in the serenity of the light, in the fulness of the joy of Christ.

45. 'That he might . . . set free all those who had been kept in slavery throughout their whole life by the fear of death' (Heb 2:15).

CPSIA information can be obtained
at www.ICGtesting.com
Printed in the USA
FSHW020510220720
71829FS

9 781925 679526